Not only have I heard Randy Frazee teach these message[s] ... [and applied] them. I am honored to partner with him in ministry, and I have no hesitation to recommend this book to you.

> MAX LUCADO, pastor and bestselling author

I'm privileged to call Randy Frazee my friend, and I know one important thing about him: he is a man of the Word. He loves the Bible, and he loves people. What's more, he's uniquely qualified to explain how our Lower Story fits into the Upper Story of God's plans and purposes. This a story you really need to read.

> DAVE RAMSEY, bestselling author and
> nationally syndicated radio show host

I love a good story. I love hearing them, reading them, and telling them. There's nothing like a good story to reach a heart, heal a hurt, kindle hope, or even cause a life to change direction. What Randy Frazee has done in *The Heart of the Story* is to masterfully weave together from the pages of Scripture the grand story of God, and he tells us the story in a way that not only gets at God's heart, but gets to our hearts as well. If you want to get drawn into a really compelling story that promises to change your life forever, read *The Heart of the Story*.

> MARK BATTERSON, *New York Times*
> bestselling author of *The Circle Maker* and
> lead pastor of National Community Church

The Heart of the Story lifted my chin, time and time again, reminding me to reckon God's promises with my problems. We so easily default to an earthbound perspective. But God is always writing a bigger story with our lives. Randy Frazee unpacks Scripture with passion, clarity, and conviction. He's one of my favorite guests on the show because he truly believes what he reads in Scripture. May the epic kingdom story come to life as you work your way through the pages of this masterful book.

> SUSIE LARSON, talk radio host, national speaker,
> and author of *Your Powerful Prayers*

I love the heart, insight, and teaching of Randy Frazee. I had the privilege of performing a song for *The Story* project—"How Love Wins"—inspired by the message of this book. The song takes the point of view of the thief alongside Jesus at the crucifixion. When Jesus shouted, "It is finished," the world thought he was admitting *he* was finished. But from the Upper Story perspective, Jesus was declaring that *his work* of redeeming us was finished on the cross, and a new beginning was born. This is just one of the life-transforming nuggets in the pages of *The Heart of the Story*. Read it, and you may just find a new beginning for yourself.

STEVEN CURTIS CHAPMAN, singer/songwriter and
author of *Cinderella: The Love of a Daddy and His Princess*

The Bible, the whole Bible, is put together and displayed as a single sweeping narrative in this extraordinary work of storytelling. Randy Frazee has invested a lifetime making God's Word useful, interesting, and accessible. This is his masterpiece!

BOB BUFORD, founder of Leadership Network
and author of *Halftime* and *Finishing Well*

Our church has grown so much going through *The Story*. I'm excited to take them through *The Heart of the Story* and see the Bible come alive for our people!

MARK HALL, lead singer of Casting Crowns and author of *Thrive*

Randy Frazee is not just a gifted leader and communicator; he is also a man with a unique ability to take the powerful things of God and present them to this generation with clarity and purpose.

LEON FONTAINE, CEO of Miracle Channel, senior pastor of Springs
Church (Canada), and television host of *The Spirit Contemporary Life*

The Heart of the Story is a brilliant work reminding us that the Bible is a collection of narratives that make up the story of God. Randy Frazee artistically guides us to discover our place in God's story. If you, like me, have always craved to know your role in the unfolding story of God, you'll want to read and share this book with others. *The Heart of the Story* is a gift.

DAVE FERGUSON, lead pastor of Community Christian Church, lead
visionary of NewThing, and author of *Finding Your Way Back to God*

The Bible is not a series of isolated fairy tales. It's one story, told in hundreds of chapters and in a compelling journey. Randy Frazee invites us—and then he takes us on that journey. And you will want to join him on it!

ED STETZER, Billy Graham Distinguished Chair, Wheaton College

As a songwriter, I've always been passionate about the power of a story. That's one of the reasons I've connected so deeply with Randy Frazee's book *The Heart of the Story*. Finding our story in the midst of the greater story that God is telling truly is the mission we're all on, and this book helps us find the heart of the story along the way.

MATTHEW WEST, award-winning singer/songwriter

If you live in the world of business, you can easily get stuck in the earthbound story of your work. Randy Frazee gently repositions our eyes and priorities toward God's grand narrative, one in which you will see yourself clearly as you live out your calling. As you ponder these stories, you'll feel God's vertical tug on your spreadsheet-driven, people-problem world and discover how to raise the cross at the center of the marketplace. In Randy's words, you'll find your story in God's story.

GREG LEITH, CEO of Convene

We live in the Lower Story. It's hard for us to see around the next bend in the road, let alone a generation or millennia. God sees everything from the Upper Story. He wrote the beginning and is orchestrating how the story ends. *The Heart of the Story* gives a glimpse into God's Upper Story and provides a road map for aligning our story to his story. Randy Frazee's teaching has deeply influenced my personal life, teaching, and the congregation I lead. It will do the same for you!

DR. BENJI W. KELLEY, founding pastor of
NewHope Church, Durham, North Carolina

ALSO BY RANDY FRAZEE

The Christian Life Profile Assessment

The Connecting Church 2.0

The Heart of the Story

Making Room for Life

Real Simplicity (expanded edition of *Making
Room for Life*; with Rozanne Frazee)

Renovation of the Heart: Student Edition (with Dallas Willard)

Think, Act, Be Like Jesus

THE HEART
OF THE STORY

DISCOVER YOUR LIFE WITHIN THE
GRAND EPIC OF GOD'S STORY

REVISED AND EXPANDED

RANDY FRAZEE

ZONDERVAN

The Heart of the Story
Copyright © 2011, 2017 by Randy Frazee

Requests for information should be addressed to:
Zondervan, *3900 Sparks Dr. SE, Grand Rapids, Michigan 49546*

ISBN 978-0-310-34936-5 (softcover)

ISBN 978-0-310-35004-0 (ebook)

Library of Congress Cataloging-in-Publication Data

Frazee, Randy.
    The heart of the story : tracing God's big idea through every story in the Bible /
Randy Frazee.
        p. cm.
    Includes bibliographical references.
    ISBN 978-0-310-33272-5
    1. Bible—Criticism, interpretation, etc. 2. Bible stories. I. Title.
BS511.3.F73 2011
220.9'505—dc22   2011012862

Scripture quotations are taken from the Holy Bible, New International Version®, NIV®. Copyright © 1973, 1978, 1984, 2011 by Biblica, Inc.® Used by permission of Zondervan. All rights reserved worldwide. www.Zondervan.com. The "NIV" and "New International Version" are trademarks registered in the United States Patent and Trademark Office by Biblica, Inc.®

Scripture quotations marked ESV are taken from the ESV® Bible (The Holy Bible, English Standard Version®), copyright © 2001 by Crossway , a publishing ministry of Good News Publishers. Used by permission. All rights reserved.

Scripture quotations marked NASB are taken from the New American Standard Bible®, Copyright © 1960, 1962, 1963, 1968, 1971, 1972, 1973, 1975, 1977, 1995 by The Lockman Foundation. Used by permission. www.Lockman.org.

Scripture quotations marked NLT are taken from the Holy Bible, New Living Translation, copyright © 1996, 2004, 2007, 2013, 2015 by Tyndale House Foundation. Used by permission of Tyndale House Publishers, Inc., Carol Stream, Illinois 60188. All rights reserved.

Scripture quotations marked MSG are taken from THE MESSAGE. Copyright © by Eugene H. Peterson 1993, 1994, 1995, 1996, 2000, 2001, 2002. Used by permission of NavPress. All rights reserved. Represented by Tyndale House Publishers, Inc.

Any Internet addresses (websites, blogs, etc.) and telephone numbers in this book are offered as a resource. They are not intended in any way to be or imply an endorsement by Zondervan, nor does Zondervan vouch for the content of these sites and numbers for the life of this book.

All rights reserved. No part of this publication may be reproduced, stored in a retrieval system, or transmitted in any form or by any means—electronic, mechanical, photocopy, recording, or any other—except for brief quotations in printed reviews, without the prior permission of the publisher.

Cover photography: Getty Images
Interior illustrations: Cally Vick
Interior design: Kait Lamphere

First printing November 2016 / Printed in the United States of America

To Mike Reilly—
you have aligned your life to God's Upper Story,
and I am one of many who have received the blessing.
May God continue to blow wind in your sails
as you press forward in your adventure in serving others.

CONTENTS

✝ MOVEMENT THREE: THE STORY OF JESUS 221

∽ MOVEMENT FOUR: THE STORY OF THE CHURCH . 269

🌳 MOVEMENT FIVE: THE STORY OF A NEW GARDEN . 295

FOREWORD
BY MAX LUCADO

Above and around us, God directs a grander saga, written by his hand, orchestrated by his will, unveiled according to his calendar. His "Upper Story" details his plan of redemption. He is creating an eternal people for an eternal place.

Without the lens of the Upper Story, the events of the "Lower Story" perplex and confuse us. They create moments of confusion in which we feel too old, too small, unqualified, or outnumbered. But in the context of his Upper Story, our Lower Story moments make sense.

Look at young Joseph in the Egyptian prison. A bright, talented youth wasting away behind bars. Imprisonment makes no sense—from the Lower Story angle. But from the Upper Story, we see something else. We see God protecting the youth in prison so he can use him in the palace. Joseph is sentenced today so he can serve God tomorrow and save the children of Israel from famine and extinction.

Or take the challenge of another Joseph. This one enters the story two thousand years later as a young carpenter in Nazareth. A seamy scandal has rocked his world. Mary, his fiancée, is pregnant. Joseph is not the father. Of this, he is sure. Of anything else, he is not. His life has taken a random turn toward chaos. But we know better, don't we? We know better because we've read the story from the Upper Level. The baby in Bethlehem's straw has convinced us that God was up to something higher, grander, and greater. Joseph's scandal was actually God's solution.

The Bible reads like this. One "aha story" after another. Prisons are actually provisions. Scandals are actually solutions. Tragedy at eye level is actually triumph at God's level.

Randy Frazee masterfully takes us to the Upper Story. I've never met anyone who better understands the big story of the Bible. I have heard Randy teach these messages at our church in San Antonio, Texas. These truths changed the perspective of our congregation, and they will do the same for you.

Not only have I heard Randy teach these messages, but I've also seen him live them. He skillfully leads our congregation and graciously guides his family. Randy and his wife, Rozanne, have invested three decades of service into the kingdom of God. They have made a difference.

I am honored to partner with him in ministry, and I have no hesitation to recommend this book to you. Let the prayer of the psalmist be yours: "Lead me to the rock that is higher than I" (Psalm 61:2). You and I need to see life from God's view, from his Upper Story. May he take us there. And may he use this book to do it.

PREFACE

I grew up in an unchurched home—which simply means that my family didn't go to church. My parents weren't against Jesus; he just didn't make the short list of priorities in their lives. But I did have two spiritual deposits in my life. The first came in the form of a ceramic prayer plaque that hung over my bed. I said this prayer every night before I went to sleep. Maybe you know it—

> Now I lay me down to sleep,
> I pray the Lord my soul to keep.
> If I should die before I wake,
> I pray the Lord my soul to take.

Let me ask you, what kind of a sick person writes a prayer like that for children? Each night as I went to bed, it wasn't sweet dreams of sugar plums dancing in my head. No, I thought, *This just might be it for me. And what are the chances the Lord will take my soul? My parents don't even take me to church!*

The second spiritual deposit was the Bible my grandmother gave me when I was a small child. I still have it to this day. It was a black leather King James Version of the Bible that sat on our family bookshelf in the hallway between our bedrooms. I remember on several occasions unzipping the Bible, lying on the floor, tucking the palms of my hands under my chin, and beginning to read with a simple faith that there was something in it I desperately needed to know. After fifteen minutes of giving it my full attention, I would close it, zip it up, and place it back on the shelf. I read it, but I didn't get it. I wanted to, but it just wasn't within my reach.

Maybe you feel the same way. You know the Bible is important. Like most people, "read through the Bible" is on your bucket list—things you want to accomplish before you "kick the bucket." It's right up there with climbing Mount Everest and jumping out of an airplane. For some, these two goals may feel more achievable than getting through the Bible. You are not alone. Forty-one percent of people who say they own at least four Bibles confess to never reading it.

That's why I'm so excited that you have picked up this book. Let me tell you why by giving you the backstory of how this book came about.

At the age of fourteen, my younger sister and I were invited by a neighbor two doors down to their church's vacation Bible school. Three days into hearing the basic message of the gospel—the good news of what Jesus did for me—I became a Christian and began my journey into discovering God's Word. At the age of fifteen, at a summer camp in New York, I dedicated my life to become a pastor. Fast-forward to age twenty-eight. After receiving degrees in theology and biblical studies, I began pastoring my first church. It didn't take long to recognize that people were struggling with the Bible as much as I did as a young boy. The search was on for solutions, but none seemed to help in a major way for the majority of people.

Now fast-forward all the way to 2005. At this point, I had been a pastor for a little more than fifteen years. I received a call from Doug Lockhart, a vice president of marketing for Zondervan. He wanted to stop by my office in Fort Worth, Texas, to show me three new Bible products. Sitting in my small conference room, Doug proceeded to show me those three products, but the one that stood out to me was called *The Story*.

The Story is an abridged chronology of the Bible. It doesn't have every word of the Bible in it, but it does put the story of the Bible into chronological order (which, by the way, is not how the sixty-six books of our printed Bibles are normally organized). All the chapter and verse references in *The Story* are omitted so that it reads more like a novel.

I thought, *This is it! This is a tool I can use to help the people of my church not only get through the story of the Bible but also really see for themselves, many for the first time, the extent to which God has gone to get us back.* The gospel didn't begin in Matthew, but in the book of Genesis. My vision was to have the whole church, ages 2 through 102, experience *The Story* together for thirty-one weeks—matching the numbers of chapters in the book. Imagine everyone on the same journey to understand the overarching story of the Bible—adults, young people, and children. Let's do this together!

The vision became a reality three years later. I accepted the position of senior minister of Oak Hills Church in San Antonio, Texas, where author Max Lucado had served in that role for twenty years. Gratefully, he stayed on with me as a teaching pastor. I remember the first time I shared the vision with Max. We were on the golf course. As he began mulling the idea over, the wheels of his creative mind started to spin and the wheels of his golf game fell off. At the end of the round, neither of us played an epic round of golf, but we did walk off the course with a vision. For my first year as senior minister of Oak Hills Church, we would anchor the people in a rich experience in God's Word. We would take the entire church on a journey through *The Story*, chapter by chapter for thirty-one weeks.

Max and I took the vision back to Zondervan to see if they might be interested in publishing all the companion tools we would need for students and children. As if it were a part of God's plan all along, they enthusiastically said yes, and off we went. At the end of the thirty-one weeks, we were amazed at the level of excitement. For the first time, many folks finally saw for themselves the one grand story of God. While we didn't go through this experience to grow the church numerically, we saw a net increase in attendees of 23 percent! This tells me that people are hungry for God's Word and his story like never before.

It wasn't until 2011 that these materials were available to other churches. We were deeply curious how other churches would respond. Well, it has been five years since the release of *The Story*. To date, more than seven thousand churches have experienced it for themselves, with nearly six and a half million lives touched. And there is no sign that things are slowing down yet. Yay, God!

One of the books I had the privilege to write for this unique encounter is the one you hold in your hands—*The Heart of the Story*. This book mirrors the thirty-one chapters of *The Story*. While *The Story* is 99 percent Scripture, *The Heart of the Story* is my chance to speak into what I have learned about each chapter and its importance in our lives. In these pages, I strive to lay out a powerful observation about the Bible you may have never seen. There are two stories being written at the same time throughout the pages of the Bible—the Upper Story and the Lower Story. The Lower Story is how the story unfolds from the perspective of humanity. The Upper Story is how the story is unfolding from God's perspective. The Bible is filled with hundreds and hundreds of Lower Stories, but it contains just one Upper Story. When you rise above and gaze at all these individual stories, you will see how God used each and every one of them to tell his grand love story of redemption. *The Heart of the Story* is designed to help you see this Upper Story in vivid color.

What God did then he is still doing now. His story isn't finished yet. Your life is unfolding even as you read these words. You see the events of your life—passing the mashed potatoes, picking up the kids, going to work, and so forth—some days better than others, some days worse—from your perspective. But know this: God is writing a story, and you are a character within it. He wants you to see your story from his perspective. He wants you to align your story to his story. The same God who was at work in the pages of the Bible is at work in your life. Seriously!

Looking back on my life from the time I was a little boy until today, I can see the story God has been writing with my life. Things are following the same pattern of most of the characters of the Bible. God takes the least likely candidate and uses them to accomplish his grand purposes. We see this over and over and over again. Why does he do this? So that when something important happens, that person (and everyone else, for that matter) will have to point to a higher power—to God—for an explanation. The goal of our life is to point people to God.

I started the journey in an unchurched home with a Bible I could not understand and a prayer plaque that frightened me almost to death. Now, God has used me in a small way to help others understand the Bible. Isn't that just like God? It is my prayer that the next time you pull your Bible off the shelf, lie on the floor, tuck the palms of your hands under your chin, and begin to read it, you will get it.

It is just like God to use a person like me all these years later to help others understand the grand story of the Bible.

Randy Frazee, San Antonio, Texas
July 2016

TIMELINE OF *THE STORY*

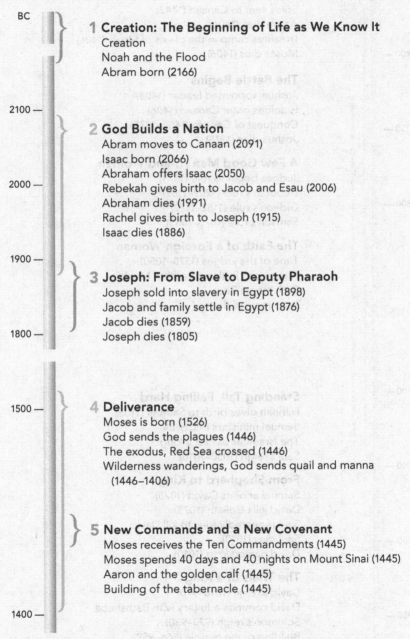

BC

1 Creation: The Beginning of Life as We Know It
Creation
Noah and the Flood
Abram born (2166)

2100 —

2 God Builds a Nation
Abram moves to Canaan (2091)
Isaac born (2066)
Abraham offers Isaac (2050)
Rebekah gives birth to Jacob and Esau (2006)
Abraham dies (1991)
Rachel gives birth to Joseph (1915)
Isaac dies (1886)

2000 —

1900 —

3 Joseph: From Slave to Deputy Pharaoh
Joseph sold into slavery in Egypt (1898)
Jacob and family settle in Egypt (1876)
Jacob dies (1859)
Joseph dies (1805)

1800 —

1500 —

4 Deliverance
Moses is born (1526)
God sends the plagues (1446)
The exodus, Red Sea crossed (1446)
Wilderness wanderings, God sends quail and manna
   (1446–1406)

5 New Commands and a New Covenant
Moses receives the Ten Commandments (1445)
Moses spends 40 days and 40 nights on Mount Sinai (1445)
Aaron and the golden calf (1445)
Building of the tabernacle (1445)

1400 —

Dates are approximate and dependent on the interpretative theories of various scholars.

BC

1450 —

6 Wandering
Wilderness wanderings, God sends quail and manna
(1446–1406)
Spies sent to Canaan (1443)
Aaron dies (1406)
Israelites camp in the plains of Moab (1406)

1400 —
Moses dies (1406)

7 The Battle Begins
Joshua appointed leader (1406)
Israelites enter Canaan (1406)

1350 —
Conquest of Canaan (1406–1375)
Joshua dies (1375)

8 A Few Good Men ... and Women
Judges begin to rule (1375)
Deborah's rule (1209–1169)

1300 —
Gideon's rule (1162–1122)
Samson's rule (1075–1055)

9 The Faith of a Foreign Woman
Time of the judges (1375–1050)
Naomi and Ruth return from Moab
Ruth meets Boaz
Boaz marries Ruth

1100 —

10 Standing Tall, Falling Hard
Hannah gives birth to Samuel (1105)
Samuel ministers under Eli
The Israelites ask for a king

1050 —
Saul's reign (1050–1010)

11 From Shepherd to King
Samuel anoints David (1025)
David kills Goliath (1025)
Saul repeatedly tries to kill David

1000 —
Saul dies (1010)
David named king (1010)

12 The Trials of a King
David's reign (1010–970)
David commits adultery with Bathsheba

950 —
Solomon's reign (970–930)
Building of the temple (966–959)

18

BC
1000—

13 The King Who Had It All
David dies (970)
Solomon's reign (970–930)
Solomon displays great wisdom
Building of the temple (966–959)
Solomon marries foreign wives and betrays God

950—

900—

14 A Kingdom Torn in Two
Division of the kingdom (930)
King Jeroboam I of Israel reigns (930–909)
King Rehoboam of Judah reigns (930–913)
King Ahab of Israel reigns (874–853)
King Jehoshaphat of Judah (872–848)

850—

15 God's Messengers
Elijah's ministry in Israel (875–848)
Elisha's ministry in Israel (c. 848–797)
Amos's ministry in Israel (760–750)
Hosea's ministry in Israel (750–715)

800—

750—

16 The Beginning of the End (of the Kingdom of Israel)
Fall of Israel (722)
Exile of Israel to Assyria (722)
Isaiah's ministry in Judah (740–681)
Hezekiah's reign (715–686)

700—

17 The Kingdoms' Fall
Manasseh's reign (697–642)
Amon's reign (642–640)
Josiah's reign (640–609)
Jeremiah's ministry in Judah (626–585)
Jehoiakim's reign (609–598)
Zedekiah's reign (597–586)
Ezekiel's ministry (593–571)
Fall of Jerusalem (586)

650—

600—

18 Daniel in Exile
Daniel exiled to Babylon (605)
Daniel's ministry (605–536)
Nebuchadnezzar's reign (605–562)
Daniel and the lions' den (539)
Fall of Babylon (539)

550—

500—

BC

550—

19 The Return Home
First return of exiles to Jerusalem (538)
Ministries of Haggai and Zechariah (520–480)
Exiles face opposition in building the temple
Temple restoration completed (516)

500—

20 The Queen of Beauty and Courage
Xerxes' reign in Persia (486–465)
Esther becomes queen of Persia (479)

450—

Esther saves the Jews from Haman's murderous plot
Days of Purim are established

21 Rebuilding the Walls
Second return of exiles to Jerusalem under Ezra (458)

400—

Last group of exiles return to Jerusalem under Nehemiah (445)
Exiles face opposition in rebuilding the wall
Jerusalem's wall rebuilt (445)
Malachi's ministry (c. 440–430)

10 —

5 BC —

22 The Birth of the King
Mary gives birth to Jesus the Messiah (6/5)
Joseph, Mary and Jesus' flight to Egypt (5/4)

5 AD —

Jesus' visit to the temple (AD 7/8)

10 —

23 Jesus' Ministry Begins

15 —

John the Baptist begins ministry (26)
Jesus baptized (26)
Jesus begins ministry (26)
Wedding at Cana (27)

20—

The woman at the well (27)
John the Baptist imprisoned (27/28)

24 No Ordinary Man
Jesus begins ministry (26)

25—

Jesus uses parables to teach (26)
Jesus gives Sermon on the Mount (28)
Jesus sends closest followers out to preach (28)
John the Baptist dies (28/29)

30—

Jesus feeds 5,000 people (29)
Jesus proclaims himself as the bread of life (29)

AD

25—

30—

35—

40—

45—

50—

55—

60—

65—

70—

90—

95—

25 Jesus, the Son of God
Jesus begins ministry (26)
Jesus teaches at the Mount of Olives (29)
Jesus resurrects Lazarus (29)
Jesus drives the money changers from the temple (30)
Judas betrays Jesus (30)

26 The Hour of Darkness
The Lord's Supper (30)
Jesus washes his disciples' feet
Jesus comforts his disciples
Jesus is arrested
Peter denies Jesus
Jesus is crucified

27 The Resurrection
Jesus is buried (30)
Jesus is resurrected
Jesus appears to Mary Magdalene and the disciples

28 New Beginnings
Jesus' ascension (30)
Coming of the Holy Spirit at Pentecost
Paul believed in Jesus as the promised Messiah (35)
James martyred, Peter imprisoned (44)
Paul's first missionary journey (46–48)

29 Paul's Mission
Paul's first missionary journey (46–48)
Jerusalem Council (49–50)
Paul's second missionary journey (50–52)
Paul's third missionary journey (53–57)

30 Paul's Final Days
Paul's first imprisonment in Rome (59–62)
Paul's second imprisonment in Rome and execution (67–68)
John exiled on Patmos (90–95)

31 The End of Time
John becomes a disciple (26)
John exiled on Patmos (90–95)
Revelation written (95)

Introduction

THE ART GALLERY AND THE MURAL

*For we are God's masterpiece. He has created
us anew in Christ Jesus, so we can do the
good things he planned for us long ago.*

EPHESIANS 2:10 NLT

Have you ever struggled to understand how the various stories in the Bible connect to one another? Or wondered how those stories relate to the story of your life today? What if the testimonies in the Bible, the lives of everyone who ever lived, and your own "story still in progress" are all connected—all part of one big divine epic?

Two of the most famous works of art in the world help us understand how the long, sweeping story of the Bible—seemingly a narrative only about God and ancient people with strange names—connects with *your* story. To view the first painting, you must travel to Paris, enter the renowned Louvre Museum, and walk past painting after remarkable painting by some of the greatest artists who have ever lived: Rembrandt, van Gogh, Monet, and, of course, da Vinci.

You climb stairs and move from one cavernous room to another until you finally spot it: *Mona Lisa* by Leonardo da Vinci—the most famous painting in the world, and the most valuable, reportedly worth $700 million. The size of the painting surprises you. Based on legend and popularity, you may have pictured it to stand two stories high, yet the dimensions are a mere 30 inches tall by 21 inches wide—about the size of a built-in microwave oven in your kitchen.

To the untrained eye, the painting appears somewhat ordinary at first. But as you gaze at the subdued colors and subtle shadows, the details, the translucency of the woman's skin and moody atmosphere of the background, it grows on you. For some reason, you are drawn to her gaze, the hint of a smile gleaming there, and you may even agree with those who say that her eyes follow you as you move.

The longer you look, the more you want to know about the woman staring back at you, so you lean closer to the guide who is explaining the painting to a group of English-speaking tourists. Ms. Lisa, you discover, was born on June 15, 1479, during the Italian Renaissance. Her husband was a wealthy Florentine silk merchant who supposedly commissioned this painting for their new home to celebrate the birth of their second son, Andrea.

Good to know, but surely there must be more to her story, you think to yourself. What was happening in her life at the time she posed for this picture? What was that enigmatic smile on her face all about? Was she happy or even amused? Or was she covering up a deep sadness?

After several minutes in front of this famous masterpiece, you stroll through the museum, stopping every now and then to study other paintings that catch your eye: *Supper at Emmaus* by Rembrandt; *Liberty Leading the People* by Eugène Delacroix; *The Virgin and Child with Saint John the Baptist* by Raphael. Each one is completely different, having its own unique tale utterly unrelated to the *Mona Lisa* story. By the time you leave the museum, you will have stood in front of dozens of exquisite paintings, each with a different and distinct story behind its creation.

To view the other famous work of art, you have to catch a flight to Rome, grab a taxi, and use your best Italian to ask the driver to take you to the Vatican. Upon arriving, you walk across a magnificent plaza and enter the Sistine Chapel and look up to see the breathtaking work of Michelangelo. You are amazed to realize that Michelangelo and Leonardo da Vinci painted their respective masterpieces during the same decade. Yet, while da Vinci isolated one person on a single canvas, Michelangelo captured the full sweep of history.

Perhaps the most famous scene from his dramatic mural shows the strong arm of God reaching out to touch the limp hand of Adam. It has been reproduced on countless posters, prints, and postcards. Now you are standing just below the original!

As you shift your gaze to take in the enormity of this stunning mural, you are mesmerized by the scope of it all. With your neck tilted so far back that it's almost painful, you recognize many of the three hundred characters painted on the ceiling of this room: Adam, Eve, Noah, Jacob, David, and many more. While each section of this massive mural depicts an individual story, they are all connected to tell a grand epic. At the highest point of the ceiling, nine scenes out of the book of Genesis unfold, beginning with God's dividing the light from the darkness and continuing on to the disgrace of Noah. Just beneath these scenes are paintings of the twelve prophets who foretold the birth of the Messiah.

Moving down the walls, crescent-shaped areas surround the chapel that depict the ancestors of Jesus, such as Boaz, Jesse, David, and Jesus' earthly father, Joseph. The entire scheme is completed in the four corners of the room with other dramatic biblical stories, such as the heroic slaying of Goliath by young David.

Each scene, each painting, tells its own singular story, stories you may have heard from childhood. Yet the artist united them to display one magnificent work of art: humanity's need for salvation as offered by God through Jesus.

The Louvre and the Sistine Chapel—two different venues for creative expression. Both display astounding art. The Louvre tells thousands of unrelated, separate stories. The Sistine Chapel, on the other hand, tells only one. On the surface, you and I—along with billions of other humans—are individual paintings hanging on the wall of some cosmic gallery, distinct and unrelated to each other. But if you look closer, you will see that your story is intricately woven into the same seamless narrative depicted by Michelangelo on the ceiling of the Sistine Chapel: God's story as recorded in the Bible. One story as seen through many lives.

God wants us to read the Bible as we would view a mural. The individual stories on its pages are connected, all entwining to communicate one overarching epic. Woven tighter than reeds in a waterproof basket, together they intersect within God's one grand story. The purpose of this book is to ponder his divine design and discover our role in it. To stand beneath an all-encompassing Sistine ceiling and see what the entire narrative from beginning to end says about us and to us as individuals.

To better understand this story, we will need to view it with a dual lens. Just as if we were wearing bifocals, through the lower lens we will gaze at individual stories from the Bible in chronological order. Think of these individual pieces as our Lower Story.

The Lower Story reveals the here and now of daily life, the experiences and circumstances we see here on earth. Goals and fears, responsibilities and reactions. In the Lower Story, we make money, pay bills, get sick, get tired, deal with breakups, and work through conflicts. These are the story elements we care about, and as people of faith, we trust God to meet our needs in this Lower Story. And he does! God meets us in each of our Lower Stories and helps us by offering us wisdom and guidance on getting through life with dignity and purpose. He intervenes and applies healing salve to our physical and emotional wounds. Like a tenderhearted Father, God loves to lavish us with his care, stretching out his arms to comfort us when we are in distress and encourage us when we are down.

But he has a higher agenda than our survival and comfort. When we rise above the here and now, look beyond the daily grind, and view each of these stories in the Bible from God's perspective, we see something much bigger. When we look up at the ceiling of the Sistine Chapel, it gives us hints that the Bible isn't filled with a thousand individual stories of God's intervention just to get people through rough times, but rather one grand story of something larger, something eternal.

This is the Upper Story. As we view the Bible through this lens, we see that God has been up to something amazing from the very beginning. He has a vision, a big idea, and it is all good news for us. When we look at the Upper Story of God—his magnificent mural—we discover where we fit in, because this story was created to deliver one singular message: "If you want to live life to the fullest and enjoy it forever, then become part of my masterpiece."

Jesus modeled this message when he said, "If your first concern is to look after yourself, you'll never find yourself. But if you forget yourself and look to me, you'll find both yourself and me."[1] In another story from the Bible, the close followers of Jesus asked him how to pray. He answered that our prayers should begin like this:

> Our Father in heaven,
> hallowed be your name,
> your kingdom come,
> your will be done,
> on earth as it is in heaven.[2]

Jesus was telling them—and us—that God's will, his grand plan for the universe, comes first. Always. The priority of our prayer should be acknowledging that God's will—his master plot, as it were—succeeds above everything else. We should long for God's Upper Story to unfold because what God wants for us will always be the best. Everything he does is for our own good. Therefore, as the grand mural is still being painted on the ceiling of the universe, we long for it to be finished.

Jesus then adds these words for us to whisper to God when we pray:

> Give us today our daily bread.
> And forgive us our debts,
> as we also have forgiven our debtors.
> And lead us not into temptation,
> but deliver us from the evil one.[3]

This is Lower Story stuff. We need to eat. Pay the bills. Avoid the little voice that says, "Go ahead; do what feels good. No one will ever know." These are the groanings of daily life, the raw clay God uses to shape us as vessels on his potter's wheel. So we cry out to God to meet us in our Lower Story, and he does. Not always according to our liking, but he is intimately involved and cares deeply about the details of our daily lives. He empowers us to live the Lower Story from an Upper Story perspective. Everything that happens to us in the Lower Story, whether good or bad, will work out for our good if we align our lives to his superior calling.

Jesus not only taught this; he lived it. In Gethsemane, the night before he was to be brutally tortured and crucified, he prayed to his Father, "My Father, if it is possible, may this cup be taken from me."[4]

Jesus is fully God, but also fully human. In his divine nature, Jesus knew the weight of taking the sins of the world on himself and having his Father turn away from saving him. In his human nature, Jesus knew how painful and humiliating the torture would be. In Jesus' Lower Story, he asked if there was any way that he could be released from the horrific experience of death on the cross. This was his cry from below. But he didn't stop his prayer there. He went on to conclude, "Yet not as I will, but as you will."[5]

Jesus knew the painless path might not be his Father's route, so he aligned his life with this Upper Story plan. If this was the only way for God's grand story to unfold, then Jesus was willing to go through with it. The cross held the only way, and Jesus accepted the journey to the cross and died a humiliating death. Jesus could accept the painful plot twist of the Lower Story because he knew the beautiful theme of redemption in the scope of the Upper Story.

As a pastor, I have the privilege and responsibility to help people understand the Bible. Over the years, it has become clear that the majority of people—even people who have attended church all their lives—view the Bible as an ancient book about what God did in the lives of people "back in Bible days." This may well explain why so many people who carry their Bibles to church seldom read them, or if they do, they come away a little confused: "What does Abimelech have to do with me?" One of my greatest joys, however, is to see that "aha!" moment when they learn that God's Upper Story in the Bible connects with their own Lower Story of going to work, caring for their families, and trying to live decent, honorable lives.

As you read through the pages of this book, you are going to encounter five movements within God's story:

Let me give you a huge clue about God's story. It does not unfold as the kind of linear story line we are accustomed to, where things keep moving forward. God's story is more like a circle:

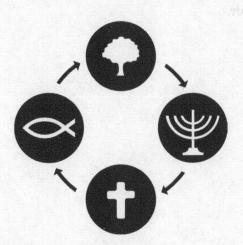

This amazing adventure ends where it began. Read the first two chapters and the last two chapters of the Bible, and you'll see they are almost identical. God's vision in the first garden is ultimately restored, and in the end, a new garden appears. Here is another fascinating discovery: God's story doesn't really have a beginning and an end, but a beginning and a new beginning.

God will use three other stories to lead us back to this new beginning—the story of Israel, the story of Jesus, and the story of the church. It is with the story of the church that we find ourselves as characters in this divine epic. Reading the Bible is not like sitting in a movie passively watching the story line unfold. No, we need to pay careful attention, because we each have a role to play that is very important to the outcome of the story. How exciting is this? God's story is a living, breathing story!

It is my prayer that when you come to the end of this book, not only will you know and better understand God's story; you will have been overwhelmed by his love for you and understand how your portrait fits on the vast canvas that he continues to paint even now.

So, as you turn the page, imagine you have just walked into the Sistine Chapel. You will see many characters in the pages to come, but they all work together to tell the one story of God. Like your own story, each of these stories will be unique, filled with drama, heartache, and joy. Taken individually, not all of them may make sense, but when viewed from God's Upper Story, they fit together perfectly.

Movement One

THE STORY OF THE GARDEN

Genesis 1–11

*I*n the Upper Story, God creates the world of the Lower Story. His vision is to come down and be with us in a beautiful garden. The first two people reject God's vision and are escorted from paradise. Their decision to disobey God introduces sin into the human race and keeps us from community with God. At this moment, God gives a promise and launches a plan to get us back. The rest of the Bible is God's story of how he kept that promise and made it possible for us to enter a loving relationship with him.

CREATION: THE BEGINNING OF LIFE AS WE KNOW IT

In the beginning God created the heavens and the earth.

GENESIS 1:1

Creation	Noah and the Flood	Abram born

BC   2166

WHAT'S HAPPENING IN THE UPPER STORY

The creator God reveals his grand purposes in writing this story: he wants to do life with us in the garden. Given a choice, the first two people created—Adam and Eve—reject this vision and are escorted out of the garden. Sin, a condition that keeps us from God's presence, is born and is passed down to all the offspring of the first couple. This is evidenced in Cain's act against his brother Abel. Left alone, humanity's collective sin nature escalates as we see the sons of God cohabitating with the daughters of humans. But God wants us back. Plan A is to start over with the best human alive—Noah. This plan fails to resolve the problem. Following the flood, Noah and his family demonstrate that the sin condition stepped off the ark with them when Noah's son disgraces him by looking at his nakedness. Humanity's condition and separation from God remain unchanged. Once again, left alone, sin escalates as evidenced in the building of the Tower of Babel. Time for Plan B.

ALIGNING OUR STORY TO GOD'S STORY

We are the offspring of Adam and Eve and therefore are conceived with the same sin virus that keeps us from a relationship with God. We demonstrate this reality in the way we treat one another. We hurt, we hurl, we hoard. We are not fit to be in God's presence and share in his perfect community. God wants us back, but the solution will not be found in us. All attempts fail. We must look for and rely on the solution God is going to provide.

*I*magine the Creator of the universe "out there" somewhere. Compared to the earth that he created, "out there" is so vast as to be immeasurable. For example, the earth is one of the smallest of the eight planets that make up a huge galaxy. But "out there" is bigger than a galaxy. In 1996, astronomers focused the powerful Hubble Space Telescope on a small and utterly black patch of space right next to the Big Dipper constellation. They left the shutter open for ten days.

What did it reveal? Three thousand *more* galaxies, each containing hundreds of billions of stars, planets, moons, comets, and asteroids. In 2004, scientists did it again. This time they focused the scope on a patch of darkness next to the constellation Orion. They left the lens open for eleven days and discovered ten thousand *more* galaxies in addition to the previous three thousand that had appeared the first time. Scientists call this the "Hubble Ultra Deep Field," and it represents the farthest humankind has ever seen into the universe. But even more is "out there," beyond our ability to see.

It turns out there are more than *one hundred billion* galaxies in the universe.

It wasn't always this way. In the beginning God came to a place that was formless, empty, and dark. The Bible tells us "the Spirit of God was hovering" over this place before he went to work creating a space where he could enjoy fellowship with you and me.[1]

Think about this for a moment. If our solar system was reduced in size by a factor of a billion, the earth would be the size of a grape. The sun would be the height of a man. Jupiter would be the size of a grapefruit, and Saturn the size of an orange. Uranus and Neptune would be the size of a lemon. Can you guess how big humans would be? The size of a single atom! We would be completely invisible to the human eye.[2]

Yet to God, we are the crowning masterpiece of his creativity.

The story of the Bible opens with a big bang, but this big bang is not an accident. God is behind or, better, above it all. The Godhead—Father, Son, and Holy Spirit—challenged each other to the mother of all science fair projects. Creation is the result.

Genesis, the first book in the story of God's interactions with and plan for mankind, provides us with an amazing starting point. The first two chapters of this book—familiar to most of us—describe how God created the heavens and the earth, and all that is contained within them. But creation is only the subplot of this book.

The *real* point of Genesis is so amazing it's almost unbelievable: God wants to be with us. The God of the universe has created a place to come down and be with a community of people. He no longer wanted only to enjoy the perfect community he had as the Trinity (Father, Son, Holy Spirit). The Ultimate Author of this grand story wanted to share it with us.

"In the beginning" God came up with a plan to perfectly connect his Upper Story with our Lower Story. He literally desired to bring heaven down to earth—first to create a paradise and then men and women in his own image, and then to come down and do life with us. Perfectly. Just as he had experienced perfect oneness as Father, Son, and Holy Spirit.

The first chapter of Genesis is like a page out of the Trinity Construction work log, except it reads more like poetry. The sequence and pattern are simple, but almost too overwhelming to take in. On days one, two, and three, God paints the places of the earth on the canvas. Then on days four, five, and six, he puts objects in each place to fill this space. Here is how the week breaks down:

Days 1 through 3	Days 4 through 6
1—Light/darkness (verses 3–5)	4—Sun, moon, stars (verses 14–18)
2—Water and sky (verses 6–8)	5—Fish and birds (verses 20–23)
3—Land (verses 9–13)	6—Animals (verses 24–25)

With the end of each day of creation, God steps back, takes a look, and records in his journal, "This is good." But while the creation of the heavens and the earth and the other one hundred billion galaxies is impressive, it is not the point of the story. Mount Everest. The Grand Canyon. The stark beauty of the Sahara, the cascading elegance of Victoria Falls. Combine these and thousands of other jewels of his creative powers, and you're not even close to identifying the core passion of God. Those are just the display cases to highlight his *real* work of art.

The pride and joy of God's handiwork, the point of it all, is revealed in Genesis 1:

> Then God said, "Let us make mankind in our image, in our likeness, so that they may rule over the fish in the sea and the birds in the sky, over the livestock and all the wild animals, and over all the creatures that move along the ground."
>
> So God created mankind in his own image,
>   in the image of God he created them;
>   male and female he created them.[3]

The perfect and beautiful world God created was incomplete without his crowning achievement—people he could enjoy and love and with whom he could communicate. Adam and Eve, you and me, and everyone in between. He had a passion to expand the wonderful community experienced by the triune God. He longed to create the perfect environment where he could hang out with real people, and we know he was proud of this final creative act, because this time he stepped back and declared, "This is very good."

With this final creative act, God's plan was in place. In his Upper Story, he experienced a perfect community. He could have continued to enjoy this total oneness forever, but he wanted to share it. He desired to bring this community to a place where it could be enjoyed by others. So the Lower Story begins with God's grand idea to set the stage and create men and women in his image and then come down and do life with us.

This is the prologue to the entire history of God and mankind. Everything begins with God. The universe, the galaxies, our little planet, men and women—all were God's idea. His vision was to spend eternity in a perfect community enjoying the fellowship of people he created in his own image. He *chose* to bring you and me into the world for his pleasure, and to this day, he yearns to be *with* you. To walk beside you and experience all of life with you, in both the deepest valleys and the highest mountains.

Of course, the big question is: *Why?* Why would God step outside of his perfect Upper Story and come down into our Lower Story?

If you are a parent, you get it.

At some point in your relationship with your spouse, you wanted to share your life with another human being—one whom you would create together. In preparation for that new little human to arrive on earth, you did your best to create a perfect environment—perhaps a special room, a sturdy crib, comfy blankets, a fuzzy teddy bear, and bright pictures on the wall. With each passing month, you grew more excited, knowing that in just a short time, you would be joined by someone so special that you would do anything to protect and nurture this new arrival. Mostly, you just wanted to be *with* that person. Finally it was time. A tiny bundle wrapped in a soft blanket entered your life, and the joy you felt when you first looked into her face was indescribable.

So it is with God, looking into the eyes of Adam and Eve and saying, "This is *very* good." And it *was* good—not just the creation of human life, but his plan for it. Just as parents dream of a bright future for their children, God envisioned not just a good life for us, but also a perfect one. It was almost as if God were saying, "This is going to be great. A beautiful garden. An abundance of food. No disease. No sadness. Even the lions and the lambs get along. And best of all, people to hang out with as they enjoy the pleasures of this world that I have made for them."

Like Adam and Eve's first chapter, your story begins with God looking into your face and saying, "This is good—this is *really* good." Like any proud parent, he wants the absolute best for you. You desire the same thing for yourself, but life doesn't always work the way you want it to. God intended for you to never suffer, but if you haven't yet, you will. He wants you to experience perfect harmony with your neighbors, but you hardly know them. He wants you to live forever in the garden he made for you, but you will one day die—and besides, you don't always feel as if you're living in a garden. God dreamed a perfect life for you, but some days you feel as if you're living in a nightmare.

So what happened?

In the midst of a perfect environment that God had created, something shifted. Keep in mind just how amazingly beautiful this place, *Eden* (Hebrew, meaning "delight"), actually was. Many scholars believe that the location of this garden was a fertile area where the Tigris and the Euphrates Rivers meet in modern-day Iraq. The Garden of Eden was a stunning acreage. Picture a lush, verdant botanical garden. Truly a perfect environment, created as a place where God could be with Adam and Eve, a perfect home where every need was met, a paradise to be shared with God forever.

When God gave Adam and Eve a perfect home in the garden, he also gave them something else: *freedom*. Rather than force them into a relationship with him, he gave them the freedom to choose whether they wanted to be with him or go it alone. To provide a way for them to accept or reject his divine vision, God set two trees in the middle of the garden. One was the tree of life, which bore fruit that when eaten would sustain life forever. The other was the tree of the knowledge of good and evil.

Even before God created Eve, he told Adam, "You can eat of any tree in the garden for food, but not this tree."[4] God told him that if he ate the fruit of that tree, he would die. What Adam didn't understand was that with his death, the plan God had envisioned for life together with him in the garden would die too because their choice would determine mankind's fate from that point on.

We are not told how much time passed between this conversation and Adam and Eve's eventual choice, but we do know that they chose to disobey God's specific command. According to Scripture, a serpent—a creature we later learn represented Satan, the very force of evil—appeared before Eve and told her that if she and Adam ate from the forbidden tree, they would be like God. This made good sense to them, so they ignored God and ate from the tree of the knowledge of good and evil.[5]

The tree lived up to its name. Evil was deposited alongside truth in the DNA of Adam and Eve—and in the DNA of every human being who came after them. At the core of this evil, which is called sin throughout the Bible, is selfishness.[6] Good looks out for others; evil looks out for self. Selfishness is the root of hatred, jealousy, violence, anger, lust, and greed. Adam and Eve are covered in it.

From that time on, the grand vision of God to dwell with us sat in ruins. Because of Adam and Eve's role as the first humans, their disobedience became an inheritance for the rest of us. Authentic love and community require both parties to choose each other, but from the beginning, mankind chose to reject God. Self-preservation became more important than anything else, and we see this played out immediately after this infamous incident.

Knowing they had done something wrong, Adam and Eve went into hiding, but God sought them out and asked if they had eaten the forbidden fruit. Instead of taking responsibility for his actions, Adam blames Eve. Eve, instead of taking responsibility for her actions, blames the snake. This brief scene depicts the now-broken community of God and mankind. Instead of walking with God in the garden, they are hiding. They do not want to be with him because they know the difference between good and bad and recognize themselves as bad. They are filled with shame, guilt, and insecurity. The relationship that God had envisioned is now broken, and God is forced to complete this chapter by banning them from the garden.

> And the LORD God said, "The man has now become like one of us, knowing good and evil. He must not be allowed to reach out his hand and take also from the tree of life and eat, and live forever." So the LORD God banished him from the Garden of Eden to work the ground from which he had been taken. After he drove the man out, he placed on the east side of the Garden of Eden cherubim and a flaming sword flashing back and forth to guard the way to the tree of life.[7]

Now why would God do this? Why would a loving God curse all of mankind with lives where we have to work hard as we live for our seventy years or so, experience disease and disappointment, and then die? How could he let a simple act of disobedience ruin the perfect relationship he desired to have with us? From our Lower Story perspective, this appears to be cruel and unusual punishment. Everybody makes mistakes, right? So these first two humans ate from the wrong tree. Aren't you overreacting, God?

Not at all. The garden—this perfect environment for doing life together with their God—had been corrupted by their rebelliousness. Prior to their disobedience, the garden was a place of joy and innocence. For a brief time it became a place of fear and hiding. To restore the garden to perfection, Adam and Eve had to leave. Selfishness has no place in a perfect community.

Their expulsion from the garden was more than fair punishment for their disobedience; it was a continuation of God's perfect plan to continue to be able to live in communion with the people he created. The garden would remain pure, and God would adjust his plan slightly to give you and me the possibility of living there with him forever. God is as passionate as ever in wanting to live with us and is willing to meet us outside of the garden and walk with us through every experience of life.

After they left the garden, Adam and Eve began their family, only to witness the pain of brother killing brother. The sin nature birthed in Adam and Eve has been transmitted to their offspring. In fact, as the population on earth grew, it became clear that when given a choice, men and women choose evil over good. According to the Bible, God saw that mankind had become so wicked that "every inclination of the thoughts of the human heart was only evil all the time."[8] Theologians call this the doctrine of depravity—a doctrine suggesting that human beings inherently will choose evil over good—that we are unable to "be good" all the time on our own, leaving us unfit for God's community.

Here is the most mind-boggling thought contained in the pages of the Bible: even in our state of blatant selfishness, God wants us back! Plan A is obvious. Start over with the best guy the human race had to offer. His name? Noah. It is one of the few times in the Bible that the most likely candidate is chosen. A tsunami from the sky falls for forty days and forty nights. Noah and his family, along with two of every kind of animal, board the massive ark on dry land in faith and are saved. Not many days after the waters recedes, Noah's son disgraces him by looking at his dad's nakedness in the tent after Noah passed out from drinking too much. Maybe you do, or don't, consider this a federal offense. One thing we know for sure is that the problem has not been resolved. Plan A fails. Even though Noah is a "good" man, he and his children are carriers of the sin virus. The solution to restoring mankind to the kind of relationship it had with God in the garden will *not* be found in us.

You would think that this would be the end of the story—that God would finally give up on us—but he didn't. He couldn't. Remember, we are his crowning achievement, created in his own image and crowned with honor and glory.[9] Regardless of what Adam and Eve, Cain and Noah did—regardless of anything *we* have done—God still wants to be with us. God's Upper Story has not changed. He still wants to do life with us in a perfect, loving community of unified fellowship. From this point in the story until the final chapter of the Bible, we see God's single passion unfolding, one story at a time. He wants to give you and me an opportunity to return to the garden, where we will live with him forever, and he will do whatever it takes to get us back. If the flood was not the way to begin again, then there must be another way. Time for Plan B.

CLUE: When God replaced Adam's and Eve's "Fig Wear" with the skin of animals, it signaled that it would take the blood of another to cover our sin.

Movement Two

THE STORY
OF ISRAEL

Genesis 12–Malachi

God builds a brand-new nation called Israel. Through this nation, he will reveal his presence, power, and plan to get us back. Every story of Israel points to the first coming of Jesus—the One who will provide the way back to God.

Chapter 2

GOD BUILDS
A NATION

*"I will establish my covenant as an everlasting
covenant between me and you and your descendants
after you for the generations to come, to be your God
and the God of your descendants after you."*

GENESIS 17:7

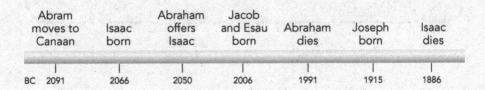

Abram moves to Canaan	Isaac born	Abraham offers Isaac	Jacob and Esau born	Abraham dies	Joseph born	Isaac dies
BC 2091	2066	2050	2006	1991	1915	1886

WHAT'S HAPPENING IN THE UPPER STORY

God's first step in providing the way back into a relationship with him is to build a new nation from scratch. Every story that unfolds will reveal God's character and his plan. God establishes this nation on the most unqualified couple—Abraham and Sarah. They are both old, and Sarah is barren. God chooses this pattern to show all people that he is behind the writing of this grand story of redemption. How will God fulfill his promise that this nation would be great and a blessing to all nations? The plan will unfold in the pages to come, but here is a clue: when God asks Abraham to sacrifice his son Isaac on the altar, it foreshadows what God the Father will do through his Son that will bless all people.

ALIGNING OUR STORY TO GOD'S STORY

God made a promise to Abraham and Sarah. They chose to follow God, even though he didn't tell them where they were going. We are in the same position. God has made us a promise, but we don't know how our story is going to unfold, how we will get there, or how long it's going to take. We would do well to believe God and just start walking like Abraham and Sarah did.

When Adam and Eve disobeyed God, he escorted them out of the perfect place he had intended for all mankind to enjoy forever. But he didn't give up on his vision of doing life with the people he created. When Adam and Eve's descendants chose to ignore God in favor of their own selfish desires, God wiped them off the face of the earth with a great flood, sparing the one righteous man on earth—Noah—and his family. Even after Noah and his son disappointed God with their behavior after the flood, God promised never to repeat this event, even though he knew that people would be inclined toward evil and that the world would never be the perfect place he had envisioned for mankind to enjoy.

Time for a different approach. Plan B.

Remember, God's original vision was to come down and live in perfect fellowship with us. That's what Eden was all about. When the first humans chose to follow their own agendas instead of God's, breaking the direct God-connection for all of us, it would have made sense for God to go back to the perfect community he had in the Trinity. At least this is what you and I might do—"Play by my rules or I'll take my toys and go home. My way or the highway." But God wasn't about to abandon his Upper Story goal of finding a way to do life with us.

He decided the best way to continue his grand vision of community with us was to establish a nation, a special group of related, like-minded people intent on knowing God as much as he wanted to know them. Through this specially chosen nation, God would reveal himself to everyone and offer a plan that would try to draw people back into a relationship with him. All other nations would be able to watch God's special involvement with this new community, be drawn to know him as the one true God, and have the opportunity ultimately to join. This new nation that God would build would be his way of saying, "I want you to return to me so we can experience the very best of life together."

Maybe you've heard the term *nation building* used by the media in referring to efforts in countries such as Iraq and Afghanistan to rebuild after the ravages of war and corrupt leadership. Among other things, the process involves forming a government, establishing an economic system, creating an infrastructure of basic services such as water and sanitation, setting up a legal and justice system, and providing protection from outsiders. Needless to say, it is a daunting endeavor with new challenges and unexpected problems springing up daily.

The way God chose to build his nation involved some of these same kinds of struggles. In fact, just to put his divine fingerprints on the process from day one, God chose to do what we would consider impossible. He chose an old childless couple to be the parents of this new nation he envisioned. Where you or I might have picked out a young newlywed couple brimming with health and the energy to have lots of kids, God makes a dramatic point by picking Abram, age seventy-five, and his wife, Sarai, age sixty-five. The real kicker is that not only were they past their prime parenting years; they couldn't even have children due to Sarai's infertility. The lineage of Abram and Sarai was at its end when they died, at least from a Lower Story perspective. But this is where God intervenes with a dramatic Upper Story plot twist. Here's how it happened.

God invited Abram to leave the comforts of his homeland, Harran (a city close to the border of modern-day Turkey and Syria), and go to a place that he would later show him. He also promised to give Abram and Sarai children and to make them into a great nation. Not only this, but this new nation would also one day be a blessing to all peoples on earth. Abram did not likely comprehend what God was saying to him—"I am going to use you and this new nation as my plan to provide a way for all people to come back into the garden."

The Bible simply says, "So Abram went . . ."[1] In Hebrews 11 we are told, "By faith Abraham, when called to go to a place he would later receive as his inheritance, obeyed and went, even though he did not know where he was going." Now there is one thing I know about most senior citizens, holding in my possession my own AARP card: they don't like change. (How many senior citizens does it take to change a lightbulb? "Change? Who said anything about change?") But this older couple—Abram and Sarai—dug down deep, got way out beyond their comfort zone, and did what God asked them to do.

Even after God had clearly intervened in their lives, their story didn't unfold as smoothly as you might have thought it would. The first order of business was to have those long-awaited kids, right? To start a nation you've got to have people. Using our Lower Story logic, you have to have at least one! Yet ten years went by—and still no children. Abram was now eighty-five, and Sarai seventy-five. It wasn't getting any easier for them.

So Sarai got to thinking, *Maybe God needs our help.* (Have you noticed how this phrase almost always leads to disaster?) To "help" God along, she concocted a plan whereby Abram would sleep with her servant, Hagar—sort of her surrogate, as it were. Abram had no objections, and Hagar delivered a baby boy named Ishmael. God came to them and said, "Uh, folks, thanks for your help, but no thanks. I will make Ishmael's offspring into a great nation, but this is not my plan for you, Abram and Sarai."

OK, so if God doesn't need their help, then what gives? Thirteen more years went by, and still no child. Abram was now ninety-nine, and Sarai eighty-nine. Think about it—this couple was pushing one hundred! How in the world could they have a baby now? It just made no sense.

Even more confusing is that God came to them and changed their names. Abram's name, which ironically means "exalted father" in Hebrew, was changed to Abraham, which means "father of many," and Sarai's name was changed to Sarah, "princess," as a mark of something new to come. Ouch! It would seem cruel to be given new names that only emphasized what they didn't have if this hadn't been God telling them their new names. Again, from our Lower Story point of view, these are impossible names to live up to. But God also told them they would have a son, exactly one year from then. Sarah burst out laughing! If you consider that this old woman was nearly a century old, wouldn't you laugh too? It was either laugh at the absurdity of it or cry from the deep loss of an unfulfilled longing. At last, could they trust God to deliver, literally, what he had promised to them?

Absolutely. Exactly a year later, Sarah had a child named Isaac, meaning "he laughs." When situations look impossible to us, God always gets the last laugh.

But their story wasn't over. When Isaac was around fifteen years old, just about to get his camel's license, God came to Abraham and asked him to do an impossible, completely crazy thing. Remember that Abraham was now 115, Sarah 105—optimal years for raising a teenager.

Here's how the story reads: "God said, 'Take your son, your only son, whom you love—Isaac—and go to the region of Moriah. Sacrifice him there as a burnt offering on a mountain I will show you.'"[2]

It's unfathomable! You don't have to be a parent to appreciate the impossibility of such a request. Talk about not being able to see beyond our Lower Story! But we must never forget how limited, and *limiting*, our viewpoint is. In fact, from a logical, rational, predictable perspective, nothing that God said to Abram made sense. In the limited vision of our Lower Story, God's ideas seldom do. "Don't eat from this tree. Build a big boat when there's no water for miles. Pack up and leave your homeland. Sell all you have and give to the poor. Love your enemies." What may seem confusing and even contradictory to us is all part of God's seamless Upper Story aimed at bringing us back to him.

Abraham obeyed. Maybe he had experienced enough of God's way of doing things that he was used to God doing the impossible. We are told in Hebrews 11 that Abraham figured God would raise Isaac from the dead. Now that's faith!

But as Abraham was bringing the knife down to take the life of his son, an angel told Abraham to stop, that God was providing a ram that was caught by its horns in a nearby thicket. Abraham sacrifices the ram and takes his son home. Talk about a cliff-hanger—whew, that was close! So what's the point? God needed to know that Abraham trusted him completely.

The same is true for us today. This is, in fact, our main part to play in God's story: to trust him even when common sense makes us scratch our head and wonder what in the world is going on. As we will see later, God was also foreshadowing, in the Lower Story of Abraham and Isaac, the big climax of his Upper Story—the sacrifice of his own Son. As a matter of fact, the hill of Moriah just happens to be in the hill of Jerusalem where Jesus will be crucified nearly two thousand years later.[3]

Spared by his father's obedience and God's grace, Isaac grew up and married a gal named Rebekah. Finally God's nation could get under way, right? Not exactly. They were married twenty years before they had their first child! Even though they didn't have to wait until they were one hundred years old, this nation-building thing was still getting off to a slow start. They had twins, Jacob and Esau. After much wrestling with God (literally and figuratively) about his part in the story, Jacob had twelve children, and from these children came the twelve tribes forming the nation of Israel. At last, some nation-building momentum!

God honored his promise to Abraham. Through the covenant he established with Abraham, God began his new approach for living in fellowship with his children through the creation of a nation, Israel. While it may not have played out exactly as Abraham and Sarah expected (or Isaac or Jacob for that matter!), their Lower Stories became major chapters intersecting with a much larger narrative, an unfolding Upper Story they could not comprehend at the time.

We struggle with this same tension today. Our Lower Story is often filled with doubt, confusion, trials, and temptations. There are times when doing things God's way feels foolish, naive, or out of touch with the rest of the world. In the midst of these challenges, we may also sense that God has become distant and silent. Like Sarah, we tend to become impatient and take over when we think God has forgotten his promises to us. We begin to conclude that maybe God needs us to help him get the plan going. While he allows us to participate through our own free will, he never asks us to take into our own hands matters that belong in his.

Yes, we find it hard to blame Abraham and Sarah for improvising. Twenty-five years is a long time to wait for God to do what he said he would do. And believing you will start a family in your tenth decade of life isn't exactly buying into the conventional wisdom of the world. But Abraham and Sarah passed the only test God cares about. The same one he still puts in front of us today.

They trusted him.

And because they did, the story continues.

Chapter

JOSEPH: FROM SLAVE TO DEPUTY PHARAOH

"You meant evil against me, but God meant it for good, to bring it about that many people should be kept alive, as they are today."

GENESIS 50:20 ESV

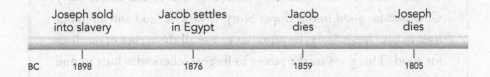

Joseph sold into slavery	Jacob settles in Egypt	Jacob dies	Joseph dies
BC 1898	1876	1859	1805

WHAT'S HAPPENING IN THE UPPER STORY

The nation of Israel is growing just as God promised. But there is a devastating famine ahead that threatens to wipe out the nation. If Israel is gone, then God cannot provide the way for all to come back to him through the offspring of Israel. So he intervenes in the most unique way. God uses the dysfunction, disobedience, sibling rivalry, and jealousy of Joseph's brothers to save Israel from extinction. When Joseph tells his brothers of two dreams in which all the brothers bow down to him, they sell him into slavery, which eventually takes him to Egypt. God orchestrated the affairs of Joseph in such a way that he becomes second-in-command of all Egypt, where, under his leadership and through God's divine insight, he prepares for the famine. Twenty-two years later, Joseph's dreams come true. His brothers leave Canaan and come to Egypt in search of food. When they arrive in Egypt, they bow down before their younger brother. Through this dramatic event, Israel is saved and their story continues.

ALIGNING OUR STORY TO GOD'S STORY

Joseph connected with God's Upper Story plan and realized how God was using him as a character in it. This enabled Joseph to forgive his brothers. He saw that what they meant for evil in the Lower Story God used for good in the Upper Story. If we love God and align our lives to his Upper Story, he promises to use all the scenes of our lives for good. This gives us the power to forgive others who hurt us and the hope to rise above our current circumstances, knowing that this is not how the story ends.

*J*ennifer, a young woman who attended the church where I pastored, had a big dream. She dreamed of going to college to become a nurse. She imagined being able to make a difference in the lives of hurting people who would benefit from her sharp mind, skilled hands, and tender heart. She knew if she realized her dream, it would be miraculous, since her family was not in a position to help her financially. In fact, if she finished, Jennifer would become the first member of her family to graduate from college.

After completing high school and earning good grades, Jennifer took the second step by applying to a college with a strong nursing program. Thanks to her grade point average, she was accepted, but this was only half the battle. Her dream would have to be deferred because she didn't have the money to pay her tuition. But she didn't give up. She got a job and began saving every penny she could from her paycheck, hoping one day to have enough for college. Week by week, dollar by dollar, she saved her money in a special box that she hid in her bedroom.

To save living expenses, Jennifer lived with her single mom and a fourteen-year-old brother. He had some run-ins with the police for stealing things and had begun to get in trouble in school. It was no secret that he experimented with drugs as well. But Jennifer loved her brother and prayed for him every day. When others accused and judged him, she always stuck up for him and encouraged him to stay on the right path. Despite the turmoil in her family, Jennifer pressed on toward her dream, getting one step closer with every paycheck.

One week, she went to deposit her money into her savings box. When she opened it, she discovered that all but twenty dollars was missing. She was crushed by the realization that her own brother had stolen from her to support his drug habit. Her dream now seemed further away than ever, and all because of her brother's betrayal.

Personal betrayal cuts us to the core. You put your trust in someone, and the very person you thought was on your side turns on you. It's bad enough when it happens between friends or colleagues at work, but when a family member betrays you, it's hard to keep going. Just ask Joseph, the biblical character known primarily for his "coat of many colors." Even if you've never read the Bible, you may know his story from the popular Andrew Lloyd Webber musical *Joseph and the Amazing Technicolor Dreamcoat*. However, his dramatic journey contains much more than any popular Broadway musical can convey, because Joseph had a starring role in saving the nation that God was building.

We are introduced to Joseph when he was around seventeen years old—the son of Jacob (renamed Israel as the forefather of God's new nation), the grandson of Isaac, and the great-grandson of Abraham. Joseph became instrumental in God's Upper Story in two significant ways: (1) saving the people of this budding nation from a terrible famine that threatened to extinguish them almost before they got started and (2) revealing God's ability to transform the worst betrayals into sparkling evidences of his own goodness.

Joseph's family certainly didn't function like a divine dynasty out of which God was building his nation. They could barely get along with each other—and we're not talking about just the normal rivalry that often happens among brothers! Joseph's brothers literally left him to die.

You see, of the twelve brothers, Joseph was Dad's favorite. He even sported a special "ornate robe" that his father gave him that left his brothers feeling more than merely resentful. "When his brothers saw that their father loved him more than any of them, they hated him and could not speak a kind word to him."[1]

To make matters worse, Joseph had several dreams that he sensed were from God. Each special dream ended with all of his brothers bowing down to him. In his oblivious innocence, young Joe shared these dreams with his brothers, who in turn soon tried to change them into his worst nightmares.

One day when Daddy Jacob sends Joseph out to see how his brothers are doing in the field, they seize the opportunity to rough him up and throw him into a pit. Over lunch, they make the decision to sell their younger brother to a band of gypsies on their way to Egypt.[2] By doing this, they wouldn't technically be guilty of murder, but Little Brother would be as good as dead.

To deceive their father and cover up their horrific betrayal of Little Brother, they dip Joseph's special robe in animal blood and return home to tell their father that his favorite son had been mauled by a ferocious animal. Needless to say, Jacob is devastated and inconsolable.

Once in Egypt, the gypsy traders sell Joseph as a slave to serve in the house of Potiphar, the captain of the guard for the mighty pharaoh. Having suffered betrayal and abuse at the hands of his own brothers, Joseph then experiences a surprising development. Immediately after the Bible reports on Joseph's new status as a slave, this simple sentence is slipped in: "The LORD was with Joseph so that he prospered."[3]

Even though God allowed his brothers to abuse him, God is now prospering him. With God's help, Joseph quickly rises in status and is put in charge of Potiphar's entire house. This would be like the United States president's chief of staff putting a janitor in charge of the West Wing! Joseph is given responsibility over everything Potiphar owns, and with Joseph in charge, the Egyptian's estate grows and prospers. In a way, Joseph is a part of the family, living on Potiphar's estate, a fact not unnoticed by his master's wife.

Just when everything seems to be back on track, it's time for another bomb—or should I say bombshell—to pop up in his story. Now, Scripture tells us that Joseph was "well-built and handsome,"[4] so you don't have to watch a steamy soap opera to figure out what happens next. While Potiphar is away at work one day, Mrs. Potiphar corners Joseph and doesn't even pretend to be subtle about her intentions: "Come to bed with me!"[5]

Have you ever been in a situation where you were tempted to do something you knew was wrong and you also knew you'd never be caught? Here we have our leading man, Joseph, young and handsome, placed in an unfavorable situation because of the cruelty of others, with an opportunity to enjoy himself. No one could have blamed him for giving in, since slaves who refused to obey orders were severely punished. From a human perspective, Joseph could have easily been on his way to the bedroom, but Joseph chooses to put his trust in God. He tells his seductress, "My master has withheld nothing from me except you, because you are his wife. How then could I do such a wicked thing and sin against God?"[6] Joseph may not have known God's Upper Story or his role in it, yet he chooses to align himself with God rather than with Potiphar's wife.

Is he rewarded for his obedience? I'm afraid not. Potiphar's wife continues to try to get Joseph in bed, and he continues to refuse, until she can't take his rejection anymore. As payback, she tells Potiphar that Joseph tried to rape her. Sent to prison for a crime he didn't commit, the young man finds himself worse off than when he started. Archaeologists and historians report that Egyptian prisons during this era were either large pits dug into the ground or fortress-like facilities where prisoners awaited their punishment, usually torture and death.

This is what awaited Joseph—and for what? Honoring God by refusing to sleep with his master's wife? From a Lower Story perspective, Joseph appeared to be abandoned by God. Where was the Lord whom Joseph refused to sin against? Did he change his mind about Joseph? Not on your life. Divine words from the Upper Story whisper, "But while Joseph was there in the prison, the LORD was with him; he showed him kindness and granted him favor in the eyes of the prison warden."[7]

Once again, God joined Joseph in his suffering. These experiences are giving Joseph training in trusting God so he is prepared to face the grand opportunity ahead. God did not spare Joseph from difficulty—even betrayal. Because of mankind's original choice in the garden, we will always have to face adversity and hardship, but even in our deepest need, God is with us.

Up, down, up, down—like a seesaw! The young Hebrew in the foreign Egyptian land finds himself on the rise again. The Story tells us that he had been in prison for two years when he is summoned by Pharaoh to interpret the leader's recurring dream. Using his prophetic, interpretive gift, Joseph explains to Pharaoh that their land is about to experience seven years of bumper crops, followed by seven years of drought. If they are to survive the famine, they must prepare out of the surplus.

Pharaoh believes him and puts him second-in-command over all of Egypt. Dressed in a fine linen suit and decked out in royal jewelry, Joseph could hardly have imagined his new role when he was curled up at the bottom of a dry well, listening to his brothers decide to sell him. Falsely accused and imprisoned, he could not have believed that he would rise to power and be second only to the king. But at each step of his journey, when it appeared that God had abandoned him, he chose to trust—to believe that God knew what he was doing. From his Lower Story perspective, Joseph's life was an unpredictable series of roller-coaster events over which he had little control. But in the Upper Story, God had a perfect plan and was in complete control.

Under Joseph's leadership, the Egyptians store tons of food over the next seven years. When the famine strikes, just as God had predicted through Joseph, people from other countries begin pouring into Egypt to beg and barter for food. Back in Canaan, Jacob sends his sons (except Benjamin, the youngest) to buy grain, oblivious to the fact that beloved Joe (whom Jacob still believed was dead at the hands of a hungry animal) is in charge of food distribution. When they arrive in Egypt, they bow down before the second-in-command of the whole land—their punk brother, Joseph—although they don't recognize him.

After several emotional encounters, Joseph reveals his identity to his brothers, assures them that he is not angry with them, and makes plans to resettle them in Egypt. Out of his position of power, he gives them the fertile land of Goshen. We're told that when his dad was getting close to Egypt, Joseph went out in his chariot to meet him. "As soon as Joseph appeared before him, he threw his arms around his father and wept for a long time."[8] Wouldn't you have loved to be at that reunion?

How did Joseph do it? How did he have such an amazing attitude through it all? How did he forgive his brothers after what they did to him? The answer is clear. Somewhere in the journey, Joseph caught a glimpse of God's Upper Story plan and his role in it. Listen to what he says to his brothers:

> "I am your brother Joseph, the one you sold into Egypt! And now, do
> not be distressed and do not be angry with yourselves for selling me here,
> because it was to save lives that God sent me ahead of you. For two years
> now there has been famine in the land, and for the next five years there
> will be no plowing and reaping. But God sent me ahead of you to preserve
> for you a remnant on earth and to save your lives by a great deliverance.
> So then, it was not you who sent me here, but God."[9]

Later he said it as succinctly as it can be said: "What you meant for evil, God meant for good."[10] When we capture and align our lives to God's Upper Story, it enables us to process all the junk we might experience in our Lower Story.

Joseph lived to be 110 years old. Yes, he went through a period of twenty-two tough years from the age of seventeen on, but we mustn't forget that he ended up with seventy-one really great ones. How rich it must have been to know he was used by God to save Israel and move the Upper Story plan forward toward completion. His chapter holds particular resonance for us today. The apostle Paul reminds us, "We know that in all things God works for the good of those who love him, who have been called according to his purpose."[11]

No matter how painful some moments seem, your story is not over. If you love God and align your life to his Upper Story purposes, everything in your life, the ups and downs, the mountaintops and the valleys, the highs and the lows, the raises and the rejections, the good and bad are all working together to accomplish good. Be patient. Trust God. Let him mold you during the difficult seasons to equip you for the assignment ahead.

Remember Jennifer, the young woman in our church whose brother stole her college tuition money? I first learned about Jennifer through a handwritten letter, you see. That morning, I spoke about forgiveness. Right in the service, she forgave her brother. Not only that, she put the remaining $20 in the offering plate. She declared through this single act of giving the equivalent of the widow's few cents that she was "all in" and would trust God to accomplish his good plan for her life. Her letter was meant for nothing else than a word of encouragement for me. As a matter of fact, she only signed her first name on the blank sheet of paper that somehow appeared on my desk on Monday morning.

I tried all week to figure out Jennifer's identity and get her contact information, but I was unsuccessful. All I had to go on was that she was a young woman named Jennifer who attended our church. No return address. Nothing. She obviously had no expectation that I would contact her. Her only motive was to share how one of my sermons had encouraged her to trust God completely, no matter the circumstances of her life.

The next Sunday at our early service, I read the letter to the congregation without revealing any names. Afterward a family came to the front of the church to see me. With tears in their eyes, they asked if they could talk to the woman in the letter. This family, along with two others, wanted to pay Jennifer's college tuition. Not just the first year, but all four!

When I read the letter in the second service, I added, "If the person who wrote this letter is here today, please come to see me." A young woman timidly approached me immediately after the service. It was Jennifer. When I told her about the families' generous offer, she wept uncontrollably—tears of disbelief and joy.

Jennifer finished college and nursing school in the top tier of her class. Today she is an oncology nurse, a loving wife, and a devoted mom. Her dream has come true, and she blesses many people with her gifts. Her Lower Story was all about betrayal, anger, and disappointment, but when she came to a place where she could trust God in spite of her circumstances, she discovered that he is indeed trustworthy and has not forgotten or abandoned her.

God's Upper Story weaves a tale of relentless pursuit. He doesn't just desire to turn whatever was intended for evil to good in your life. He wants *you*. To be with you. To have fellowship with you. He refused to allow a famine to destroy the nation he was building, just as he refused to let a brother's selfishness destroy Jennifer's dream.

We have no idea what betrayals and injustices await us today or may confront us tomorrow. All we know for sure is that in our lifetimes, we will have many occasions to wonder if God has forgotten us. Life is filled with disappointment, but when it hits, we must rise above it in the strength of God's goodness, hearing him whisper that he loves us and will never abandon us, no matter what. If we look beyond what seems to define our Lower Stories and trust that God is writing something much bigger, then we can trust that the ending will be much more than "happily ever after."

It will be like coming home.

Chapter

DELIVERANCE

*"Commemorate this day, the day you came out of
Egypt, out of the land of slavery, because the LORD
brought you out of it with a mighty hand."*

EXODUS 13:3

Moses born	The plagues	The exodus, Red Sea crossed	Wilderness wanderings
BC 1526	1446	1446	1446–1406

WHAT'S HAPPENING IN THE UPPER STORY

God told Abraham that the land he promised would not be ready for another six hundred years. They would need a place to stay where they could grow, prosper, and maintain their purity as a nation from other religious influences. God had told Abraham that for four hundred years, that place would be Egypt. In the story of Joseph, we see how the children of Israel got to Egypt. For the majority of those four hundred years, Israel was free and grew great in numbers. Egyptians considered shepherding an abomination, so they refused to marry the Israelites, keeping their lineage pure. God had also warned Abraham that for a period of time, the Egyptians would enslave and mistreat them, but God would deliver them. All this came to pass just as God said. God used the fear and evil of the Egyptians in the Lower Story to reveal his name, power, and Upper Story plan to redeem all people through the Passover Lamb.

ALIGNING OUR STORY TO GOD'S STORY

Moses was saved from Pharaoh's edict to kill every son born to a Hebrew family. God adds a twist in the Lower Story and uses Moses to issue an edict for the death of the firstborn sons of Egypt. Often when God saves us from tragedy, it is because he has a special assignment for us to fulfill. Live with the sense that God has a special plan for your life, because he does. You may feel unqualified for the assignment, but say yes to God. He will give you the strength and power to see it through.

As God's plan to build the nation of Israel continued to unfold, he consistently chose the unlikeliest of people to play leading roles, just as we saw in the story of Joseph. However, few people, at first glance, are as unlikely a leader as our next character in the story.

After Joseph died, things gradually got worse for his descendants, the Israelites, the people God was using to build his nation. Under Joseph's leadership, they had settled into Egypt and began to grow in numbers. But after he died, they had no leader to mediate between them and the Egyptians. Their numbers had grown so large that the new pharaoh[1] began to fear that they might take over the land. To keep the power with himself and the native people, Pharaoh enslaved the Hebrews, putting cruel slave masters over them who forced them to work from sunup until sundown, building such massive structures as the now-famous pyramids.

What happened to God's great Upper Story plan for a new nation? From a Lower Story perspective, it appeared that Pharaoh controlled the world of the Israelites. Did this development take God by surprise? Not at all. In fact, more than five hundred years earlier, God told Abraham this would happen: "Know for certain that for four hundred years your descendants will be strangers in a country not their own and that they will be enslaved and mistreated there."[2]

As we've already seen, a lot of the real plot of God's story unfolds in ways that seem hidden (or even contrary) to our limited viewpoint and information. What seems like a long time to us is only a moment to our infinite, timeless Creator. And the time had finally come for him to deliver the Israelites and restore them to the path fulfilling his promise. It was time once again to reveal his name, his power, and his plan. He just needed the right point person.

He finds his man, Moses, out in the wilderness, minding his own business as he tends his father-in-law's sheep—good Lower Story living. There in the wilderness, Moses is visited by God, represented by a burning bush, with an Upper Story proposal for him. God wants Moses to return to the city and stand in front of the mighty pharaoh and give a speech that essentially commands Pharaoh to let the Hebrew people go.

Moses, feeling overwhelmed and unqualified, musters up the courage to respectfully decline: "Pardon your servant, Lord. I have never been eloquent, neither in the past nor since you have spoken to your servant. I am slow of speech and tongue . . . Pardon your servant, Lord. Please send someone else."[3]

Now before we get too hard on our buddy Moses, let's consider his situation:

- **Fact #1:** People fear public speaking more than dying. It is terrifying for most people to stand in front of a group of people and speak, let alone address the pharaoh of Egypt, who thinks he is a god and doesn't particularly like you.
- **Fact #2:** To my knowledge, Toastmasters doesn't have a chapter in the middle of the Midian Desert. Sheep aren't the most responsive audience when you're trying to hone your verbal skills.
- **Fact #3:** Moses had some Hebrew skeletons in his Egyptian closet that he knew would not help the cause. He had burned some bridges and consequently would not be the best candidate to deliver a hard message.

You may recall that Moses had a rather unusual cross-cultural childhood. As a baby, he was spared Pharaoh's death edict against all males born into a Hebrew family, thanks to the wise stealth and crafty ingenuity of his mom. Rather than watch him be killed, she places little Moses in a papyrus basket and launches him into the shallow part of the Nile where Pharaoh's daughter often bathed. Sure enough, the Egyptian princess discovers the tiny boy, and her maternal instinct kicks in. She adopts him and raises him as her own, a royal prince in her mighty father's palace. Not a bad series of "lucky breaks," wouldn't you say?

However, as Moses reaches adulthood, his privileged treatment ends. One day he sees an Egyptian soldier abusing a Hebrew slave. Fueled by his outrage, Moses kills the Egyptian and then flees to the countryside for his life. He knows that if he steps foot back in the royal city limits, he will be arrested and killed before the first word of the Lord comes out of his mouth.

So our guy Moses stammers and can't talk well. Has no leadership experience or communication skills. And he is wanted for murder charges in the very place he'll have to go deliver God's message! I don't know about you, but these seem like three pretty good reasons Moses is not a good candidate to be the new secretary of state for the nation of Israel. It's something like the United States president choosing a migrant worker who picks berries in California to lead a special delegation charged with securing a peaceful release for millions of Americans enslaved by a foreign dictator. Not something we're likely to see, right?

God sees it differently.

In Lower Story logic, Moses isn't qualified for such an important task. But in Upper Story understanding, God sees Moses' weaknesses as providing the best conduit for God's strength. There is no way for Moses to take any of the credit or for those around him to think his dynamic personality and speaking skills could get the job done. No, the only possible way is through God's divine power and miraculous provision.

As with our lives, the best thing we can do, even when we don't feel equipped or adequate, is to say yes to God. So despite his own objections, "Moses took his wife and sons, put them on a donkey and started back to Egypt."[4] Back to the land where he had a bounty on his head. Back to the land where his people toiled as slaves for Pharaoh. Not on a chariot accompanied by an army, but on a donkey. Not as a celebrated ruler who had fought and won battles, not as a skilled orator and experienced teacher, but as a humble husband and father, as a lowly shepherd.

From our Lower Story perspective, it makes absolutely no sense to choose someone like Moses and entrust him with such an important mission. But our perspective is limited. We seldom see things the way God sees them:

> "For my thoughts are not your thoughts,
>   neither are your ways my ways . . .
> As the heavens are higher than the earth,
>   so are my ways higher than your ways
>   and my thoughts than your thoughts.

As the rain and the snow
   come down from heaven,
and do not return to it
   without watering the earth
and making it bud and flourish,
   so that it yields seed for the sower and bread for the eater,
so is my word that goes out from my mouth:
   It will not return to me empty,
but will accomplish what I desire
   and achieve the purpose for which I sent it."[5]

Moses was one of the unlikeliest people God could ever choose, but as we will see, he is by no means the last. Our job qualifications are a little different from God's. While we may focus on externals—education, work experience, wealth, and charm—God looks on the inside. The only qualification he looks for in order to accomplish great things through his people is a willing and obedient heart. No matter how many or what kind of obstacles loom in your way, if your heart is humble, open, and willing, God promises you exactly what he promised Moses: "I will be with you."[6] A powerful promise, especially when you are facing the showdown of a lifetime.

Eye to eye with Pharaoh, Moses reveals God's message to the Egyptian leader and backs it up with impressive evidence. How does God reinforce his message through Moses in a way that no one can doubt or ignore? Simple: ten very ugly plagues. As the plagues unfold one at a time, Pharaoh becomes so overwhelmed by their impact that he agrees to let the Hebrew people go. But he keeps changing his mind. In fact, the Bible tells us that God hardened Pharaoh's heart just so he would change his mind. God wanted to display his power in an overwhelming and undeniable way. He also wanted to foreshadow more of his ultimate plan to restore fellowship with his children. The apostle Paul later summed it up nicely in his letter to the Romans: "For Scripture says to Pharaoh: 'I raised you up for this very purpose, that I might display my power in you and that my name might be proclaimed in all the earth.' Therefore God has mercy on whom he wants to have mercy, and he hardens whom he wants to harden."[7] Even people who do not follow God are used by God to accomplish his Upper Story plan—even though they don't often know it.

The tenth plague is both devastating and revealing. God tells Moses that at midnight, his angel will sweep through the entire kingdom of Egypt and take the life of every firstborn male. However, this angel of death will "pass over" any home that has the blood of an unblemished lamb brushed across the doorframe.

So on that fateful night, all the firstborn sons of Egypt, including Pharaoh's son, die as the appointed angel makes his rounds. However, the Hebrew sons are saved because Moses has instructed God's people to apply the blood of a lamb to their doorposts. Jews today still celebrate Passover. And as followers of Jesus Christ, we get a sneak peek at the way in which God will fulfill the need for a perfect, unblemished Lamb in order to provide the blood of salvation over the doorposts of our lives. But I'm getting ahead of our Story.

Ironically, the edict that Pharaoh unleashed on the Hebrew baby boys at the beginning of the story is reversed and unleashed on his people at the end of the story. In the wake of such intense loss, Pharaoh says, "Go!" God allowed his heart to soften just long enough for the Israelites to begin their trek toward the Red Sea. Many scholars estimate that somewhere between one and three million Hebrew people marched victoriously out of Egypt that day. Can you imagine the depth of their joy to be free? Or their gratitude to God for doing what appeared to be the impossible?

Maybe you have a pharaoh in your life right now—it may be a person, a circumstance, or a conflicted situation. It may feel like this personal pharaoh is completely in charge of your life, enslaving you to its harsh demands. *Do not lose heart.* Don't give up, no matter how the odds seem to be stacked against you. Just remember, in the Lower Story it may appear as though Pharaoh is in control, but your plight has not surprised God as he reveals and enacts his Upper Story in your life. He is completely in charge, fully in control.

Mike Sharrow moved to San Antonio, Texas, to be closer to his wife's family. After relocating, he connected with a family that had a family member in the military hospital at Lackland Air Force Base. Mike began visiting the hospital quite frequently to minister to his friend. Although Mike was in business, he was a licensed and trained minister, so the base offered him a chaplain pass to make it easier to get on and off the premises.

The first day after he received the chaplain pass, his mom called from Alaska to see how he was doing. He immediately told her about the chaplain's pass to Lackland. The line went silent. After a long pause, his mom said, "How could you?" and then hung up.

A few days later, Mike was able to reach his mother to see why she had reacted so negatively to his comment. An emotional hand grenade went off. Tearfully she said, "First you move to San Antonio and then you're at Lackland and then you're visiting people in the hospital. How could you do that to me?"

Mike was unaware of the backstory that his mom was now letting him in on after so many years. She said, "I was in the Air Force and did my basic training at Lackland. That was where I was raped and got pregnant. I was in that hospital. Everyone encouraged me to abort the baby. And while I didn't know what was going to happen, I did know that God valued life—and Mike . . . you're that baby. I swore the one place I'd never go back to was San Antonio—particularly Lackland Air Force Base."

Mike said, "Mom, because you chose life that day, I'm here. Now God has brought me back to the very city and the place where this evil thing occurred so I could do this good work."

What God did for Moses and Mike, he is doing for you as well. He is working out his plan for your life. If you love God and align your life to his Upper Story plan, God promises that everything is going to work out for the good. One way or another, you will cross the Red Sea as well. God always keeps his promises. He always provides a way through obstacles that seem insurmountable to us. It may seem a bit scary, but always say yes to God and you will see for yourself.

You can count on him!

Chapter

NEW COMMANDS AND A NEW COVENANT

"Then have them make a sanctuary for me, and I will dwell among them. Make this tabernacle and all its furnishings exactly like the pattern I will show you."

EXODUS 25:8–9

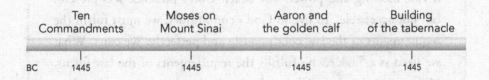

Ten Commandments	Moses on Mount Sinai	Aaron and the golden calf	Building of the tabernacle
BC 1445	1445	1445	1445

WHAT'S HAPPENING IN THE UPPER STORY

It's time for Israel to move into the promised land of Canaan, a garden-like land flowing with milk and honey. And for the first time since Eden, God comes down and lives among his people. In preparation, he instructs the Israelites to build a tent called the tabernacle. A thick curtain separates his dwelling place, the Most Holy Place, from the rest of the tabernacle. While the people do not have direct access to God because their sins have not been atoned for, his presence and power are nonetheless at the center of their camp to guide them. Rules for ongoing animal and grain offerings are established to symbolically represent the payment for their sins, a cost that will ultimately be paid by Christ's death on the cross. The innocent dying for the guilty will become a familiar theme to God's people. Israel is given commandments to guide them on how to love God and their neighbors in a manner appropriate for God's community. Their inability to keep these commandments reminds them of their need for a Savior. Everything points to the first coming of the Messiah.

ALIGNING OUR STORY TO GOD'S STORY

Having the presence of God at the center of our lives is the secret to divine blessing and power. For Israel, God's presence was present, but not accessible. To live in God's community, we must fulfill the requirements of the law continuously and perfectly. We can't. What we need is a Savior who fulfills the requirements of the law for us. His name is Jesus. In Christ, the barrier has been removed and we now have direct access to God. When we seek God for guidance and follow his leading, it leads to blessing.

ou will recall that God's Upper Story started in a garden. A perfect environment where he could walk and talk and enjoy a relationship with the people he created. He made everything available to them except one thing, and they chose this one thing that was forbidden, forever banishing themselves—and us—from the garden.

So God took another approach to doing life with his people. He would create a nation and reveal himself among them. After preserving his people during a famine and rescuing them from slavery in a foreign land, God was ready to lead his people—through Moses—into another garden. Canaan. The promised land. A land gardenlike, flowing with milk and honey. This would be the place where he could build a nation out of which he would reveal his presence, his power, and his plan for all people to come back into a relationship with him.

As the Israelites wandered in the wilderness, God was getting ready to put them into this new garden and meet with them again. This was huge! Although God had continued to interact with his people after he expelled Adam and Eve from the garden, it was always from a distance. This time, however, he so wanted his people to get it right that he decided to come down personally and dwell with them again. His desire for intimate relationship with us is the heartbeat of the Upper Story: God desperately wants to experience life with us. God tells Moses that three things had to be worked out in order for God to dwell among the Israelites.

First, God insisted that his people must live by a set of guidelines. He envisioned a community in which people are treated with full respect and dignity, but he had seen how poorly people on earth treated each other. So he developed clearly stated rules—we know them as the Ten Commandments—for the sole purpose of creating a community where everyone got along with each other and with God.

As a general rule, we don't like rules! Or more precisely, we think rules are necessary for everyone else but ourselves. Rules get in our way, and we don't like anyone forcing us to stay within any boundaries other than the ones we set.

Whenever I think about following rules, I'm reminded of the five-year-old girl who was having one of those "can't stay out of trouble" days. Her mother had reprimanded her several times for being disobedient and finally lost her patience with her daughter's willful behavior and sent the child to a chair for a time-out. The little girl went to the chair and sat down. After a few minutes she called to her mother, "Mommy, I'm sitting down on the outside, but I'm standing up on the inside!" It is in our human nature to stand up on the inside and to defy authority when other people tell us what to do.

Of course, we like rules when they are enforced on someone else's behavior toward us. I want the police to catch people who speed by my front yard where my kids are playing, but when *I* drive a little over the speed limit, I am the exception. After all, I'm in complete control of my car and can stop on a dime if I need to. "So no need to write that ticket, Officer." This is the Lower Story as the Israelites lived it: *I can do whatever I want whenever I want. It's all those other people who need rules.* The only problem is that living by their own rules consistently got the Israelites into trouble. In God's Upper Story, he was telling them, "I want to be with you, but first you have to learn how to treat each other, which is why I'm giving you these rules." But when everyone thinks the rules apply to others and not themselves, then no one follows them.

It is no wonder, then, that many people take exception to God giving us the Ten Commandments. They see him as a distant judge sentencing lawbreakers or a mean old principal who lives only to catch truant students. They see God hurling all these rules and regulations at people and then watching them and eventually catching them only so he can punish them—and even enjoying the entire process. A sadistic, cosmic killjoy.

Such a distorted view couldn't be further from the truth! The commandments are a gift from a God who knew that without these guidelines to show his children how to live, they would continue to make life miserable for themselves and others because they just would never figure out how to get along. Since God was trying to build a nation based on the same type of perfect community he enjoyed within the Trinity, he knew that before he could come down and join his people, they had to learn how to live the same way. He intended the Ten Commandments to be indispensable tools for improving every aspect of our lives.

The first four commandments apply to our vertical relationship—how we relate to God. All four ask us to treat God with ultimate respect. We are to worship only him; we are not to create our own gods by making images or idols; we are not to misuse or trivialize the name of God; we are to honor him by observing a day of rest, just as he rested from creating the world and everything in it. In these first four life-rules, God invites his followers to be "all in." He wants their hearts, minds, and bodies focused exclusively on their relationship with him—there can be no "God plus someone or something else." For God's perfect community to work, it has to start with this level of respect.

The rest of the commandments guide us in our horizontal relationships—how we treat each other. After telling us to honor our parents, God prohibits us from murder, adultery, stealing, lying, and coveting what doesn't belong to us. When it comes to living harmoniously with others, God instructs, "Don't do anything that would hurt or harm anyone. This is the way I planned it in the first place. This is the kind of community I envisioned—one that has your best interests at heart."

Later in God's story, Jesus summarizes these ten guidelines for living: "Love the Lord your God with all your heart and with all your soul and with all your mind . . . Love your neighbor as yourself."[1] Love God. Love each other. Don't hurt anyone. Don't take advantage of anyone. Obey these commandments, and we will all get along.

Viewed through our Lower Story lenses, these commandments are God's way to catch us in the act of doing something wrong just so he can punish us, but from an Upper Story perspective, they set the boundaries for the only kind of community God desires for his special nation—one in which everyone is treated with respect. More important, this is the only kind of community where God can return and live with us.

He knows better than we do what's best for us.

Second, God needed a place to stay. After giving the Israelites the rules for how to treat him and each other as part of his special nation, God pointed to a second condition to be met so he could come and dwell among them. He needed a place to stay: "Then have them make a sanctuary for me, and I will dwell among them. Make this tabernacle and all its furnishings exactly like the pattern I will show you."[2] The word *tabernacle* means "tent" or "place of dwelling," and it is the place where God would meet his people.

Exactly one year after Pharaoh released the Israelites to leave Egypt, this large portable tent with ornate furnishings was erected in the wilderness according to the detailed instructions God gave the people. Built out of wood (not just any wood, but *acacia* wood), the chest was to be covered with gold inside and out. Using not just "finely twisted linen," but linen made with blue, purple, and scarlet yarn, the tabernacle would then be covered with a protective layer of ram skins dyed red.[3]

From the Lower Story perspective, the Israelites might have thought such an elaborate blueprint a bit excessive. Or they might have thought Moses was pulling a fast one on them because they were required to fund this project with their personal gold and silver and any other valuables they had lying around. Put yourself in their shoes. In the wilderness, just one year out of slavery. Your leader claims to speak for God and tells you to give him all your valuables because God wants to build a church in the middle of nowhere. It may seem tough to swallow.

However, the tabernacle represented much more than just a fancy place to worship. Through its construction, God wasn't just building a sanctuary; he was building a nation. He needed to know if the Israelites would obey him completely, and he needed a place to stay that reflected his power and majesty. Earlier in their wanderings, the Israelites' dedication to God seemed quite shaky. Since they felt abandoned by God because they couldn't see him, and since Moses was nowhere to be found—up on some mountain talking to this mysterious God about his special rules—they decided they needed something more concrete in which to place their trust. They demanded that Aaron, the brother and helper of Moses, build them a golden calf—a visible "god" they could worship. God was outraged, and then some! After all he had done for them—miracle after miracle, gift after gift—this was how they responded. Had it not been for Moses' pleading with God, the Israelites might have been destroyed right then and there. But like the loving Father he is, God kept his commitment. With the tabernacle, he would have a place to dwell among the Israelites, and they would know he was with them because, according to

Scripture, when he was present, a cloud covered the tent and "the glory of the LORD filled the tabernacle."[4]

Third, God required a way to restore fellowship between a holy God and a sinful people. The new nation God was building received guidelines for living with him in community and for preparing the place where God would dwell with them. One more thing had to happen before God could dwell with his children: the gap between his perfect holiness and their flawed selfishness had to be overcome.

He desperately wanted to reconnect with the people he had created, but their sin stood in the way. You see, God and sin cannot peacefully coexist. He is a pure and holy God, so much so that when he was present in the tabernacle, no one could enter where he was staying because all humans are corrupted by sin. Even the priests, who were ceremonially washed and then anointed and covered with consecrated robes, could not enter the special place where God resided in the tabernacle because, despite their priestly assignments, they too were infected with sin and therefore prohibited from seeing God face-to-face.

God devised a way for his people to pay for or atone for their sins: animal sacrifices. Many consider the book of Leviticus to be one of the most boring books in the Bible, and from a Lower Story perspective, it's not exactly a page-turner. But it is one of the most important books in the Bible because it lays out what has to happen before sinful mankind can be reconciled to God. Like the tabernacle itself, all the elaborate instructions on how to sacrifice animals without blemish so their blood can atone for the Israelites' sins have a greater significance. God is essentially telling his children, "The one thing separating us is your sin. I want to do life with you, but the only thing that will cover your sin is the blood of the purest and most valuable animals you have."

In our current age, the idea of animal sacrifices seems primitive and cruel. But for the Israelites, tied directly to hunting for their survival, it was their only way to bridge the gap between themselves and God, and the symbolism was humbling and meaningful. A pure, innocent animal of great value in essence took their punishment. Instead of the sinful person being struck down for his sins, the lamb accepted the punishment so that the person could live and enjoy a relationship with God Almighty. Unfair? That's exactly the point God was making: "Yes, it is totally unfair that an innocent creature gets what you deserve. But it's the only way because you cannot get rid of your sin by yourself. But because I want so much to be with you, I am providing a way for you to pay for your sins."

What began in a garden—God's vision for perfect community with his creation—now found itself played out in a wilderness with a nation that wanted a relationship with God but didn't know how to go about being that community. From a Lower Story perspective, it seems ritualistic and ponderous—all the commandments, the tabernacle, the animal sacrifices. Why should we have to jump through all these hoops just for God to be willing to come back down to earth and live with us?

In the Upper Story, God gives a hint of what is to come in his vision for a perfect community where he can finally be with his children forever. Based on the fact that sin has permanently infected the people he created, God made a way. No matter how hard we try to be "good," we can never be good enough on our own. So he gave the Israelites a way to atone for their sins—the blood of a perfect lamb, innocent of any wrongdoing. If you peek ahead in the story to the book of Hebrews, you will see that these animal sacrifices were only temporary. They would offer a way for the Israelites to deal with their sin until another Lamb was sacrificed—one who would actually defeat sin and death and prepare a final community where God's grand vision for his people will be fully realized.

With a new set of practical guidelines to help them become the nation God had promised Abraham, and a way to atone for their sins when they broke God's rules, all the Israelites had to do was follow God, who now lived with them. During the day, he appeared as a cloud, and at night, a blazing fire.

What could be easier, right?

Chapter 6

WANDERING

Then Moses entreated the LORD his God, and said,
"O Lord, why does Your anger burn against Your
people whom You have brought out from the land
of Egypt with great power and with a mighty hand?"

EXODUS 32:11 NASB

Wilderness wanderings	Spies sent to Canaan	Aaron dies	Israelites in plains of Moab	Moses dies
BC 1446–1406	1443	1406	1406	1406

WHAT'S HAPPENING IN THE UPPER STORY

From God's point of view, the sin of the Amorites (Canaan's current residents) has reached its full measure. Everything is on the track with the timetable God laid out for Abraham more than six hundred years ago. Israel can conquer the land, not because they have the strength to overtake the residents, but because God does and because it is a key part of his Upper Story plan. Once they take the land permanently, the surrounding nations will be able to see how Israel's God keeps his promises and how he has a plan to provide a solution to include even them. Israel, overwhelmed by the task ahead of them, refuses to take the land. God sends them back into the wilderness until the unbelieving generation dies. Once the forty years has passed, God will give the next generation another opportunity to enter.

ALIGNING OUR STORY TO GOD'S STORY

Israel's spies brought back clusters of plump grapes to prove the land of Canaan was a beautiful and lush garden. They also brought back a description of the giants living in the land and discouraged the people from moving forward. Whenever God lays out his will for our lives, we need to charge ahead, believing that God is bigger than the giants we face. If we refuse, we miss an opportunity to play our role in God's Upper Story.

There's nothing like taking a road trip for vacation. The destination can be the Grand Canyon or Yellowstone National Park; maybe the beaches of Destin, Florida; or even a fall foliage tour through the Northeast. While it is a great feeling to arrive at your destination, part of what makes a road trip so special is the process of getting there. Well, this is true in theory at least.

When I was a kid, our family traveled in a wood-paneled station wagon (really!). All six of us crammed into the car that was loaded down with a week's worth of stuff. There were no TVs, video games, or iPods to occupy our time. We would wiggle and fidget, nudge and tickle each other, get into each other's space, laugh and argue, all with a constant refrain every few minutes to our dad behind the wheel: "Are we there yet?"

After about the tenth time, my mom or dad would first reach an arm to the backseat and give us a little swat on the leg. After about a dozen more times, my dad would blow a gasket and say, "If you don't stop asking, I am going to turn this car around and head back home." He never did, but we always knew he was capable of it.

The second major problem with road trips occurs when the driver makes a wrong turn that takes you way out of your way. This happened to Rozanne and me years ago. We were traveling back to Fort Worth from San Antonio. I turned the wheel over to Rozanne so I could take a nap. I told her to simply stay on this road until we arrived in Fort Worth. How hard could that be? Several hours later, she woke me up, saying, "Are we supposed to be in Houston?" Now, I'm usually a pretty easygoing guy, but this was beyond my capacity to fathom. How could she have made such a huge mistake? This wrong turn cost us *five hours*. I resumed control of the wheel and started heading back, only to discover we had made the wrong turn when I was driving. I hate when that happens!

What would you do if you were in the middle of the wilderness with a bunch of people, and the guy who is leading the way keeps repeating a promise he says was handed down from his ancestors for the past 650 years? When you ask him where you're going and when you'll get there, he tells you to just be patient because we're going to end up at a really neat place. Talk about not having GPS back then!

Moses was the driver; the children of Israel were in the backseat. Unlike my dad, who had four kids to manage, Moses had at least a million—some scholars estimate the nation of Israel had grown to approximately three million people. It must have been like herding cats. He was leading them across the barren Sinai Peninsula to the fertile land of Canaan, also called the promised land, which the Bible describes as flowing with milk and honey. I live in San Antonio, along with more than a million other people. The city of Dallas lies about 275 miles north. Imagine what it would be like if I tried leading the entire population of San Antonio—on foot—to Dallas, which is about the distance from where the Israelites were in the wilderness to Canaan. I'm doing my best to lead these million people to Dallas, only to occasionally take a wrong turn, adding more miles to our dusty road trip. And all we had to eat was bologna sandwiches. Bologna for breakfast, bologna for lunch, and bologna for supper. And then there was that humongous tent we had to take down and set up all the time.

And I thought my parents had their hands full with four kids in the backseat! Poor Moses had an impossible job.

At first there must have been the same sense of expectancy we've all experienced when we're about to embark on a trip. Keep in mind, they had camped in the same place in the wilderness for more than a year and were probably a little stir-crazy, but this changed as Moses prepared to lead them to a new location. To bring some order to such a large group of people, God instructed him to divide them into twelve tribes, each tribe named after the twelve sons of Jacob (who had been renamed Israel, you will recall) and visually represented with giant banners. He also told Moses to have two trumpets made of hammered silver that would be used to signal the time to pack up and leave. So after all their waiting, imagine their excitement when, "on the twentieth day of the second month of the second year,"[1] the trumpet blast echoed throughout all twelve campgrounds and a divine cloud rose from the tabernacle for them to follow. (They had something better to follow—a divine GPS, "God's Positioning Satellite.")

Finally, it was time to leave. Time to gather all the children, pack up the tabernacle, and follow the cloud that would finally lead them into the lush, bountiful land God had promised them. As at the start of many road trips, everyone was happy. I bet Moses could hardly contain himself as he turned around and saw a million people following him: "It's really happening! They're actually following me. God is showing the way, just as he said he would, with that huge cloud ahead of us. We're getting out of this wilderness, and soon we will be able to let our sheep graze in green pastures and grow more crops than we could ever use. And best of all, we will finally be that great nation that God said we would be."

Such happy thinking lasted for about three days.

The contrast couldn't be clearer. In one chapter, the Bible paints a glorious picture of each tribe leaving its camp, marching proudly under its banner, and the very next chapter begins, "Now the people complained about their hardships."[2] For the briefest time they were able to enter the Upper Story of a God who keeps his promises. As a "nation," they had started out with just seventy people when they arrived in Egypt four hundred years earlier, and just as God had promised, they had grown in number. They had been promised their own land and were now on their way to occupy it. But all too soon, they fell back into the tunnel vision of their Lower Story. *It's hot. It's dusty. We're tired. It's taking a lot longer than we thought it would.*

Remember how I mentioned that when my siblings and I complained in the station wagon, my parents would reach back and try to swat us into behaving? Well, God did one better. According to the Bible, he sent fire down from heaven and it singed the outskirts of their campsites. No one got burned, but it was a clear signal that God wanted his nation to behave. He knew the journey would be much more enjoyable if the Israelites would just trust him. The fire got their attention, but not for long.

When the Israelites fled from the Egyptians, they complained to Moses because they didn't have any food. God responded by miraculously providing a bread-like substance called manna. Each day, enough manna appeared to feed the entire population of God's special nation, with a double portion provided on the sixth day of the week so that the people would not have to work on the Sabbath to collect food. But shortly after they began their journey to the promised land, they started complaining about the lack of variety in their diet. They not only whined about their food; they started longing for the "good old days" when they were slaves in Egypt: "We remember the fish we ate in Egypt at no cost—also the cucumbers, melons, leeks, onions and garlic. But now we have lost our appetite; we never see anything but this manna!"[3]

You've probably heard the expression "You can't have your cake and eat it too" in reference to someone who is spoiled—a person who has everything she needs yet still wants more. This describes the Israelites. The Bible tells us they want meat, but it's clear that what they want is *control*. They don't want to have to trust God with something as basic as their daily menu. They want control so badly that they start reminiscing about the "good old days" when they were slaves in Egypt!

What happens next reminds me of a story a friend told me about how he got caught smoking when he was a teenager. In a combination of wisdom and humor, his dad produced an entire pack of cigarettes and said, "So you wanna smoke, huh? Start smoking." After my friend puffed away at the first cigarette, his dad handed him another one. And another one. After about three cigarettes, the poor guy started throwing up and claims to this day that he gets sick when he smells tobacco smoke. I think his dad may have heard about God's response to the Israelites' demand for meat!

When God hears his people complaining about the manna and asking for meat, he gives it to them. Bushels of it. You know you're in trouble when God says he's going to give you so much meat that you'll be eating it "until it comes out of your nostrils and you loathe it."[4] But this is exactly what he says because he wants to show his ungrateful children what can happen when they insist on having it their way instead of God's way.

You would think that after the firestorm and a few nights of indigestion from too much meat, the Israelites would have gotten the message: *God does what he says he will do so that we can relax and enjoy his presence.* When they were slaves in Egypt, they worked from dawn to dusk, were beaten if they didn't work hard enough, and, worst of all, felt completely abandoned by God. Consequently, he not only rescued them from their misery; he made his presence known to them in a tangible way. The cloud that hovered over the tabernacle was like a giant billboard that read, "I'm right here with you, and all you need to do is follow me and everything will be great!"

Still they complain. After the almost humorous incident with the meat, Moses' own family members begin to question the whole "journey to the promised land" thing. Even though God made it abundantly clear that his plan was to communicate to the Israelites through Moses, Aaron and Miriam—his brother and sister—aren't buying it. They grumble among themselves and come to the conclusion that God also spoke through them. This outburst is more than just a little sibling rivalry, because to God it again reveals a lack of trust. Not only did they challenge God's plan of choosing Moses to lead their nation; they must not have really believed that God was with them. If they had, they would not have dared to openly question God's wisdom. But he *was* with them, and he heard them and could not let such an act of rebellion go unnoticed.

He tells Moses to bring Miriam and Aaron to the tabernacle and meets the three of them there in the form of a great cylindrical cloud. God begins by declaring, "Listen to my words." It was God's way of letting them know that what he was about to say was extremely important, and I can only guess that it got their attention as much as a burning bush would have. As they stand next to Moses, God continues:

> "When there is a prophet among you,
>   I, the LORD, reveal myself to them in visions,
>   I speak to them in dreams.
> But this is not true of my servant Moses;
>   he is faithful in all my house.
> With him I speak face to face,
>   clearly and not in riddles;
>   he sees the form of the LORD.
> Why then were you not afraid
>   to speak against my servant Moses?"[5]

Then God leaves, but not before inflicting Miriam with leprosy. Aaron begs Moses to intervene with the Lord—clearly he got the message that God had a special relationship with Moses. Moses cries out to God for Miriam's healing, and God relents.

Despite all the follies, foibles, and foolish deeds, the Israelites finally make it across the desert to a city called Kadesh Barnea, just south of the promised land. It is time to enter. The sin of the Amorites, the current residents, has now reached its full measure according to God's standard. The divine court of justice has declared it time to take the land away from the evil occupants and give it to his people Israel. Moses sends out twelve spies, one from each of the tribes of Israel, to scope out the land and bring back a report.

Forty days later, they return and give their report: "Yep, this land is flowing with milk and honey alright, just as God said."[6] To prove it, they even brought back a branch bearing a cluster of grapes so heavy it took two men to carry. Canaan was a garden—a welcome sight after being in the desert. But the spies also reported that the people were huge—giants really. And there were a bazillion of them! Ten of the twelve spies recommended Israel not enter the land. The people concurred, and the decision was made: we will not enter the land God promised to give us.

From the Lower Story perspective, the giants were bigger than the God who delivered them from slavery through ten powerful plagues, led them through the Red Sea on dry ground, crushed Pharaoh and his army, provided food and water in the desert, and guided them with a cloud during the day and a pillar of fire at night! But in their moment of fear, they forgot to align their lives to God's Upper Story. Joshua and Caleb, the two spies who voted to enter the land, believed they could do it because God, who had proven his trustworthiness and power, said it was time to take it. But the people wouldn't change their minds. They even thought about stoning Moses and Aaron, finding a new leader, and heading back to Egypt. As a Bible historian once wrote, "It was one thing to get the Hebrews out of Egypt and quite another to get Egypt out of the Hebrews."[7] It's not that Israel liked their life of slavery; they had just gotten comfortable with it. They wanted freedom in the garden of Canaan, but they just couldn't trust God and his promise enough to go in.

And God lamented their unbelief: "The LORD said to Moses, 'How long will these people treat me with contempt? How long will they refuse to believe in me, in spite of all the signs I have performed among them?'"[8] In the end, God gave in to their Lower Story wishes, but with this caveat: they would not get another opportunity to enter until that entire adult generation died in the wilderness. Forty more years of desert dwelling! As the 1970s' song "Walkin' Sinai" has it, "Go on and take another lap around Mount Sinai till you learn your lesson." When we know God and have seen his mighty hand at work, the fear of God should keep us from the fear of anything else, including giants.

When we read about these incidents from a Lower Story perspective, it can be tempting to conclude that God is mean-spirited and enjoys punishing people. So what if Miriam and Aaron were a little jealous because God chose their brother as his leader and spokesman? Can you really blame them? And what's the harm in grumbling about it to each other? And shouldn't God cut them a little slack for being afraid of giants? As it turns out, from the Upper Story view, this is a big deal. God is building a special nation—one that is different from any other. One that is worthy of his presence. People in other nations complained. People in other nations were never satisfied, no matter how good they had it. People in other nations got jealous. God's nation had to be different because it would reflect the very character of God to all others, attracting them to the one true God.

Such a nation could only succeed if the people placed their complete trust in this God, even when things did not make sense to them. For the Israelites, wandering in the wilderness with only manna to eat was not their idea of "a chosen nation." Their Lower Story expectations and fear got in the way of the Upper Story's development. Can you relate? Maybe it's unemployment, a troubled marriage, a painful illness, a stress-inducing debt. The Israelites kept forgetting that God always keeps his promises. The land of milk and honey would be theirs, and while the journey might be long and difficult, he was right there with them along the way—just as he is right here with us in the midst of our own often difficult journeys.

Fast-forward nearly forty years. Almost all of the unbelieving generation has died. As Moses approaches the end of his life, he gathers the Israelites to give them what will be his final speech. For a guy who tried to convince God not to choose him as a leader because he couldn't speak very well, he crafts one of the most beautiful and inspiring messages in the entire Bible. Dale Carnegie didn't have anything on this guy's pep talk! The Israelites are going to get another shot at entering the land that God had promised to Abraham more than 650 years earlier. Moses knows these people well and has watched them turn away from God countless times when things didn't go according to their plans. So he presents them with two alternatives: love God and obey him and enjoy a prosperous life, or turn away from God and disobey him and suffer destruction. And then he concludes this speech with these words:

> This day I call the heavens and the earth as witnesses against you that I have set before you life and death, blessings and curses. Now choose life, so that you and your children may live and that you may love the LORD your God, listen to his voice, and hold fast to him. For the LORD is your life, and he will give you many years in the land he swore to give to your fathers, Abraham, Isaac and Jacob.[9]

Choose God, trust and obey him—and you will have "the good life." Choose your own way, live by your own rules—and you will face destruction. Why *wouldn't* you want the good life?

My dad was not a mean or angry man. He looked forward to family vacations because he really enjoyed hanging out with his kids, laughing with us, and watching us have fun. He knew the trips in the car were long, and that our fighting and arguing would only make things worse. He wanted us to enjoy the journey as much as the destination, and when we refused to do that, he corrected our behavior. He wanted the very best for us, even if it meant the temporary discomfort of being disciplined.

Our life is like a road trip. God wants to lead us every step of the way from his GPS. God sees the picture from the Upper Story and wants the best for us. He wants us to make it to our final destination. He wants us to enjoy the journey. But we have to trust him. When he calls out, "Left," we need to go left. When he tells us, "Right," we need to go right. When he says, "Stop," we need to halt dead in our tracks. When he urges, "Go faster," we need to put the pedal to the metal. When he implores, "Bust through the barrier, no matter how big and bad it looks," we need to charge ahead in faith—like a scene out of an old *Knight Rider* episode!

We also need to be reminded that whatever choice we make, there are others who are in the car with us. They will experience either the blessings of our good decisions or the pain of our destructive decisions. God has a place of blessing to which he wants to take us. In this place, as we live our lives for him, we will also be a blessing to the people around us—as we serve them and allow them to share in God's blessings in our lives. As others see God working in our lives, they will want to follow God too. This will be the biggest blessing of all. But to get to this place, we must trust him.

So are we there yet?

No, not yet. But just sit back and enjoy the ride. Our heavenly Father knows exactly what he's doing, and he will keep his promise to be with us always.

Chapter

7

THE BATTLE BEGINS

"Be strong and courageous. Do not be afraid;
do not be discouraged, for the LORD your God
will be with you wherever you go."

JOSHUA 1:9

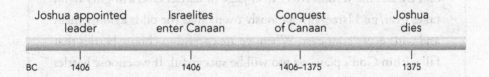

Joshua appointed leader	Israelites enter Canaan	Conquest of Canaan	Joshua dies
BC 1406	1406	1406–1375	1375

WHAT'S HAPPENING IN THE UPPER STORY

Forty years have gone by, and the unbelieving generation that refused to enter the land God promised to give Israel has died in the wilderness. Under the leadership of Joshua, the next generation has a fresh opportunity to trust God. They press forward across the Jordan River and, through several military campaigns, are successful in securing and distributing the land to the tribes of Israel. From the Upper Story, God is patient with the residents of Canaan, giving them more than six hundred years to stop the escalation of evil among them. God, at just the right time, deals with all forms of evil by applying a just sentence against them. This fertile land will now set the scene for God to bless his people and to establish his Name so that all people from all nations will know he is the one true God who desires a relationship with them. As promised, he will make this blessing for all possible through Israel.

ALIGNING OUR STORY TO GOD'S STORY

God told Joshua that if he was careful to align his life to the word and will of God, turning neither to the right or the left, he would be successful. Taking the land of Canaan at this time was the will of God. Strong and courageous, Joshua makes the move of obedience and crosses the Jordan River to engage in battle. God's mighty hand takes over, and Israel miraculously overcomes the odds against them and wins every conquest. When we are careful to choose battles that fall within God's plan, we too will be successful. If we choose battles that fall outside of the word and will of God, we are on our own and the outcome is unpredictable.

On June 5, 1944—the day before the Allied Forces stormed the beaches at Normandy—General George S. Patton gave a speech to the Third Army that left no room for failure:

> I don't want to get any messages saying, "I am holding my position." We are not holding . . . We are advancing constantly, and we are not interested in holding on to anything . . . Our basic plan of operation is to advance and to keep on advancing, regardless of whether or not we have to go over, under, or through the enemy.[1]

Can you imagine the fear that must have been racing through their minds and hearts as these men prepared to jump into the water and charge the shore? The fate of the Free World was truly riding on their shoulders.

The Israelites faced a similar overwhelming, "defeat is not an option" military challenge. The time had come for them to enter the land that God promised to give to them more than six hundred years earlier. It was time to start the next chapter in God's Upper Story.

Just before Moses died, he appointed a man named Joshua to succeed him as the leader of the nation God was building. Some forty years earlier, Joshua was one of twelve spies whom Moses selected to sneak into Canaan (the promised land), check it out, and report back. When they returned, the diligent dozen brought back the proverbial "good news and bad news." Yes, it really was a land flowing with milk and honey. A single cluster of grapes was so big that it had to be carried by two men! The bad news? The Canaanites had been supersized to match the size of the grapes!

The native people were big, tall, scary-looking warriors. The spies said they felt like grasshoppers compared to the gigantic people in Canaan and gave this recommendation to Moses: "We can't attack those people; they are stronger than we are."[2]

Two of the spies—Joshua and a man named Caleb—vehemently disagreed with this hopeless assessment. They recommended an immediate attack, but the other spies had already started spreading the bad news throughout the entire community. All night long, the Israelites grumbled against Moses, once again longing for the good old days of slavery under the pharaoh. In fact, they even suggested choosing a new leader and returning to Egypt.

Joshua and Caleb tried desperately to change their minds with a passionate plea:

"The land we passed through is exceedingly good. If the LORD is pleased with us, he will lead us into that land, a land flowing with milk and honey, and will give it to us. Only do not rebel against the LORD. And do not be afraid of the people of the land, because we will devour them. Their protection is gone, but the LORD is with us. Do not be afraid of them."[3]

But the people wouldn't listen. So the stubborn Israelites got their way, and then some. Not only did they *not* cross over into the promised land, as Joshua recommended; they stayed in the wilderness for the rest of their lives. Sometimes the best punishment is to give someone exactly what they want, and this is what God did. He banished an entire generation of his people from entering the promised land, except for two people—Joshua and Caleb.

Now, with Moses dead, God told the courageous captain Joshua, "Get ready. It's time to go in."

Nothing on the other side of the Jordan River had changed since Joshua and the other spies snuck in to check things out. If anything, the cities would have been even more heavily fortified. And the people would still be big. Forty years earlier, Joshua had been young and strong—maybe even a bit naive and impetuous. Older and wiser, he clearly knew the odds were against him. Their first major challenge was simply getting all the Israelites across the river. It's one thing to have a few spies float across the river, but getting more than a million people across a river with no bridges seemed impossible.

Then there was the special rite of circumcision that God commanded them to perform before they went into battle. Circumcision was an outward sign of God's covenant with his people, and this younger generation of Israelite men had not been circumcised. Not to be indelicate, but performing a circumcision on an adult male is not exactly the best way to prepare him to go into battle. And we're not talking stainless steel scalpels here, but knives made out of flint. Yes, as in *stone*. These poor guys were about to be in a world of hurt a few days before the major conflict.

If a major river crossing and the prospect of being circumcised weren't enough, God's battle plan for their first conquest—at the walled city of Jericho—had to give Joshua pause: march around the city, blow your trumpets, and shout. That's it. God's divine battle plan was to march and make noise.

As a leader, I've occasionally had to challenge the people in my church to do something difficult, and they have always come through. But I'm not sure I could go to my people and lay this plan in front of them: "Folks, we're going to cross that raging river on the edge of town without any boats or bridges. Once we get to the other side, I want all the guys to meet me in this big tent. Bring your knives and a Band-Aid. When we're finished there, we're all going to form a big column and parade around that huge walled fortress where soldiers will be waiting to ambush us. No need to bring any weapons, except for seven of you. Bring your trumpets. When I say the word, make some noise—and I think that'll do it. Are you with me?"

When we read this story with our Lower Story eyes, it would be funny if there wasn't so much at stake. God's chosen nation had waited for more than six hundred years to enter the land he had promised them. They almost made it forty years ago, but their fear of the enemy and stubborn refusal to trust God blocked their entry. Finally, after years of wandering in the barren wilderness, God is giving a new generation the opportunity to claim this rich and bountiful land as their own. *Just cross the river, perform delicate surgery on all your men, and then march around a well-fortified city inhabited by giants.*

Nothing about God's plan made sense. At least not from the Lower Story perspective. And as we've already seen, it seldom does. God's ways are not always our ways, and this is because he always has his Upper Story front and center in his mind. The community in which he can dwell will be unlike any other community because its citizens will obey God rather than follow their own logical judgments and subjective desires. And one way in which God determines our level of trust is to test us. Our "swords and spears" may seem like the best weapons to fight God's battles, but he asks us to do it *his* way—even when his way appears to be a sure recipe for failure.

God knew exactly what he was asking Joshua to do. He also knew that Joshua was human, so to encourage him in this task of leading the Israelites into a dangerous battle, he gave him a little pep talk. Three times he repeated these words: "Be strong and courageous." Perhaps sensing a little nervousness from Joshua, he added, "Do not be afraid."[4] This encouragement is a major Upper Story theme. Variations of the phrase "do not be afraid" appear more than one hundred times in the Bible. The community God is creating for us will not be characterized by fear, despite the fact that we will face many fearsome moments.

During this pep talk with Joshua, God asked him to do something else that on the surface doesn't seem to have anything to do with the battle ahead:

> Be careful to obey all the law my servant Moses gave you; do not turn from it to the right or to the left, that you may be successful wherever you go. Keep this Book of the Law always on your lips; meditate on it day and night, so that you may be careful to do everything written in it. Then you will be prosperous and successful.[5]

The law—the guidelines God established for his unique community—had nothing to do with fighting a battle. Instead, it was given to the Israelites so that they could get along with each other and be the kind of community God could inhabit. As he was about to give them the land he had promised, however, he wanted to make sure they did not forget how they were to live, because he was intent on doing life with them. Obeying the law, then, created the conditions for God's final reassuring message to Joshua on the eve of leading his first battle: "I will be with you."[6]

The key to victory was found not in superior weapons and conventional strategy but in obedience. God was essentially saying to Joshua, "Don't be afraid. Trust me. Do exactly what I ask you to do. Live according to the guidelines I have given you, and you will defeat anyone who stands against you."

It worked.

Joshua, facing an uncrossable river, a well-fortified city, and an unpopular request to make of every male in his army, does exactly as he is told. When he tells his officers about God's plan to defeat Jericho, they respond, "Whatever you have commanded us we will do, and wherever you send us we will go."[7]

Led by priests carrying the ark of the covenant, they approach the Jordan River, and when one of the priests steps into the river, God miraculously stops the flow of the water so that the entire nation can cross over into Canaan. They then obey God by circumcising every male before setting out on their notorious march around the city of Jericho. For six days they march—once around the city each day. Then on the seventh day, they circle the city seven times before the trumpets blast and Joshua gives the command: "Shout!"[8]

And the walls come a tumblin' down. Just as God had promised.

The rest of the story of Joshua is all about conquest. They conduct a southern campaign, wiping out five kings and their armies that banded together to fight the Israelites. Then they head north and take on an alliance of fourteen kings and their armies, wiping them out too. I mean, they didn't just defeat a city; they eliminated it. No survivors. No prisoners. These weren't a handful of rogue soldiers, but God's chosen nation obeying God's orders. Many people read this part of the Bible and conclude that God is heartless and cruel. Why would God have to completely eliminate the native people in these cities?

The answer comes from the Upper Story, where God is preparing a perfect environment in which to dwell among his people. He wasn't so much giving the Israelites Canaan as he was taking it away from those who were living there, the Amorites, and here is where we see the consistency of God's Upper Story. After giving the Israelites the Ten Commandments that God inscribed on stone tablets, Moses delivered a major speech to prepare them for their eventual conquest of Canaan: "It is not because of your righteousness or your integrity that you are going in to take possession of their land; but on account of the wickedness of these nations the LORD your God will drive them out before you, *to accomplish what he swore to your fathers, to Abraham, Isaac and Jacob.*"[9]

Way back more than six hundred years before, when God first met with Abraham and promised to make a great nation out of his family, he set the conditions for the land he would give them to build their nation: "In the fourth generation your descendants will come back here, for the sin of the Amorites has not yet reached its full measure."[10]

The very land that God had chosen to be the home of his new community was being desecrated by the wickedness of its inhabitants. After four generations, their wickedness would become so detestable that he would have just cause to take the land from them by force. What seems brutal and excessive in the Lower Story is a statement about God's justice and righteousness in his Upper Story kingdom. God is patient and long-suffering. He gave them more than six hundred years to change their ways. If they had, God would have changed his mind. God cannot tolerate the kind of widespread evil that had infected the entire Amorite population.

He cannot reside in a land with people who worship other gods and even practice prostitution in the worship of their gods. It may seem unfair to us that God would order an entire population to be wiped out, but their evil behavior had reached a point at which he had to put a stop to it. "They do all kinds of detestable things the LORD hates. They even burn their sons and daughters in the fire as sacrifices to their gods."[11] Something had to be done.

The Upper Story message is clear: the community God envisions for his people—the environment in which he wants to come down and live with us—cannot tolerate evil. Who would want to live in such anarchy? When the Israelites capture the land and destroy the cities, justice is served in a dramatic fashion. But there is another reason God gave this land to his people. He wanted to establish his name in Canaan so that everyone could know the one true God. At just the right time—when the wickedness of the Amorites reached its peak—God gave the land to this now big and great nation called Israel so that others would be drawn to this God who wants to be intimately involved with his people.

God continues to call us to be the same kind of unique people who will attract others to him. He is calling us to live distinctive, wholesome lives that stand out from lives characterized by selfishness, greed, and materialism. He is calling us to face the giants of a lousy economy and personal setbacks in ways that reflect our trust in him as a Father who always provides for his children.

He is calling us to choose life, to value those whom society rejects, to counter hatred and prejudice with love for all God's people.

Just like the Israelites, we will need to be brave and courageous if we are to live the way God wants us to live. We will need to become people of the Word so that we know God's ways and can follow his guidelines for getting along with him and with each other. And whenever we have the inner sense that he wants us to do something difficult for him—whether walking across the street to introduce ourselves to a neighbor or adopting a child who may not otherwise be given a chance to live—we should do it so that others can see the one true God.

In the Lower Story, the giants are bigger than the Israelites. In the Upper Story, God is bigger than the giants. We all face battles in our own lives. Like Joshua and the children of Israel, we need to be faithful people. We need to look intently into God's Word to discover his will for how we should proceed—so we can find courage and strength. We need to remember that more is unfolding than what we can see.

We need to be people of prayer. We need to ask God if we should move forward or hold our position. Prayer involves listening to God. If he is in it, charge. If he is not, hold your position.

We need to be people identified with God. If we have come into a relationship with God through Jesus Christ, we need to publicly declare our allegiance to him by being baptized—unashamedly identifying ourselves with our God both privately and publicly. We need to live our lives obediently so others will be drawn to our loving Father.

Success was already declared before the first foot was placed into the Jordan River. Why? Because this battle belonged to the Lord. When we are careful to choose battles that fall within the word and will of God, we too will be successful. If we choose battles that fall outside of the word and will of God, we are on our own and the outcome is unpredictable. Choose the Lord's battles and then charge!

Chapter 8

A FEW GOOD MEN . . . AND WOMEN

*"How can I save Israel? My clan is the weakest
in Manasseh, and I am the least in my family."*

JUDGES 6:15

Judges begin to rule	Deborah's rule	Gideon's rule	Samson's rule
BC 1375	1209–1169	1162–1122	1075–1055

WHAT'S HAPPENING IN THE UPPER STORY

In the Upper Story, God is revealing his character and his plan to provide the way for all people from every nation to come back into a relationship with him. He is accomplishing this mission through the nation of Israel, who now resides in the promised land of Canaan. Over the course of the next 330 years, Israel finds itself in a long season of disobedience. Six times we see a cycle throughout the tribes of Israel—sin, oppression, repentance, deliverance. God allows Israel to fall captive to other nations so they can be tutored in the ways of God. When they repent, God is faithful to raise up judges who lead Israel's deliverance from oppression. He continues to rescue them because he made an unconditional promise that the blessed solution for all people to come back into a relationship with him would come through Israel.

ALIGNING OUR STORY TO GOD'S STORY

Like God wanted with Israel, he wants us to make his name known by the way we live our lives. We can avoid discipline by following God's ways. However, if we do sin and fall into trouble, we should confess our sins, and Christ, our deliverer, will forgive us and cleanse us from all unrighteousness.[1]

*H*ave you ever felt that no matter how hard you try, you just can't win? You can't get ahead financially. A downturn in the economy catches you holding too many bills with too much debt, and now you're sinking. Creditors are chasing you day and night, no escape in sight. You can't get a break. The small business you started doesn't stand a chance against the big guns in town, who can slash prices and drive you out of business.

You are in sales but can't make a sale. Can't even get your foot in the door. You haven't seen a decent commission check in months.

You are surrounded by people who are better looking than you are. It's hard to compete and get noticed in a world filled with thin, buff, pretty, younger people. They're everywhere, making it hard for you to get a date or a job.

You can't finish your education—even through those special degree-completion programs. You need a degree to get a better job, but you're working long hours to support your family and don't have time to take even one class a semester. You feel trapped, and there is no end in sight.

You love sports and the thrill of competition, but others are faster, stronger, and more coordinated than you are. Injuries plague you and prevent you from training at your full potential. Unless something changes, you may as well forget about running the race or staying in the game.

If you've ever felt outnumbered, unqualified, or disadvantaged, you will be encouraged by Gideon's story. It begins at a time when Israel had been living in the land of Canaan for nearly three hundred years. God has given them everything they need to be a great nation: a set of guidelines on how to live, his presence in the tabernacle, a way to atone for their sins, and land he had promised their ancestors. But it isn't enough. The children of Israel cannot stay focused on the Upper Story. Specifically, they are addicted to worshiping other gods, a blatant violation of the very first guideline God gave them.

God severely punishes this behavior by allowing other rulers to oppress them, often scattering the Israelites into the mountains to hide in caves. Eventually they reach a point of utter desperation and call out to God to rescue them, and

God responds by sending judges to free them from their oppressors. While we tend to think of judges as older men or women wearing robes and listening to court cases, God's judges are warriors who wear helmets and carry swords.

When a judge is in charge, the Israelites repent, which in the Hebrew language literally means they turn back from the direction they are heading and return to God. They experience a period of prosperity as they observe God's guidelines and begin to resemble the community he has always envisioned for his people. But when the judge dies, they turn their backs on God and his guidelines, and another oppressor conquers them. God in his mercy raises up another judge, and the Israelites clean up their act. But after the judge dies, they return to their old rebellious habits.

This cycle of lather, rinse, repeat (or sin, judge, repent) occurs six times in the book of Judges. Of the 330 years that make up this period of Israel's history, they spend 111 of them in oppression. After all they had been through as God's people! They really did have it all, but it wasn't enough.

During one of those periods when the Israelites are suffering under an oppressive regime—in this case, the Midianites—they again repent and cry out to the Lord. This time God chooses a guy named Gideon to deliver them from their oppressors. Remember the guy in high school who got voted "Least Likely to Succeed"? This is our hero, Gideon. Even *he* is surprised when God gives him the prestigious assignment of saving the nation.[2] He is the youngest in his family, from the weakest tribe, the runt in a family known for being weak. The weakest link in a paper-link chain. Not exactly gladiator material.

Gideon has a hard time believing that God really would choose him to save Israel, and who can blame him? This sounds to him like the ultimate prank, and he isn't about to fall for it, so he proposes a plan to God that will prove whether he really is the man God wants to lead Israel into battle. Gideon decides that he will lay the fleece of a lamb on the ground overnight, and if it is soaked with dew while the ground around it remains dry, then he will know that God indeed has selected him. Sure enough, when he awakens the next morning and goes to retrieve the fleece, it is so wet he squeezes a whole bowl of water from it, but the ground is bone-dry.

"There must be some mistake," Gideon apparently concludes, thinking so little of himself that he wants further proof. He asks God to reverse the order—this time the ground will be wet with dew while the fleece will remain fluffy and dry. God must have really wanted Gideon, because instead of getting angry or impatient with him, he does exactly what Gideon asks him to do. When Gideon goes out in the morning, the ground is covered with dew, yet the fleece is dry. People today still talk about "putting out a fleece" in order to receive confirmation for something they feel compelled to pursue.

Once Gideon is firmly convinced that God has chosen him to lead Israel out of its oppression, he gathers the Israelite army—thirty-two thousand strong—at an encampment overlooking the valley where the Midianites are entrenched. God whispers to Gideon, "That's too many. Let any soldier who's even the least bit fearful leave." Twenty-two thousand soldiers depart, which isn't exactly a rousing endorsement of Gideon's leadership. But God tells him he still has too many and helps him sift through the rest of the troops until he has only three hundred dedicated warriors left.[3]

No one knows for sure the size of the Midianite army, but historians agree that it was quite formidable. The Bible records that "it was impossible to count them or their camels," such was their great number.[4] A conservative estimate is two hundred thousand soldiers, which is a ratio of 666:1. You don't have to be a military strategist to know that regardless of how strong and skilled the three hundred Israelite soldiers were, they would be no match against two hundred thousand Midianites. At least from a Lower Story point of view. Why would God, then, put Gideon at such a disadvantage? If anything, Gideon needed *more* soldiers. If anything, God should have allowed him to keep all of his original soldiers, thirty-two thousand, which, when pitted against two hundred thousand opponents, would still be lousy odds.

But God knows his children well. He knows that if the Israelites defeat the Midianites with their full army, they will become boastful and think their superior military strength and strategy saved them. Just as Adam and Eve thought they could be as wise as God, the Israelites would believe they were as strong as God. In the Upper Story, the only way we can be in a relationship with God is to acknowledge that he is God, and we are not. And like the Israelites, we still need to be humbled and reminded of this reality. If the Israelites were to pull off an upset and defeat the Midianites with just three hundred men, they would know that their salvation comes from God, not from their own hands. Not only would *they* know, but so would everyone else.

The Midianites knew there was *no way* Israel could defeat them. Gideon lays out God's military strategy to his ragamuffin band of soldiers. He tells his tiny army to light torches and then hide them inside jars of clay. Each soldier carries the clay pitcher in his left hand; in the other hand, following Gideon's instructions, each carries a trumpet. They sneak up on the Midianite army at night, and at Gideon's signal, they smash the pitchers and blow on their trumpets. Gideon has the soldiers shout in unison, "A sword for Yahweh and for Gideon."[5] The flash fires and horn blowing confuse and frighten the Midianites so greatly that they literally run around like chickens with their heads cut off! They must be thinking, *If Israel has that many torchbearers and troubadours, just think how many soldiers they must have.* They try to flee, but in the darkness they turn on each other with their swords. The battle is over before it started. When the Midianites said, "No way," Gideon had the men shout, "Yahweh."

Gideon, the runt of the weakest family in the weakest tribe, leads a minuscule army of three hundred men to victory over the mighty Midianites. And under his leadership, Israel enjoys forty years of peace and prosperity.

Unfortunately, after Gideon died, the Israelites fell back to their old ways: "No sooner had Gideon died than the Israelites again prostituted themselves to the Baals. They set up Baal-Berith as their god and did not remember the LORD their God, who had rescued them from the hands of all their enemies on every side."[6]

You would think that after such a miraculous victory, the Israelites never would have wanted to do anything less than serve God faithfully forever. But in their Lower Story lives, they always ended up putting their own selfish interests ahead of God's wonderful provision for them. Instead of trusting that God knew what was best for them, they became resentful and concluded that following God's ways would keep them from getting what they wanted. Like a spoiled kid who demands a new toy because all the other kids have one, the Israelites wanted what everyone else had. All the people from other nations got to worship Baal—an idol—so they wanted to worship him too.

If this sounds familiar, it's because even today, it's difficult for followers of God to remain focused on him when everything is going right. For some reason, in times of prosperity and abundance, we often grow distant or ignore God completely, feeling self-sufficient in our temporary happiness. Conversely, some of the most inspiring stories of devotion to God come from the poorest and most oppressed communities of faithful Christians.

Like the Israelites, we forget that the same God who saves us from our distress wants to walk with us and enjoy a relationship with us *all* the time, not just when our backs are against the wall. As you study the history of Christianity in the Western world, you see periods of spiritual lethargy—even rebellion against God—followed by great "awakenings" in which people cry out to him and he answers with great power, reclaiming his children who have wandered from him.

Our Lower Story rebellion against God is always met with his Upper Story invitation to return to him. We can try it our way, until we get into such a mess that the only way to turn is toward God, and then he always takes us back. Regardless of what you have done, no matter how long it has been since you have turned away from him and followed your own selfish desires, you are never too far from God.

God is always ready to welcome *anyone* who calls out to him to be saved.

God was able to use the runt of the weakest family in the weakest tribe in Israel to rescue his nation from oppression. He will go to whatever lengths are necessary to reclaim his people so that he can do life with them.

As for those who are willing to do exactly what he wants them to do, God will use them like he used Gideon's jars of clay, as vessels to pour out his blessings and to build his nation, even if they are cracked pots—small, insignificant, and overlooked by others!

As Christians, we get ourselves into all sorts of trouble because we want to live life the way we want, not the way God wants. We think in our Lower Story nearsightedness that God has abandoned us, turned his back on us. But in the Upper Story, God's 20/20 vision always keeps us in his view. He is always waiting for us to return to him when we stray. Like the loving Father he is, God opens his arms and says, "I will take you back. *Always.* No matter what you've done. I will deliver you because I love you."

Chapter 9

THE FAITH OF A FOREIGN WOMAN

"Praise be to the Lord, who this day has not left you
without a guardian-redeemer . . . He will renew
your life and sustain you in your old age. For your
daughter-in-law, who loves you and who is better
to you than seven sons, has given him birth."

RUTH 4:14–15

Time of the judges	Naomi and Ruth return from Moab	Ruth meets Boaz	Boaz marries Ruth

BC   1375–1050

WHAT'S HAPPENING IN THE UPPER STORY

During the period of the judges, God surprisingly highlights a story of a single family. In the Lower Story, Elimelek and Naomi, with their two sons, arguably make an unwise decision and move their family from Bethlehem to the foreign land of Moab in search of food during a time of famine. Israel was forbidden to marry foreigners, not because of their race or skin color, but because of the temptation to follow other gods. This event is an important part of God's Upper Story. When Elimelek and his two sons tragically die in Moab, Naomi, filled with bitterness, returns home to Bethlehem. Ruth, a Moabite woman who married one of her sons, declares allegiance to Naomi's God and returns to Bethlehem with her. While there, Ruth marries a relative named Boaz, whose mother was Rahab, the Canaanite harlot who hid the Israelite spies. Ruth and Boaz have a son who not only brings joy to Naomi but who will also become the grandfather of King David in the direct lineage of Jesus. God intentionally seeks out these women from foreign nations who give their allegiance to God to signal his love and redemption for all people.

ALIGNING OUR STORY TO GOD'S STORY

From a Lower Story perspective, Elimelek and Naomi are just trying to make a decision to provide for their two boys. When everything falls apart, Naomi assumes that God has turned against her. Instead, God is using their choices to write his Upper Story of love and redemption. God is still in the business of taking our Lower Story decisions that put us in special places at special times and using them to tell an even greater story. Look for it. Expect it. Be amazed by it.

Every time Rozanne and I decide to watch a movie, we are faced with a decision: guy movie or chick flick. Now, don't get me wrong. I like a good shoot-'em-up, martial arts, espionage, "save the world against all odds," really Balboa movie. However, as I have gotten older and my heart mushier, I fall for the great love story. Movies like *Sleepless in Seattle* and *Breakfast at Tiffany's* leave me crying like a baby.

The story of Ruth starts out with our plot already in progress. You almost need a flowchart to keep track of the characters and dramatic events. During the period of the judges (see the last chapter), a married couple from Bethlehem—Naomi and Elimelek—move with their two sons to a region called Moab, which is not part of God's special nation. Shortly after they arrive in Moab, Elimelek dies. Eventually, Naomi's two sons marry Moabite women—Orpah and Ruth—and then ten years later the sons die. Are you still with me?

Naomi decides there is no reason for her to stay in Moab. The only reason they had moved there in the first place was the famine in their homeland. She has since learned that the famine is over, so she packs her bags and sets out for Bethlehem. When she sees that her daughters-in-law are following her, she tells them to return to their own mothers and then kisses them good-bye. Naomi must have been a great mom-in-law because the two younger women weep and beg to go to Bethlehem with her. She again tells them they will be much better off staying in their own country where they can easily find a couple of nice Moab boys and remarry.

Orpah reluctantly and tearfully agrees to stay in Moab, but Ruth holds fast, refusing to stay behind, with one of the most beautiful declarations of loyalty and love ever recorded: "Don't urge me to leave you or turn back from you. Where you go I will go, and where you stay I will stay. Your people will become my people and your God my God. Where you die I will die, and there I will be buried."[1]

Aside from the simple power and beauty of Ruth's speech, it is remarkable on another level. Historically, Moab had been an enemy of Israel. Although the two nations enjoyed a rare period of peace at this time, enemies have long memories. Ruth had to have known that it was risky for a Moabite to enter Bethlehem, but this didn't stop her. Neither did the fact that both she and her mother-in-law were widows. Life for her would be difficult at best because Naomi had nothing to offer her. If Ruth were to stay in Moab, she would at least have her extended family to take care of her.

And this God she had pledged would be her own? As a Moabite, Ruth would have been taught to worship the god Chemosh, an act that the Israelites considered not only idolatrous but also abominable. Ruth was willing to turn from the god she worshiped and believe in the God who must have appeared cruel or at least indifferent to her and Naomi's plight. According to her mother-in-law, this God was responsible for allowing Elimelek's death.

In trying to dissuade Ruth from returning to Bethlehem with her, Naomi warns that things will be bad because God has turned against her. When they finally arrive in Bethlehem, Naomi complains to some old friends who recognize her: "I went away full, but the LORD has brought me back empty . . . The LORD has afflicted me; the Almighty has brought misfortune upon me."[2]

Yet there she is—a widow from enemy territory in Bethlehem with a desolate woman whose God has apparently abandoned her.

And these events are only the first episode! From the Lower Story view, Ruth's plotline has some kinks in it. First, Naomi and her husband made a poor decision to settle in a pagan country that had once been a vicious enemy. Second, her sons violated God's teaching that the Israelites must not marry anyone from other nations. Finally, it made no sense for Ruth to travel with her mother-in-law to Bethlehem. If you have been paying attention, you know that when things get a little fuzzy, God is usually up to something.

And he certainly is in this instance. The two women arrive in Bethlehem during the harvest season, which offers a way for these two poor women to earn some money. According to God's instructions, wealthy farmers were required to let the poor glean the fields—follow behind the harvesters to pick up scraps of grain they missed. Ruth convinces Naomi to let her go to a field to glean, a sure recipe for trouble. Bethlehem is a relatively small town where everyone knows everyone else and especially takes notice of strangers. A single woman gleaning in a field presents a certain risk, but a single woman from an enemy state would make her a certain target for harassment—or worse. Imagine if a woman wearing a burka stopped to pick leftover corn in a farmer's field in Iowa. Can you say "homeland security"? If God is really up to something, then it's going to require some risks on the part of our heroine.

As it turns out, of all the fields surrounding Bethlehem, Ruth unknowingly chooses one that is owned by a relative of the father-in-law she never knew—Naomi's deceased husband. This relative's name is Boaz, and when he discovers that she is the Moabite widow who accompanied Naomi back to Bethlehem, he showers her with kindness. He invites her to glean all she wants and to drink from the jars of water he provides to his workers, and he warns his men not to lay a hand on her. He even tells his workers to deliberately leave a little extra grain behind so that Ruth won't have to work so hard.

Ruth is stunned! She knows her status. Foreigners were never treated so well, and when she rushes home to tell Naomi her news, the older woman begins to taste hope for the first time in many years. She immediately catches God's vision for a happy ending, one of those intersections where both the Lower Story and the Upper Story seem to fit together beautifully. So the old woman takes on the role of a Jewish matchmaker straight out of *Fiddler on the Roof.*

She tells Ruth to take a shower, splash on a little Chanel No. 5, and put on her Sabbath best. She must then head over to Boaz's place that night and play the part of Cinderella. She has to wait until he finishes eating—never approach a man with an empty stomach. After he goes to bed, she is to sneak in, uncover his feet, and lie down at the foot of his bed. Boaz will understand exactly what Ruth is doing.

And Ruth follows her mother-in-law's inspired instruction to the letter. Don't worry—it isn't as seductive as it sounds. Her behavior is actually a respectful, nonverbal way of conveying her availability and interest in marriage. She is not throwing herself at him or propositioning him like a sugar daddy. Ruth is definitely being more "bold and beautiful" than "young and restless"!

When Boaz awakens, startled at the sight of this stranger camped at the foot of his bed, he asks who she is, to which his secret admirer replies, "I am your servant Ruth . . . Spread the corner of your garment over me, since you are a guardian-redeemer of our family."[3] The word for "garment" in Hebrew is the same word for "wing." When Ruth first met Boaz, he referred to God's wings providing her a place of refuge. Ruth is now asking Boaz to become God's wing for her permanently. And he accepts. He exercises his obligation, and they become married! He buys not only Ruth's deceased husband's land but also his brother's land and Elimelek's as well. Risking his own estate, he redeems them all.

What drives Boaz to turn his attention from his own selfish needs and wants in order to reach out to an outsider? *As it turns out*, Boaz, the now strong, wealthy, respected man in Bethlehem, knows what it is like to be an outsider. We learn in Matthew 1 of the New Testament that Boaz's mother is Rahab, the harlot.[4] Rahab was the Canaanite prostitute who provided cover for Joshua's spies when they were scoping out the land. She risked her life and as a result was adopted into the family of Israel.[5] Boaz has it in his heart to reach out to someone else who stands on the outside looking in. *As it turns out*, that person is Ruth.

Ruth and Boaz have a little boy together. The little lad doesn't know it, but he inherits the land of his "father" Mahlon (Naomi's son and Ruth's deceased husband), whom he never met. As a result, he carries on the family name because of the kind act of Boaz.

The women of the town said to Naomi, "Praise be to the LORD, who this day has not left you without a guardian-redeemer."[6] In the Lower Story, Naomi thought her life was over; she believed that God had given up on her. She was mistaken. Naomi took her grandson and cuddled him in her lap, living proof of the God who never abandoned her. The little heir's name was Obed, which simply means "worker." Naomi was forced to sell the land because she was unable to work it. God has provided for the worker she needed to tend to her Lower Story ground.

As overwhelming a turnaround as this is, the good news doesn't stop here. There's more going on in the Upper Story. At the end of the book of Ruth, we are given the genealogy of Boaz's family. Here we learn that Obed grew up and had a son named Jesse. Jesse grew up to have a son named David. Twenty-eight generations later, a little baby named Jesus was born in a stable in the town of Bethlehem.

Jesus is the ultimate Guardian-Redeemer. He will redeem all who want his wings of forgiveness to cover them, even outsiders. Jesus came from the family of an outsider named Ruth!

God was working above the scenes of Ruth's and Naomi's lives in the Lower Story to provide them with a son who could redeem the land. God was also working above the scenes of Ruth's and Naomi's lives in the Upper Story to provide them with a Son who could redeem the world.

God went out of his way to include an outsider, a pagan Moabite, in the lineage of Jesus. This is a clue to us that God's salvation will be for all people. In the Lower Story, life seemed hopeless, with no chance of acceptance for outsiders. In the Upper Story, God redeemed their lives and accepted them as his own, and he continued to carry out his plan to bridge the gap between himself and his children. More and more, the Bible foreshadows the coming Messiah, God's beloved Son, who will sacrifice himself once and for all so that we can enjoy a restored relationship with the Father.

You know, right now your story may seem a little hopeless and bitter to the taste. It may feel as though you are living in a real-life soap opera, with crisis after crisis and constant relational turmoil. Just remember, though, if we love God and align our lives to his purposes, then, just as we are reminded in Romans 8:28, God is working out everything for our good. Since we know how the story ultimately ends, we can wait patiently for God to unfold his good plan for us!

Chapter **10**

STANDING TALL, FALLING HARD

For the foundations of the earth are the LORD's;
on them he has set the world.
He will guard the feet of his faithful servants,
but the wicked will be silenced
in the place of darkness.

1 SAMUEL 2:8–9

Samuel born	Samuel ministers under Eli	The Israelites ask for a king	Saul's reign
BC 1105			1050–1010

117

WHAT'S HAPPENING IN THE UPPER STORY

In the Upper Story, God wanted to be Israel's only king. With no human layers between God and his people, he could best govern, guide, and reveal himself and his plan to provide the way for all people to come into a relationship with him. In the Lower Story, Israel wanted a human king so they could be like the surrounding nations. Our sovereign God finds a way to honor the free will of Israel's request for a king without altering the trajectory of his ultimate objective. Israel would have their human king. If the new king was careful to follow the plan of God, things would go well. If, on the other hand, he got off course and misrepresented God's name and plan, God would intervene. Saul, from the tribe of Benjamin, is selected as first king of Israel. He is the people's choice—tall, dark and handsome. To give Saul the best possible chance to succeed, God places his Spirit inside Saul to guide and empower him. Despite a strong start, Saul failed in his mission to represent God and created long-term consequences in the life of Israel. God intervenes and removes Saul from the throne.

ALIGNING OUR STORY TO GOD'S STORY

Israel wanted to be like the other nations, which resulted in long-term consequences. Don't align your life to the culture, but to God's good plan for your life. Saul fudged on carrying out God's instructions and lost his role in God's story. In the same way, if we deny full obedience to God, he will continue to advance his story without the role and the blessing that was designed for you from the beginning of time.

As a middle school student back in the 1970s, I paid the price for looking cool, just like everyone else. The fashion gurus of that era included long hair, bell-bottoms, earth shoes, and wide lapel shirts on their list of must-haves. I didn't want to stand out from the other kids, so I wore the uniform of cool. At the time, I thought I was pretty hot stuff. Looking back at pictures, I cringe at how silly I looked.

In fact, the styles back then were so ridiculous that I never thought I'd see their return in my lifetime. No one would fall for those crazy outfits a second time, would they? Just when I thought it was safe to retire my peace symbol, I see my college-age kids strut their bell-bottom jeans and tie-dyed T-shirts. It all comes around. No doubt, their generation will look back on these fashion decisions with the same disdain I now feel.

So much depends on looking cool and fitting in, though, especially in the early teen years. We want everyone to know that we're as cool as they are, have the same hip taste, can afford the latest styles, and know where to shop. As we're about to see, it's not just schoolkids who want to fit in. The children of Israel went through their own middle school phase, since all they could think about was being like everyone else.

This new chapter in the saga of God's construction of a nation begins with a happy ending. God opens the womb of a woman named Hannah and provides her with the child she so longed to have. She appropriately names him Samuel, which in Hebrew means "heard by God." Hannah knew that God had listened to the cries of her heart and had given her this new life, this beautiful baby boy. She experienced the joy that comes in our Lower Story when God gives us our hearts' desires.

Once the child was weaned, she gave the boy to Eli, a priest in the temple, to be trained there. Every year Hannah would make a little robe for her son and take it to him. While she missed seeing Samuel on a daily basis and watching him grow up, she had her hands full with the five other children God bestowed on this once-barren woman.

Just as Samuel's mom-made robe got a little bigger each year, so did the assignment God had in mind for him. In the Upper Story perspective, God was preparing the young man to lead Israel through its own awkward adolescence.

Samuel comes on the scene during one of those periods of disarray for God's chosen nation. They have been attacked twice by enemies known as the Philistines, who, during the second battle, stole the ark of the covenant. God allowed the Israelites to be defeated because of their widespread disobedience and corrupt leaders. Samuel has taken over from his mentor Eli, who died when he learned that the sacred ark was in pagan hands.

By now, it's probably starting to sound like the proverbial broken record. Just when things settle down and God's people are behaving themselves, they fall off the wagon. Samuel had appointed his two sons to lead the nation, and they essentially made Capitol Hill politics look like a Sunday school picnic. What a disappointment they must have been to Samuel, for they were anything but godly. According to the Bible, they "accepted bribes and perverted justice" and used their position to line their own pockets.[1] Maybe the leaders of all the other nations were corrupt, but God's nation was called to be different.

Samuel's spiritual advisers know the two brothers have to be removed, and they call a meeting to convince him to make a change. They have the right diagnosis but the wrong solution: "Your sons do not follow your ways; now appoint a king to lead us."[2]

Samuel takes this as a personal affront—a challenge to his own leadership—so he seeks God's advice. Essentially, God tells him, "They're not rebelling against you but against me, and they've done it repeatedly since I rescued them from Egypt. Tell them they can have their king, but that it's going to cost them." When Samuel goes back to his advisers and tells them that life under a king will limit their freedoms and press their children into the king's service, they still ask for a king, finally giving the real reason: "Then we will be like all the other nations."[3]

It's a bit comical but mostly sad, isn't it, the price we're willing to pay to be like everyone else? In the Lower Story, all the other nations surrounding Israel have kings, but the Israelites just have priests and prophets leading them. Religious people. Kings wore regal robes and jeweled crowns; priestly garments were quite simple and drab in comparison. Kings could make decisions on the spot; religious leaders checked in with God first and conferred among themselves. Kings commanded massive battalions of horse-drawn chariots that carried warriors dressed in armor and brandishing swords and spears; religious leaders told their men to blow horns and shout or carry candles in clay pots.

Why can't we be like everyone else?

Simple. In God's Upper Story, he wants something better for us. He wants us to be so different that we attract others to him and his ways. "Everyone else" indeed have their kings, but they also have rampant idolatry and barbaric behavior. They worship pagan gods and seek no guidance from the one true God on how to live with and treat each other. If the Israelites were to become like "everyone else," how could God build his nation? How would they be able to attract others to him?

Despite Samuel's warnings, the people still want a king, and as we learned earlier, sometimes God gives you what you want, even if it's not what he wants for you. He always prefers that in our Lower Story we do things his way, not because he has to have his way but because he loves us. He knows that his way will always make our lives better, and this is all he has ever wanted for his special nation.

But we don't always do things his way, which only makes our lives miserable. This doesn't fluster God because it won't change the outcome of his Upper Story one bit. He *is* going to build his nation, whether we obey him or not. Ultimately, he will find a way to do the one thing he has always wanted to do—live with us in perfect community forever.

So it falls to Samuel to find a king. God directs him to a man named Saul, a man who clearly has kingly potential. He is "as handsome a young man as could be found anywhere in Israel, and he was a head taller than anyone else."[4] God may not have wanted the Israelites to have a king, but when he finally relents, he gives them exactly the kind of king they want. A king who looks like a king on the outside. In our day, we would say that Saul looked "presidential."

Samuel meets with Saul over a big meal and explains that God has chosen him to lead the nation of Israel. He then sends him off on a spiritual retreat to prepare him for his daunting assignment. When Saul returns, Samuel calls the nation together and introduces him as their new king. After a brief celebration, he is put to the test. A neighboring nation threatens to gouge the right eye out of everyone in Israel as a way to disgrace them. (War is never pretty, but in ancient times, it was downright ugly.) Saul responds swiftly and dramatically. His first battle as king of Israel is a resounding victory, and the nation, with both eyes intact, is back on its way to establishing God's reputation throughout the land.

Just to make sure they won't mess things up again, Samuel calls the nation together and gives what amounts to his farewell speech as their leader—his final instructions to a nation that had finally gotten what everyone else had. It is a brilliant speech that takes them all the way back in their history to their escape from Egypt and reminds them of the many times they forgot God and suffered for it. Then he chides them for going against God's wishes by asking for a king. He must have been quite convicting, because they begin to repent for committing such a grievous sin against God. But Samuel reassures them that if they obey God and faithfully serve him with all their hearts, everything will be just fine because God still loves them and will not reject them. After all, he gave them their king, didn't he?

After Samuel's powerful speech reminding the Israelites that God has given them a second chance and all they have to do to receive his blessings is to honor and obey him, Saul takes the reins as king and promptly forgets everything Samuel said. Throughout his reign, the Israelites wage a bitter war against the Philistines. Then, at God's instruction, his attention turns to another enemy, the Amalekites. Several hundred years prior, the Amalekites had ambushed the Israelites as they were fleeing from Egypt, and God had told Moses to write down these words: "I will completely blot out the name of Amalek from under heaven."[5]

God has a score to settle. He tells Saul to attack the Amalekites and completely take them out. He is to take no prisoners, nor is he to take anything that belongs to these people. But Saul cannot resist. The enemy king would be a great trophy, so Saul spares his life and plunders his flocks. And when Samuel confronts him about his disobedience, Saul tries to rationalize on the run, claiming he took the animals not for himself but to be used as sacrificial offerings to God.

Samuel isn't buying it: "To obey is better than sacrifice."[6] It is the beginning of the end for Saul.

It is easy to read this account from a Lower Story perspective and be troubled by God's insistence that the entire Amalekite nation be destroyed. What possible Upper Story message can we glean from this? More important, how does this message apply to the here and now—the way we live our lives today?

I believe we see two Upper Story messages here—one a warning, the other an instruction. Samuel shares the warning with us when he tells Saul, "He who is the Glory of Israel does not lie or change his mind."[7] God will do what he says he will do, and it is to our peril that we forget this truth. The Amalekites had ambushed God's chosen people when they were vulnerable slaves trying to escape from Egypt. God's declaration that the Amalekites would be destroyed spread far and wide and was passed down from generation to generation. To let Saul off the hook for disobeying God would have made God a liar. While it is true that God is merciful, he is also just. He will always welcome us back, but he will not protect us from the consequences of our rejection of his ways.

The other Upper Story message is that God's people are called to be different, to stand out in contrast to others by reflecting his very character. Saul not only disobeyed God, but his actions misrepresented God. As the new king of God's chosen nation, he caused people to get the wrong idea of what God was really like. By plundering the prized possessions of the Amalekites, he became like all the other kings—nothing special about *this* nation.

Like it or not, those of us who trust Jesus Christ are his visible witness. Just as Saul and the Israelites were God's representatives, so we, the New Testament people, are the representatives of God today. As we will learn later in this story, the New Testament church is called the "body of Christ." Most of the people in our world will get their take on God from us. We may be the only Bible they ever "read." Our interactions with them may be all they glimpse of God's grand design in his Upper Story.

Whether you are in middle school or coveting a new sports car just like the one your neighbor drives, it is a lot easier trying to be like everyone else. But God wants us to be different. Not weird or eccentric, but different. His Upper

Story tells of his relentless pursuit of people to join his perfect community, where they will spend eternity with him. By living splendidly *unlike* "everyone else," we give others a glimpse into what life in this community will be like. God doesn't want us to be just like everyone else; he wants us to be known by our love. He wants us to look like Jesus.

Chapter

11

FROM SHEPHERD TO KING

*"The LORD does not look at the things people
look at. People look at the outward appearance,
but the LORD looks at the heart."*

1 SAMUEL 16:7

Samuel anoints David	David kills Goliath	Saul tries to kill David	Saul dies	David named king
BC 1025	1025		1010	1010

WHAT'S HAPPENING IN THE UPPER STORY

A significant shift takes place in the Upper and Lower Stories. In the Lower Story, God is going to replace King Saul with a young shepherd boy from the tribe of Judah named David. David is a man after God's own heart. If there is a human king who can represent God, David is as close as you can get. From the Upper Story, God sees the evil pattern of Israel and their persistent violations to the law he gave through Moses. Their evil will continue to grow and distort the witness of God to the surrounding nations. God would be just in removing his blessing from them, but he had made an unconditional promise to Abraham: the way for everyone to come back into a relationship with God will come from this nation. God always keeps his promises. So he narrows his scope to the tribe of Judah, with a new unconditional promise made to David. The promised Messiah will come from this tribe.

ALIGNING OUR STORY TO GOD'S STORY

When Samuel came to Bethlehem to see which of Jesse's sons would be the next king of Israel, Jesse didn't even put the young, glowing-with-health David in the lineup.[1] But when others only saw a shepherd boy, God saw the king of a great nation. God sees more in you than others see—and perhaps more than you even see in yourself. Remember that! David was anointed king of Israel as a young boy. He would not be inaugurated king until after fourteen years of being chased by King Saul like a fugitive. God uses this long season to grow David's dependency on him. God often brings us through difficult seasons to prepare us for bigger challenges ahead.

According to legend, the custom for many years on the Hawaiian Islands was for a suitor to pay for the right of asking his beloved's hand in marriage by giving her father cattle. Most young women of marrying age would require two, sometimes even three, cows. If a daughter was a special catch, she might fetch four cows. It is rumored that one father in the distant past received an unfathomable *five* cows for his amazingly gorgeous and charming daughter.

An islander named Sam Karoo had two daughters, and he faced a serious dilemma. No one on the islands considered his older daughter beautiful. Aware that her shyness and plain features were not assets for a proposal, Sam had accepted many years earlier that he would not likely fetch three cows for her. He dreamed of two, but would settle for one. In fact, if he knew the man would treat her well, he would let her marry without receiving any cows. He felt fortunate that everyone agreed his *younger* daughter was definitely a three-cow kind of girl.

Then one day, Johnny Lingo, a wealthy landowner, came to pay Sam a visit. Everyone knew Johnny was ready to settle down and assumed he was coming to propose to Sam's younger daughter. But to the surprise of the whole town, and to Dad's delight, Johnny came a callin' for his older daughter.

It was more than Sam could've hoped for. *I may get three cows for her after all.* Then he let his imagination get the best of him and thought he might even receive four cows from the wealthy suitor. You can imagine Sam's shock when Johnny brought him *ten* cows for his daughter.

When the happy couple came back from a yearlong honeymoon, the villagers were amazed at the difference in the young wife's presence. She was strikingly beautiful, graceful, poised, confident, and self-assured. Everyone thought Johnny got a bargain paying only ten cows for her hand in marriage.

It was clear that Johnny had viewed Sam's older daughter differently than her father and the other villagers. He saw beyond her outward appearance and recognized the beauty of her heart and character. The value he placed on her true beauty helped her realize her true worth. The moment he paid ten cows for her, she became a ten-cow wife!

Sometimes someone else has to tell us what we're worth before we can realize it ourselves. Such was the case with a certain young shepherd boy named David, the one who discovered his true identity as a man after God's own heart.

In the previous chapter, we learned that Israel wanted a king so they could be like the other nations. God allowed it, and they selected Saul—"as handsome a young man as could be found anywhere in Israel"—a five-cow king for sure!

Unfortunately for the people of Israel, Saul didn't align his life with or rule the nation according to God's guidelines. Saul refused to accept his role in the Upper Story. His disobedience sent a contradictory message about the nature and character of the God of Israel. Instead of the surrounding nations seeing God as holy, just, loving, and full of grace, through Saul's leadership they saw God as cruel, vindictive, and greedy. Of course, God cannot allow this, so he communicates to the prophet Samuel that it is time to find another king—one who will represent God's heart and passion.

On the direct order of God, Samuel is sent to the house of Jesse from Bethlehem. God makes it clear that one of Jesse's sons will become the next king of Israel. Samuel fills his horn with oil and leaves on what appears to be a fairly straightforward assignment.

When Samuel arrives and explains his mission, Jesse lines up his seven sons from oldest to youngest. Samuel goes through the lineup but doesn't feel led to anoint any of them as the next king of Israel. Perplexed, Samuel asks, "Are these all the sons you have?"[2]

Jesse admits he has an eighth son named David but hasn't thought to bring him off the field from tending sheep because he doesn't see him being even a possibility. The Hebrew word Jesse uses to describe his youngest son can be translated in English as "runt." Like Sam Karoo's unattractive daughter, David is the "runt of the litter," a good boy but not a contender for a cow, let alone a kingdom.

David comes in from the field to meet the famous prophet, and before he knows it, Samuel pours oil down the boy's head. God confirms that David will be the next king of Israel: "This is the one."[3] David is a mere sixteen years old.

And there is a big difference in being anointed as king and being inaugurated as the king. David is God's pick, but the young man has to wait for a date in the future to actually become king. However, the benefits begin immediately. We are told that from the time David is anointed with oil, the Lord is with him.

So what is it that God sees inside of David? What is it that God looks for when he gazes into *your* heart? "I have found David son of Jesse, a man after my own heart; he will do everything I want him to do."[4] This is the kind of person with whom God wants to build his nation. He wants our priorities to be his priorities, our allegiance to be completely to him. Saul was *almost* totally committed, but he kept a little part of life to control for himself. He withheld his allegiance just a little, thinking it wouldn't matter. But it does.

Almost never works with God. Why? Because he knows we can never experience his fullest blessing if we hold back even a little from him. I'm not a gambler, but I confess to occasionally landing on one of those televised poker tournaments as I'm channel surfing. To be honest, it seldom holds my attention because I don't have a clue what's going on except that a lot of money is at stake and the actual skill comes in how well you can "bluff" your opponents. But there is one move I get—the time when one of the players says, "All in," and shoves his entire pile of chips to the center of the table. It's all or nothing. Win big or go home.

With poker, "all in" is a huge risk. With God, it's a sure thing. It's the transaction God proposes to us that is rewarded with life itself. To this day, most Jewish people regularly recite this "all in" declaration, which is referred to as the Shema: "Hear, O Israel: The LORD our God, the LORD is one. Love the LORD your God with all your heart and with all your soul and with all your strength."[5]

Throughout the Bible, this "all in" proposition of total commitment to God is repeated to remind us that "almost" does not work with God. But unlike poker, where all you lose is money, failure to go "all in" with God has devastating consequences:

> Now what I am commanding you today is not too difficult for you
> or beyond your reach . . .

> See, I set before you today life and prosperity, death and destruction.
> For I command you today to love the LORD your God, to walk in obedience
> to him, and to keep his commands, decrees and laws; then you will live
> and increase, and the LORD your God will bless you . . .
>
> But if your heart turns away and you are not obedient, and if you are
> drawn away to bow down to other gods and worship them, I declare to
> you this day that you will certainly be destroyed.[6]

Saul refused to go all in, and it cost him his throne. When God looked into
the heart of David, he saw an "all in" kind of guy. Where others saw a shepherd
covered with dirt and grime, God saw a boy who went the extra mile to protect
and care for his father's sheep. As we get to know David better, we learn that
on two occasions the flock he was tending was attacked by wild animals—a
bear and a lion. Risking his own life, he fought off these beasts with his bare
hands and rescued the sheep. That's the kind of king God was looking for. If
he would go to such lengths to rescue an animal, just think how far he would
go to guide and protect God's special nation.

As it turns out, it didn't take long to see David's heart at work on behalf
of Israel.

Israel was at war with the Philistines, and things weren't going well. The
Philistines had what we might call a "ringer," a kind of secret weapon. For
example, let's say all the teams in your recreational basketball league have players
who are about the same age and ability—except for one team that went out
and recruited a former college basketball star who is six inches taller than your
tallest player. This guy would be considered a ringer, and the Philistines had
one in an extremely large guy named Goliath.

You probably already know how this story goes. Goliath mocks Saul's
army every day because they are too cowardly to fight him. Jesse sends David
to the front lines to deliver some home-cooked food to his brothers. David
hears Goliath taunting the Israelites and offers himself to Saul to go out and
fight the obnoxious giant. When Saul finally gives in, David refuses his offer of
royal armor and instead picks up a few smooth stones and grabs his slingshot.

The rest, as they say, is history. One shot, and the nine-foot giant, Goliath, falls dead. Israel defeats the Philistines because a teenager trusts God. As Goliath prepares to crush David, the shepherd shouts his confidence to the enemy: "You come against me with sword and spear and javelin, but I come against you in the name of the LORD Almighty."[7]

Talk about being "all in"! David doesn't *mostly* trust God. He doesn't ask a few soldiers to back him up with their spears. To him, it is a no-brainer: *God will save us.*

Between being anointed by Samuel and then slaying the enemy's secret weapon, you would think David would be coronated on the spot. However, this isn't in God's plan yet. David is only sixteen years old. Over the course of the next fourteen years, he will learn more about how to persevere and trust in God as Saul, jealous and further rejecting God's ways, tries to kill him. But eventually he is inaugurated as king of Israel and proves to be the great leader God wanted for his kingdom. Even during this interim time, David could have easily demanded royal privileges or played the part of a celebrity hero, but he doesn't. He just keeps tending his father's sheep and writing poetry (maybe you've heard of the psalms?), acting more like a cowboy than a king. He courageously trusts God with his life when facing a giant. And David humbly trusts God during the "in-between" time of waiting until he becomes king.

In our Lower Stories, we often look at ourselves as if we're undeserving, no-kind-of-cow little runts. Like we're just dirty field hands who are only good enough to tend sheep. We're not king material. We think, "God can't possibly use me to build his perfect nation because I don't have a seminary degree." Or you aren't a dynamic speaker. Or you are unemployed. Or your marriage just fell apart. Or you haven't been a follower of Jesus since childhood.

But God still has giants to kill. He still has big, hairy, audacious plans to accomplish that require someone like David to get the job done. The shepherd boy's unlikely rise to power reminds us that in the Upper Story, God often uses underdogs to advance his plan. He is not impressed with titles or rank or status but looks inside the heart to find people he can use. He knows that with *our* willingness to go all in for him and *his* power to transform shepherds into kings, nothing is impossible.

Chapter

12

THE TRIALS
OF A KING

> *Create in me a pure heart, O God,*
> *and renew a steadfast spirit within me.*
> *Do not cast me from your presence*
> *or take your Holy Spirit from me.*
> *Restore to me the joy of your salvation*
> *and grant me a willing spirit, to sustain me.*
>
> PSALM 51:10–12

David's reign	David and Bathsheba	Solomon's reign	Temple building
1010–970		970–930	966–959

BC

WHAT'S HAPPENING IN THE UPPER STORY

God's plan of redemption is moving forward. Israel is established in the land of Canaan and has become a great nation, just as God promised. David, as God's chosen king, is blessed with God's presence and prosperity. Everything he sets his hand to do is successful. God made an unconditional promise to David that the Messiah, the King of all kings, would come from his family. Even with David's moral failure—his adultery with Bathsheba and the murder of Uriah—the plan presses forward in the Upper Story, even though the Lower Story consequences in David's life are severe. Demonstrating his forgiveness and grace, God promises that the next king will be Bathsheba's son.

ALIGNING OUR STORY TO GOD'S STORY

Saul and David both sin against God. Saul does not complete the assignment God gave him to destroy the Amalekites and then does not wait for Samuel to offer the sacrifice. David commits adultery with Bathsheba and covers it up by murdering her husband. Yet Saul is rejected, and David is accepted. The difference seems to be found in their hearts. When confronted, Saul rationalized and made excuses; David comes clean with God and repents. When we make mistakes, no matter how grave, come clean with God, and he will forgive and restore you.

Many years ago, a little boy lived in the country, out in a rural part of West Texas (you're probably thinking, *Isn't all of West Texas rural?*). His family had to use an outhouse, and the boy hated it because it was hot in the summer and cold in the winter, and it stunk all the time. The outhouse sat on the bank of a creek, and the boy fantasized about pushing their permanent porta potty over the edge and into the water someday.

Well, one afternoon after a hard spring rain, the little creek became so swollen that the boy decided it was his perfect chance to get rid of the much-hated outhouse. He got an old two-by-four from the barn and used it as a giant crowbar, prying and pushing until the outhouse toppled backward into the creek and floated away.

The boy wondered how long it would be before the "outhouse hit the fan," so to speak, and it didn't take long. That evening, his dad told him they were going to the woodshed after supper. Weighing his options, the boy decided to play innocent and asked why. His father replied, "Someone pushed the outhouse into the creek today. It was you, wasn't it, son?"

The boy thought for a moment, switched strategies, and answered, "Yes." After a quiet pause, he continued, "Dad, I read in school last week that George Washington chopped down a cherry tree and didn't get into trouble because he told the truth."

His dad said, "Well, son, George Washington's father wasn't in that cherry tree!"

While you may have never pushed an outhouse into a creek with your dad in it, all of us can identify with this story in at least three ways. First, there is something inside us that wants to do things our own way, no matter what the consequences. The Bible refers to this as the realm of "the flesh." Second, our lack of goodness affects other people, not just us. And similarly, most of us have been in a lot of outhouses that have been pushed over by sinful people. Finally, none of us get away with keeping our sinful acts secret. In fact, we often end up sinning more—lying and deceiving—to cover up the reality of our bad choices.

As we check in on David's progress as king of Israel, we discover that he has his own issues with getting what he wants. At first, things couldn't have gone better for David or for Israel. After he is anointed as king, it seems as if everything he attempts turns out just right. Israel has been plagued with attacks from invading armies, but under his leadership his army racks up an impressive string of victories over Israel's enemies, including twice defeating the ferocious Philistines and even freeing Jerusalem from the iron hand of the Jebusites. In one battle alone—against the Arameans—David's army kills forty thousand foot soldiers. So impressive is this victory that all the other kings who supported the Arameans surrender and make peace with Israel.

But David is more than a great military leader. Remember, God chose him because of his heart for the Lord, and it is this tender heart that enables David to lead his people spiritually as well. Under his leadership, the ark of the covenant is returned to Jerusalem—such a huge event that the Israelites celebrate with a parade to rival anything Macy's has done on Thanksgiving Day. The Bible says that "David was dancing before the LORD with all his might" as the ark entered Jerusalem.[1] Now the city is not only the national capital of Israel but its spiritual capital as well.

All because of David's heart for the Lord.

David the dusty shepherd boy has become Israel's Renaissance man. A fierce warrior, gifted poet, and compassionate king who loves God and serves him with intense passion. Under his leadership, Israel prospers. His army continues to defeat any enemy that dares to attack. Life is good for David.

Until he decides to topple the outhouse.

It happens one spring evening when David can't sleep. After tossing and turning, he gets up and walks out onto the roof for some fresh air and suddenly notices "the girl next door." She is taking a bath, and she is beautiful—and David can't help but notice her.

At this point, I believe we can cut David a little slack. He isn't out on the roof with binoculars or camera, scoping out the neighborhood. If he noticed this beautiful woman and returned inside without further reaction, I suspect he would have done nothing wrong.

But David not only stares at her; he immediately has to have her—right then and no matter the cost. So he sends one of his servants to find out who she is: Bathsheba, the wife of Uriah, one of his loyal soldiers off fighting a war for his king. Next, the situation becomes a biblical episode of *Desperate Housewives*. David sends a messenger to bring her to him; he sleeps with her; she goes back home. A short while later, she sends word to David that she is pregnant.

It happened just that fast.

One minute, David is God's treasured king of the special nation he is building—a righteous and holy man with a heart for God; the next minute he is going his own way to satisfy his own appetites. What was he thinking? How could someone so dedicated to God let his guard down so quickly? It's one of the oldest Lower Story tragedies, and it still happens to this day.

You've probably heard the expression "the bigger they are, the harder they fall." One of the great dangers of success is that it lulls us into thinking we don't need God anymore. Think back to all of the leaders in government, business, entertainment, and sports who have fallen because of their own immoral choices. In almost every case, these men and women had it all, just like David. Success, money, power, fame. When things are going great—when everything is working out better than we ever could have expected—watch out. That's when we are most susceptible to taking matters into our hands and thinking we deserve to have what we want, however we want it. We think we can topple an outhouse without anyone ever noticing.

And with David it only gets worse. This poet-king who once wrote, "Turn from evil and do good,"[2] finds himself in a scandal and does what most people do when they've done something wrong and fear being exposed: he plans a cover-up—one that ranks right up there as one of the most diabolical schemes anyone could conceive. He sends Uriah—Bathsheba's husband and a loyal soldier of great integrity—into battle and then secretly tells his commander to put him on the front line, where he will surely be killed. With Uriah out of the picture, David marries Bathsheba, she delivers a son, and David dodges a bullet.

Not exactly.

With God, there are no cover-ups, and in David's case, his secret isn't hidden for long. A prophet named Nathan confronts him with his sin, reminding the king that his sin is not just against Bathsheba and Uriah but also against God himself. David has blown it and has made matters worse by trying to cover it up, as if he could be above God's law.

So David's secret comes out, just like all sinful actions emerge eventually. So just like Saul, he blew it and ruined his ability to lead the nation of Israel, right? No, there's a crucial difference, and it has to do with David's response.

When Saul was confronted by Samuel about his disobedience, he tried to rationalize his behavior and make up excuses. He never fully owned up to his sin. Even though his sin seemed to be less egregious than David's (although there is no hierarchy of sins in God's eyes since we all fall short of his holiness), Saul was too proud to admit he did wrong.

David, on the other hand, responds to Nathan's accusation with six simple words: "I have sinned against the LORD."[3] He tells the truth. He takes full responsibility for the error of his ways, admitting that he has done wrong. In seeking God's forgiveness, David writes one of the most beautiful poems in all of Scripture. It begins:

> Have mercy on me, O God,
>   according to your unfailing love;
>   according to your great compassion
>   blot out my transgressions.
> Wash away all my iniquity
>   and cleanse me from my sin.[4]

God knows we will break his rules—rules that he established to help us live well and treat each other with kindness and respect. It breaks his heart when this happens, but it doesn't prevent him from giving us the most remarkable gift he can give: *forgiveness*. But he can only do this if we acknowledge what we've done and refuse to rationalize our way out of it. One of the great promises in the Bible is this: "If we confess our sins, [God] is faithful and just and will forgive us our sins."[5] God is more interested in how we respond to breaking the rules than in simply punishing us for disobeying. He wants to know what is in our hearts. Are we humble and teachable and willing to learn from our mistakes, or are we proud and defensive and oblivious to our need for God's mercy and love? Despite his horrendously sinful behavior, David realized he had sinned most of all against his God.

If you fast-forward to the New Testament book of Hebrews, you will find a section often referred to as the "Hall of Faith"—a list of the godliest and most faithful men and women in the Bible—and right in the middle of the list is David. There is no asterisk by his name with a footnote that reads, "Not counting his sinful behavior with Bathsheba and Uriah." Disobedience is disobedience, but what David did was so deceitful, so perverse that you would think his name would be on another list: the Bible's "Hall of Shame." Instead, he is right there alongside Abraham, Moses, and Gideon.

Why would God let this happen? Why is David still revered as Israel's greatest king and remembered for his heart for God, and not his moral meltdown? More important, what is the Upper Story message for any of us who are living in ways that displease God?

The answer begins back in the garden. Try as we may, we cannot be perfect. Through the choice of Adam and Eve, all of us will struggle with temptation and sometimes give in to it. I wish I could tell you that as a pastor, I have never sinned, but then I would be committing the sin of lying. Even when God chose David to lead his nation as king, he knew that David was human and therefore could not be perfect.

I'm convinced there is another reason that David's sin, and how he handled it, landed him in God's Hall of Faith. One of the tragic truths about sin is that it has consequences. God's forgiveness restores us into a right relationship with him, but it doesn't erase the consequences of our actions. If you look at David's life, you will see that everything is good for him up until his encounter with Bathsheba. From this point on, everything goes downhill. His baby dies. His daughter is raped. His son Absalom mounts a rebellion against him and tries to take his throne. Then that son dies, followed by yet another attempted rebellion against him.

David could have been bitter and angry at God for not stepping in and preventing him from having to deal with all of these crushing blows, but he wasn't. Instead, he faced the consequences of his sin with dignity. Even though so many things turned sour for him, at the end of his life David is still deeply in love with God. His final prayer in front of his assembled nation is one of praise and thankfulness to God.

Now here is the best part of this story. Because David owned up to his sin and accepted the consequences of his behavior, God continued to bless him in other ways, including allowing him to have more children with Bathsheba. One of these children was Solomon, who would continue the lineage of David as king of Israel.

It is a head-scratching demonstration of God's grace. While the decisions that David made brought a string of negative consequences, God deposits a sweet drop of grace in David's life. David had more than one wife, which was a common practice in that day. God wouldn't be open to criticism if he were to tap one of David's other wives to bring us the next king of Israel. But he doesn't. He chooses the relationship born out of adultery, murder, and deceit. Not only is Bathsheba's son, Solomon, to sit on the throne by divine appointment, but it also means that Bathsheba is now a part of the lineage of Jesus Christ.

This is just the way God works. He would love it if we could all be like Uriah, the loyal soldier who selflessly served his king. He exhorts us to be like Nathan, having the courage to confront a friend who has taken a wrong turn in life. But if, like David, we do something horribly wrong, he still loves us and can use us to draw others to him if we have the character to own up to it, accept the consequences, and continue loving him with all our heart, soul, and mind.

There are few worse feelings than those that accompany seeing flashing lights in the rearview mirror. No one likes to get caught doing something wrong. When it comes to speeding, the consequences are a ticket, a fine, and some embarrassment. When it comes to our relationship with God, a lot more is at stake. When we violate God's standards for us, our human tendency is to hide, to try to talk our way out of it, to pretend it isn't a big deal. Each time we do this, we fall farther away from God and run the risk of forever being excluded from the perfect community he is building.

In the Lower Story, David messed around with another man's wife. In the Upper Story, God finds a way to use a deeply flawed man to serve him. By confessing that what he did was indeed a big deal and accepting the consequences of his behavior with dignity, David gives a glimpse of how we can rise above our own sinfulness.

On any given Sunday morning, there are men and women in our church who have messed up at some point in their lives. Men who have cheated on their wives. Women who are alcoholics. People of all ages who have been trapped in the grip of drug addiction. They may be singing in the choir or working with our young people. They may be greeting visitors or rocking babies to sleep in the nursery. These are modern-day members of the "Hall of Faith"—people who experienced a devastating fall from grace but today serve God with a passion and purity that are infectious.

Maybe this is the point. Maybe the reason David remains one of the most celebrated characters in God's story is to highlight this message for ordinary people like you and me: If God can redeem a man who did something this awful and restore him to such a lofty position, imagine what he can do for us!

Imagine what he can do *through* you for his kingdom.

Chapter
13

THE KING WHO
HAD IT ALL

Pride goes before destruction,
a haughty spirit before a fall.

PROVERBS 16:18

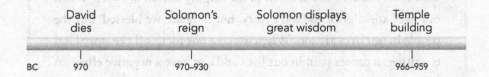

David dies	Solomon's reign	Solomon displays great wisdom	Temple building
BC 970	970–930		966–959

143

WHAT'S HAPPENING IN THE UPPER STORY

God is keeping his promise to David by passing the kingdom of Israel to his son Solomon. Solomon receives the throne from his father in the best possible condition. In the early years of his reign, Solomon makes wise decisions that are in alignment with God's will, and the nation is blessed beyond measure. Royalty from other nations visit to see this amazing success for themselves. Credit is given to the God of Israel. As planned, God is revealing his name, his power, and his plan to other nations so they can be blessed as well. At points during Solomon's reign, he lost his way. This is most evident when he married foreign women who worshiped other gods, which ultimately led him to compromise Israel's witness of a holy God to the surrounding nations. From the Upper Story, God decides to divide Israel into two weaker kingdoms, but for the sake of David, he waits until after Solomon's reign ends.[1]

ALIGNING OUR STORY TO GOD'S STORY

Solomon started strong, and God blessed him and his people. Somewhere along the way, Solomon lost his focus and forgot the wise counsel he wrote in the book of Proverbs. This slow descent away from God's story caused the division of the mighty nation of Israel. When our lives are aligned to God's story, not only are we blessed, but the people in our lives are too. When we take our focus off the story God is writing, it causes pain in our lives and can have a negative effect on other people, even on generations to come.

*H*ave you ever been tempted to drive through those exclusive neighborhoods in your city just to see how the other half lives? You know what I'm talking about. You're not really snooping—just driving past the lovely homes to admire the architecture. And if it happens to be at night and you can see over the fence and into the house through the large picture windows, who can blame you for taking a peek? Maybe you can see a grand piano or beautiful artwork on the walls, elegant furnishings, maybe even catch a glimpse of the "king and queen" of the manor being waited on by servants.

Human beings seem to have a fascination with wealth and glamour, particularly royalty. In November 2010, the entire world was captivated by the engagement of a guy named William Mountbatten-Windsor, otherwise known as Prince William, to a beautiful young "commoner" named Kate Middleton. Will's father, Prince Charles, stands in line to be the next king of England when his mother, Queen Elizabeth II, dies. Then, because William is Charles's oldest son (you may know his mum was Princess Diana), he stands in line to inherit the throne after his father dies.

At this point in history, royal succession in England is orderly and predictable. Not quite the case in ancient Israel. As King David grows feeble with age, one of his sons named Adonijah sees an opportunity to replace Dad and makes his move. He calls some friends together and essentially declares himself king. Remember Nathan, the prophet who confronted David about his sin? He sees what is going on and knows that David has already decided he wants the first surviving son he had with Bathsheba to be king, namely, Solomon. So once again, Nathan has to give David some bad news: Israel has a new king, and his name isn't Solomon.

Even though David is feeble, he isn't timid. He goes into crisis mode and declares Solomon as his choice for king, finds a priest to join Nathan to anoint Solomon, then plans a major celebration with trumpets blasting and the people shouting, "Long live King Solomon!"[2] Adonijah is just finishing up his own celebration and hears the roar of the crowd, and when he learns what has happened, he has one of those "uh-oh" moments, knowing that Solomon's first royal act may be directed at him.

When Solomon learns that Adonijah is hiding in fear, he makes one of those decisions that contributed to his reputation for wisdom: "If he shows himself to be worthy, not a hair of his head will fall to the ground; but if evil is found in him, he will die."[3] As David passes the leadership baton to Solomon, Israel is in great shape. Financially, they are strong and prosperous—no trillion-dollar debt hanging over them. And they are at peace—no wars with neighbors in the Middle East to drag down Solomon's popularity rating. If ever there was a good time to be king of Israel, this was it.

God approaches Solomon early in his reign and tells him he can have everything he wants. Can you imagine what this would be like? God, who can provide *anything*, comes and says, "Whatever you want is yours. No boundaries. No rules. Ask for anything, and I'll give it to you."

Be honest. If you could have anything by just asking for it, what would it be? Many people who come into huge sums of money—whether they are professional athletes who sign multimillion-dollar deals or lottery winners who become rich overnight—think they need to look like a millionaire so they waste no time buying a tricked-out luxury automobile and a new bazillion-square-foot house. Me? I'd like to think I would give all my money to the poor or build orphanages or hospitals or churches. But when you think about it, wouldn't it be cool to have your very own golf course?

Solomon asks for wisdom.

What is astonishing is that his request is not so much for himself but for insight to fulfill his duties as the leader of God's people. He essentially tells God, "You are giving me this awesome privilege of serving you, but I'm a mere child and this nation is huge, so please give me the wisdom to be a just and righteous king."

Now I'm *really* feeling embarrassed about wanting that golf course.

God honors Solomon's request, and it doesn't take long for the new king to put his gift from God to work. One of the duties of a king is to resolve disputes, and shortly after Solomon becomes king, two women come to him with a baby. Both claim to be the mother of the baby, and it is Solomon's job to decide what to do. You or I might have flipped a coin or chosen the woman who looked more like a mother to us. Solomon has a better idea. With both women standing before him, he asks one of his attendants to cut the baby in half and give each mother half of the baby. The first mother thinks this is a great idea, but the second mother is horrified and rescinds her claim on the child. Knowing that the real mother of the baby wouldn't allow any harm to come to it, Solomon gives the baby to the second mother.

When I tried this trick, it didn't work out quite the same way. When my boys were small, they came to me fighting over who had the rights to a Hot Wheels car, each trying to clutch the tiny red Camaro. Seizing the opportunity to have a Solomon-sized teaching moment, I asked them to go get my hacksaw so we could cut it in two. They both yelled, "Cool, Dad! Awesome!" and ran to get more Hot Wheels. Not quite what I had in mind. It takes wisdom to know how to use wisdom.

Not only did Solomon desire wisdom for himself so he would lead God's nation well, but he also wanted every citizen to have wisdom and apply it to their everyday lives. So he wrote down hundreds of wise sayings that are included in the Bible in a book called Proverbs. Perhaps the best definition of a proverb comes from Solomon's own words describing a proverb as necessary "for receiving instruction in prudent behavior."[4] These short, simple instructions offered practical guidance to help everyone in God's community live well and prosper:

A gossip betrays a confidence; so avoid anyone who talks too much.[5]

The plans of the diligent lead to profit as surely as haste leads to
poverty.[6]

A fortune made by a lying tongue is a fleeting vapor and a deadly snare.[7]

An inheritance claimed too soon will not be blessed at the end.[8]

Sluggards do not plow in season; so at harvest time they look but find
nothing.[9]

If all this weren't enough, his father, David, raised all the money to build a temple for God. Not just any temple, but one worthy of God's very presence so that as his people worshiped him they would be reminded of the awesome and majestic God they served.

According to the biblical record, it took 180,000 workers seven years to build this temple. When the temple was finished, God's very presence took up residence in a sacred section called the Most Holy Place and then God approached Solomon with further instructions to help him develop into a great leader.

It is the same Upper Story message God has been telling his people from the beginning: If you just do what I say and make me the Lord over everything in your life, I'll be able to come down and live with you and give you everything you ever need. Forever! And by this time, Solomon begins to see that God is delivering on his promises, because things couldn't be going better for Solomon and the entire nation of Israel.

The lavish temple and the prosperity throughout the land attracted exactly the kind of attention God intended. Word traveled fast that something big was happening in Israel. People came from all over just to see these people and their temple—including a glamorous royal from a neighboring kingdom, the queen of Sheba. She had heard all about Israel's great wealth but had to see it for herself because she couldn't believe any nation could be *that* rich, or any leader *that* wise.

So the queen enters Jerusalem with a large caravan of camels carrying gifts for Solomon. During her visit, she continually takes note of the surroundings and sees that the nation's prosperity is even greater than she had been told. Her final conversation with Solomon is Exhibit A for what God is trying to do with the community he is building: "Praise be to the LORD your God, who has delighted in you and placed you on the throne of Israel."[10] God wants *everyone* to become part of his perfect community. What the queen sees in the people and prosperity of Israel is a reflection of the God they serve.

With celebrities like the queen of Sheba "tweeting" about her visit, dignitaries from all over the region came to seek Solomon's advice and present him with gifts of gold, silver, weapons, spices, and horses. He had a fleet of ships that sailed the world, returning every three years loaded down with riches. According to the Bible, he accumulated more than twenty-five *tons* of gold, which along with all his other possessions made him "greater in riches and wisdom than all the other kings of the earth."[11]

Solomon seemed to be the perfect king, a rock star for God and his nation. But you know what's coming, right? In the course of any good story, it seems that life can't go smoothly for too long before conflict rears its ugly head. This was the case for Solomon as well. By the time his reign drew to an end, he had faced rebellion from within and attacks from outsiders who once thought he hung the moon. The changes didn't happen overnight, but in a succession of events that came together like dominoes toppling. The wise, humble, unfathomably rich king tumbled off his throne and found himself running for his life.

You've probably heard about the phenomenon of putting a frog in a pan of boiling water. He will immediately jump out to save his life—just like when you touch scalding water and instantly jerk your hand away. Our little green friend has the same reaction, only with spring-loaded legs. But if you put this same frog in a pan of lukewarm water, he will sit there as happy and content as tourists in a Jacuzzi. Then as you gradually turn up the heat on the stove, our buddy Kermit only relaxes all the more. As the water gets warmer and warmer, he doesn't realize that his warm bath has become a boiling cooker until it's too late.

The same thing happened to Solomon. He got cooked. In addition to having palaces filled with the most exquisite and expensive stuff, Solomon also had a lot of wives. I'm not talking about two or three here. I mean seven hundred wives and three hundred concubines (fancy word for "more wives"). According to the cultural customs of that time, this wasn't necessarily unusual or wrong in God's sight. But Solomon took wives from other nations, disobeying one of God's rules for living well. He had warned the Israelites not to marry people from other nations because it could lead them to worship foreign gods. Solomon probably thought he was too wise to let any of his wives turn him away from God, and from all evidence, he was right. At first. We don't know if his fall started after twenty years of ruling Israel or thirty years into his reign. But eventually the water got too hot. All the Bible tells us is that "as Solomon grew old, his wives turned his heart after other gods."[12]

In all of my years of ministry, I've never met anyone who jumped into a pot of boiling water. I've never met anyone who woke up one morning and declared to himself, "I'm going to ruin my relationships with my family and commit adultery today." I've never met a businessman who just out of the blue decided to embezzle from his company. I've never met a woman who decided to become an alcoholic. But sadly, I've known men who lost their marriages and their businesses. I've known women who had to be committed to rehab. If you could talk with them, they would tell you, "The water didn't seem too hot at first."

In our Lower Story lives, it can seem like everyone else is having all the fun. Everyone else can do whatever they want to do, but I'm stuck with these "rules" from God that keep me from having any fun. Solomon probably thought those women from neighboring countries were so exotic and beautiful that he deserved to enjoy them as wives while having the willpower to reject their gods. But God's Upper Story never changes, nor is it influenced by what we want. He may allow us to have what we want, even if it violates his standards for enjoying life with him. But ultimately he is building a perfect community in which people treat each other with respect and honor him as the one true God.

What about you? Do you find yourself tempted from time to time to dive into that lukewarm water? We must keep in mind that what feels warm and soothing to us today may well become the cauldron that cooks our goose (not just our frogs!) tomorrow. How we live our lives matters. Our prayer must be that we will not only start strong, but also finish strong. The best advice Solomon offers us is to be extremely careful about jumping into "harmless" pots of water. But if we have—and we're already feeling cooked—then we must remember that with God it is never too late to come back to him even though we may be a bit overdone and wrinkled. True wisdom leads us to depend on God and humbly trust that he knows what is best for us.

Chapter 14

A KINGDOM TORN IN TWO

*"Your father put a heavy yoke on us, but now
lighten the harsh labor and the heavy yoke
he put on us, and we will serve you."*

1 KINGS 12:4

Kingdom divided	King Jeroboam I	King Rehoboam	King Ahab	King Jehoshaphat
930	930–909	930–913	874–853	872–848

BC

WHAT'S HAPPENING IN THE UPPER STORY

From a Lower Story point of view, it appears the nation of Israel is divided because of the immature response of Solomon's son Rehoboam. But from the Upper Story point of view, we learn that the division comes as a part of God's plan.[1] The life and behavior of Israel are a witness to the name and character of God. People look at this community and draw conclusions about God. Israel had consistently compromised their pure worship of God with the worship of other gods and their disobedient actions. God made an unconditional promise to Abraham that all nations would be blessed through Israel. Then God told David that the Messiah would come not just from Israel, but specifically from David's family, the tribe of Judah. When you see things unfold from the Upper Story, it is not surprising that the twelve tribes of Israel are divided this way—the kingdom of Israel to the north comprised of ten tribes, and the kingdom of Judah to the south comprised of two tribes. From here until the arrival of Jesus, the focus shifts to the story of the tribe of Judah.

ALIGNING OUR STORY TO GOD'S STORY

God's decision to divide the nation of Israel was already set in motion years before it actually happened. Some of the things that occur in the world are completely out of our control. We can't avoid the consequences set in motion by the previous generation. We can, however, choose to live according to God's will in the hope of putting ourselves in the best possible position to receive God's blessing and promise for the next generation.

ilitary aviators have an interesting saying about imminent plane crashes that provides significant insight into this part of God's story: "The accident has already occurred; we are just waiting for the plane to arrive at the crash site."

What does this mean? The accident occurred miles before the actual crash when a pilot or a member of the plane's crew made a fatal decision—perhaps before the plane ever left the ground due to a manufacturing or design flaw or even a maintenance oversight. That's when the mistake was made. Now it's just a matter of waiting until the plane crashes because of a previously made mistake.

This is precisely what is happening in the story of Israel. As Solomon approaches the end of his reign over Jerusalem, two new characters enter the scene, whose names couldn't be much more confusing or fun to say out loud—Jeroboam and Rehoboam. At this particular point in our story, you'll recall that God was using the nation of Israel to reveal his character to the rest of the world so they would want to do life with him. When they all got along well and prospered, foreign nations caught a glimpse of what it would be like to be part of God's family. When they turned their backs on God and lived selfishly, God disciplined them because he needed to make sure his nation accurately reflected who he was and the kind of community he was building.

God's reflection was becoming distorted, which meant Israel was about to be disciplined, and it started with Jeroboam, one of Solomon's officials. After Solomon died, his son Rehoboam became king. Apparently, Solomon accumulated much of his wealth the old-fashioned way—high taxes and forced labor. Thus the first Tea Party. Jeroboam and a huge crowd of angry citizens went to Rehoboam and asked for a little relief. King Rehoboam replied, "You ain't seen nothin' yet." Jeroboam and his many followers then said, "We're outta here."

They retreated to their tribal regions in the north and made Jeroboam king over all of Israel since they represented ten of the twelve tribes of the nation.

Rehoboam remained king, but only over his tribe of Judah and the tribe of Benjamin. What was once a proud and prosperous nation was now a divided kingdom—Israel to the north and Judah to the south.

This internal strife and national division has all the makings of a great epic movie, one of those with a cast of thousands and all kinds of cool special effects. The Lower Story point of view of this movie is as old as time itself. A king mistreats his people. A courageous revolutionary leads a rebellion against the king. A struggle for power ensues, and eventually the kingdom is divided. And as you dig deeper into this Lower Story, you learn that Rehoboam could have avoided the rebellion if only he would have listened to the right people.

Remember when Jeroboam came and asked for a kinder, gentler treatment of Israel's citizens? As it turned out, Rehoboam first consulted with some of his father's elders, or trusted advisers, and they told him that if he lightened up, his citizens would be loyal to him forever. Then he went to some of his contemporaries—younger friends he had grown up with—and they told him to rule with an even harsher hand than his father did.

Who could blame Jeroboam, then, for leading a rebellion and setting up his own kingdom to the north? And who could blame Rehoboam for mounting his troops and readying them for battle to regain the territory from Jeroboam's rebel forces? You can almost hear the music build and see the horses galloping northward, soldiers grabbing the reins with one hand and waving their swords with the other. Sort of like *Ben-Hur*, *The Ten Commandments*, *Gladiator*, and *Troy* all rolled into one.

Except there was no battle, and to understand why, we need to look at this movie from another point of view: the Upper Story. Or to put it another way, what in the world was God up to in this apparent chaotic series of events with his chosen nation? Did he just take a break and let the plot unravel on its own, or does this "movie" somehow figure into his grand plan to bring us all back into his perfect community?

Lower Story logic tells us that Rehoboam should have launched a massive battle against the northern rebel kingdom, and he was just about to do that when God stepped in and offered a glimpse into his plan with these four simple words: "This is my doing."[2] It was as if he was saying, "I was behind this from the beginning. I knew you would heed the advice of your yes-men instead of that of your father's wise elders. I knew Jeroboam would rebel against you. And I knew you would do everything in your power to bring your divided kingdom back together. But it's in my power, not yours. So go home. Your role in this movie is just about over."

If God indeed did this—if he orchestrated it all along—the question remains, *Why?* For the answer, we turn to the theme of this movie. By the time we reach the end of a well-written and well-directed movie, we discover it contains a theme or message. On the Lower Story level, the theme of this movie is obvious: leaders who treat their followers poorly will face rebellion. Rehoboam is clearly the bad guy; Jeroboam is the hero. This is a great message, one that God would surely support, but it isn't *his* message in this story. The Upper Story theme has little to do with tyrannical rulers or rebellion. It really has little to do with the main characters or even the setting and plot. If you want to sum up God's message in a short phrase, it is this: *I keep my word.*

He does what he says he will do because he longs to give everyone the opportunity to reside in his perfect community.

As we learned in previous parts of this Story, God made promises or covenants with his people. He promised Abraham he would make a great nation from his offspring, despite the fact that Abraham and his wife were beyond childbearing age. God kept that promise. He promised Moses that if the people of Israel kept the laws he gave them, he would bless them, but if they turned away from these laws, he would discipline them because he wanted people to see that he is a just and fair God. He kept that promise.

He made a third promise—this time to David—one that built on the promises to Abraham and Moses to make Israel a great nation. But he took it one step further with David. He promised David that his tribe—the tribe of Judah—would be established forever. Why? Because in God's plan to invite us back to him, Jesus, the Messiah, will come from the line of David, and he will reign forever as King of kings. Because of David's great love for God, the perfect community God is building will be traced back to David's tribe.

In the Lower Story it appears that Rehoboam is being disciplined for his actions, and that the southern tribe of Judah is the one that has been weakened and will eventually fade away. Rehoboam goes to the wrong people from whom he gets the wrong advice so that he ends up making what appears to be the wrong decision regarding Israel. The winner here clearly is Jeroboam and the ten northern tribes, except for one small problem. If the northern tribes prevail and Judah perishes, God is made out to be a liar. Who could ever trust a God who can't keep his promises?

Remember the great U2 song "With or Without You"? It comes to mind when I read this story of Jeroboam and Rehoboam because it summarizes how God is going to establish his perfect community—with or without you and me. Both kings eventually turned their backs on God, but it didn't matter. His plan to give us relief from the sinful nature we inherited from Adam and Eve was going to come to fruition through Judah—with or without the cooperation of Jeroboam and Rehoboam.

This U2 song still warns each of us today. In the New Testament part of God's story, God gives us another promise when he declares, "I will build my church."³ He doesn't say, "I *might* build my church," or "I *hope* to build my church." He declares a nonnegotiable truth. He *will* build a church that will demonstrate the good news that everyone in the human family—all races, all colors, all nationalities—is included in the perfect community he is forming. And he will do it *with or without you.*

Nothing harms the church more than when its people reflect the wrong image of who God is. We do this whenever we treat others unkindly—especially the poor, the widows, and the strangers in our midst. We do this whenever we conduct our business dishonestly or let our anger get the best of us. These actions harm the church, but they don't stop it. God *will* build his church. With or without you.

Wouldn't you prefer that he did it *with* you? What a privilege God gives us to show others what he is like! Imagine knowing that the way you live today may result in someone changing their negative ideas about God and being drawn to find true life in him.

We have opportunities every day to live obediently so that everyone around us can see who God is and what he is like. If I choose to disobey and live according to my own selfish interests, that's OK. God did not force Rehoboam to "do the right thing" and treat his subjects better. Instead, he allowed Rehoboam's behavior to help fulfill a promise God had made to David.

Maybe you are the victim of a crash set in motion by another person. I am sorry. I understand this is one of the hardest things to accept. Our goal should not be to contribute to the mistake, but rather to live a life that helps us get back on track with God. For sure, we do not want the decisions of our lives today to cause an accident later in the days ahead. Wouldn't you prefer to be used by God because of what you do for him rather than in spite of your disobedience?

If you're part of the church today—just as those who were part of Israel in Bible times—remember that the story will continue on with or without our cooperation. God will accomplish his mission to bring people into relationship with him in perfect community through Israel and the church. One particular tribe or one particular church may not make it, but Israel and the church will make it because God made a promise. And God always keeps his promise.

Chapter

GOD'S MESSENGERS

"I will heal their waywardness
and love them freely,
for my anger has turned away from them."

HOSEA 14:4

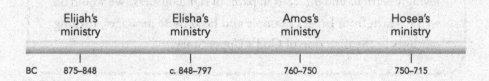

Elijah's ministry	Elisha's ministry	Amos's ministry	Hosea's ministry
875–848	c. 848–797	760–750	750–715

BC

WHAT'S HAPPENING IN THE UPPER STORY

The mighty and blessed nation of Israel is divided into two weaker nations—ten tribes to the north called the kingdom of Israel and two tribes to the south called the kingdom of Judah. For God to fulfill his unconditional promise to Abraham and David, only the southern kingdom of Judah needs to survive, for it is from the tribe of Judah that the Messiah will come. God positioned the northern tribes to be removed from the rest of the story due to their serial disobedience. In fact, the books of 1 and 2 Chronicles retell the story of 1 and 2 Kings but leave out the kings who reigned in the north. Yet more than 150 years before the northern kingdom's scheduled destruction, God, out of his intense love for Israel, sends messengers to warn them in the hope that they will return to a place of pure worship.

ALIGNING OUR STORY TO GOD'S STORY

God sent messengers to the northern kingdom of Israel to warn them of the danger they were in due to their careless worship of other gods. Over the course of 208 years, he will send nine prophets who have the same basic message. God is doing the same for us today. He has sent his message through his word, the Bible, and through his followers to lovingly warn us and direct us in paths of righteousness. We would do well to learn from Israel's example and heed these messages, turning our lives in the direction of God's Upper Story.

On April 10, 1912, the British passenger liner called the *Titanic* took off on its maiden voyage from Southampton, England, to New York City. At 11:40 p.m. on April 14, just four days into the trip, the *Titanic* hit an iceberg. At 2:20 a.m. on the 15th, the massive ship sank into the Atlantic Ocean. Only an estimated 705 of the 2,224 passengers survived, making it one of the deadliest commercial peacetime disasters in modern history.

On the evening of April 14, the *Titanic*'s wireless operators received several messages from nearby ships, warning them of icebergs ahead. One such message came from a steamer called the SS *Mesaba*. Here is the message:

To Titanic:

Ice report in lat 42n to 41.25n Long 49w to long 50.30w saw much heavy pack ice and great number large icebergs also field ice. Weather good clear[1]

The message gives the exact location of the fatal iceberg, but the message was ignored. An operator from another nearby ship, the *Californian*, also attempted to send messages warning of the iceberg ahead, but Jack Phillips, the *Titanic* operator, was focused on getting passengers' messages out. He sent this reply to the *Californian* operator: "Shut up. Shut up. I am busy."

No one imagined such a big, powerful ship like the *Titanic* could be sunk. Warning messages were sent in time to avert the fatal blow, but they were ignored.

What happened to the passengers of the *Titanic* in AD 1912 also happened to the kingdom of Israel in 722 BC. With all the success and prosperity that Israel enjoyed for so many years, no one thought it could sink. It did, but not without warning. More than 150 years earlier, God had raised up messengers to warn them of the upcoming "iceberg" that was going to destroy them if they continued in the direction they were going.

After God divided Israel into two kingdoms, things went from bad to worse through years of spiritual decline and unprecedented immorality—208 years, to be exact. According to the Bible, during this 208-year period, the combined kingdoms had thirty-eight different kings, and only five were good; the rest were described as evil. Imagine what that would be like.

In the United States, we've had forty-four presidents over a period slightly longer than the divided kingdom's 208 years. A few of these leaders may have been less than stellar, but I don't know of anyone who would describe any of our presidents as outright *evil*. In fact, in my lifetime I can think of only a handful of rulers in the world whom we would consider evil.

But Israel was God's special nation, his chosen people through whom God would reveal himself to the rest of the world as part of his plan to create a perfect community. Yet for most of this period, evil kings allowed abominable practices to go on, making this a particularly dark time in this part of God's story. Over and over, we read tragic words like these, describing Israel's kings: "But you followed the ways of Jeroboam and caused my people Israel to sin."[2]

What would you do if you were God? What would you do if the nation you chose to reflect your character repeatedly turned away from you, worshiped other gods, and allowed immorality to run rampant throughout the land? I would think this would be the perfect time for a "reset." "Let's wipe these rebellious and evil people who are giving me a bad name off the face of the earth and start over." But as you recall from Noah's story, God did that once and promised never to do it again because the next group would only do the same thing.[3] God never breaks his promises.

Besides, God loves his chosen people, even if they don't reciprocate. It's the part of the Upper Story that is so difficult for us to comprehend: God loves us no matter what, and despite our rebellion, he wants nothing more than to call us back to him so he can live with us.

So for 208 years, he patiently waited for his children to return to him, but he didn't wait passively. He sent special messengers, or prophets, to call them back to his ways. These messengers used their bullhorns to implore Israel to return to God's ways and trust him as the one true God.

In the northern kingdom alone, God raised up nine prophets during this 208-year period to try to convince the people to turn from their wicked ways.

One of these prophets, Elijah, challenged the wicked king to a supernatural duel of sorts. The king at the time was notoriously evil. His name was Ahab, and according to the Bible, he "did more evil . . . than any of those [kings] before him."[4] In fact, he considered the sins of his predecessors to be trivial. Child's play. And if his own depravity wasn't enough, he married a woman named Jezebel, who was so bad that to this day her name symbolizes promiscuity and immorality.

It was Jezebel who convinced Ahab to turn away from God and begin worshiping Baal, a false god popular among neighboring wicked nations, along with other gods. Clearly an enemy of God, Jezebel—with Ahab's full support—executed several prophets, which seems to have triggered Elijah's challenge to Ahab: Gather all the prophets of your pagan gods (he had 450 of them), and let's see how they do against me and the God I serve.[5]

The plan is for each side to build an altar, slaughter a bull on it for a sacrifice, and then call on their god to send down fire and consume the sacrifice. Ahab goes first, leading to the first biblical record of trash talk. The prophets call out to Baal. *Nothing.* They shout at Baal, demanding that he answer them. *Not a word.* They start dancing around the altar as they beg Baal to show up, and that's when Elijah gets in their faces with a little sarcasm: "Maybe your god is hard of hearing and you have to shout louder! Maybe he's just too busy for you or on vacation. Maybe he's asleep. Nice god you got there, guys."

Who says God doesn't have a sense of humor?

No matter how loud they shout, nothing happens. Can't you almost see that meat on the pile of stones in the heat of the day? Flies buzzing around it, the unmistakable smell of rotting flesh. But the poor prophets of Baal keep at it throughout the entire day, cutting their own skin until blood flows down their arms and chests in an effort to get their god's attention. The Bible describes their actions as "frantic."[6]

Then it is Elisha's turn.

Do you know what it means to "showboat"? In sports, when a star player decides to grab the spotlight and make the game all about him rather than the team, he is called a showboat. In a movie or play, sometimes an actor will "steal the show" from her fellow cast members by dramatically elevating her character's role above the others. She is a showboat. Elijah, this deeply spiritual prophet of God, uses the occasion to showboat just a bit himself. I don't know any other way to describe it. He essentially kicks his own challenge up a notch by ordering his assistants to pour water over the altar. Three times.

He wants to make sure that anything combustible is soaked. He even has them dig a trench around the altar and fill it with water. Both his own followers and those who worshiped Baal must have thought he was crazy. Even a Boy Scout troop with propane torches wouldn't have been able to get a fire going anywhere near this altar. Or maybe he is just giving himself an excuse if nothing happens when he calls out to God.

But something *does* happen. Something big.

When Elijah calls out to God, fire rains down from above, turning the watery mess of an altar into an inferno. The flames burn and burn, consuming everything. Even the water in the trench vaporizes in a fiery blast from God. When all the people see this dramatic demonstration of God's power, they cry over and over, "The LORD—he is God!"[7]

In our Lower Story lives, we are vulnerable to the same sin that plagued the northern kingdom of Israel: we want to worship gods of our own choosing. None of us would ever admit to idol worship, but consider how much time, energy, and money we spend on things that have no eternal value—and compare it to the time, energy, and money we devote to God. Every November, I marvel at the lengths people go to in order to be the first in line for "Black Friday"—the day after Thanksgiving—when stores lure shoppers inside with discount deals and special sales. (Tragically, a couple of years ago a worker opening the door at a large retail store was crushed to death by the incoming rush of shoppers. I don't recall anyone being run over by people rushing to get inside the church.) And it's not just "things" that become our gods. I know people who will adjust their schedules to make sure they are home to watch a TV program ironically called *American Idol*. We often chase our sports, hobbies, and pleasures as if they are worthy of our worship. I'm not judging anyone who shops on Black Friday or watches reality TV shows or plays golf three times a week. I'm just speaking for myself and a few others I know.

In the Lower Story, the one true God is often shoved aside for our little gods. In the Upper Story, God invites us to enjoy all the blessings of life he has given us, but to worship *him* only. And while he no longer sends fire from heaven to get our attention, he pursues us just as relentlessly. He uses whatever it takes to get our attention and bring us back into a relationship with him.

If Ahab's story gives us an idea of how God will use supernatural events to call his people back to him, Hosea shows us just how far God will go to reclaim us. As one of God's prophets, Hosea pleads with Israel to return to God, but to no avail. Israel continues to worship other gods and live in ways that displease God. But then God does something that seems strange to us who live in the Lower Story. He asks Hosea to marry a prostitute.

I've counseled a few young men regarding their desire to find a good wife, and I've never even considered asking them to marry a prostitute. In fact, if I ever recommended this, I'd likely lose my minister's credentials and be banished from ministry forever. But this is exactly what God does, which I find absolutely amazing. But what is even more amazing is that Hosea does as he is told.

Just let this sink in for a moment. Imagine being a single guy who prays earnestly to God and seeks his guidance. You ask God for direction and then just listen and meditate, and a thought enters your mind: *Go downtown to the corner of State and Division. When a shady lady in leopard-print tights and stiletto heels struts over to your car and asks if you want some company, ask her to marry you.* If something like this happened to me while I was praying, I would beg God's forgiveness for letting my mind stray where it shouldn't be going and try praying a little harder. I'm quite certain I wouldn't conclude that this thought was put there by God.

But Hosea knows it is God, and he obeys. He marries a prostitute whose name is Gomer.

So what could God be up to in his Upper Story? It is possible that God wants Hosea to marry the prostitute so he can help her turn her life around and become a follower of God. Except this isn't what happens. Despite her marriage to Hosea, Gomer keeps her night job. And despite her brazen unfaithfulness, Hosea continues to support her, even as she leaves him for days at a time to practice her trade.

After more time passes—we don't know exactly how long—God tells

Hosea to find his wife and show her that he still loves her. The Bible isn't clear about the details, but I can imagine Hosea asking around and learning that Gomer is working out of a dingy apartment building on the wrong side of town. As he approaches the place, he hands over some money to her "office manager" just so he can talk to her. When Gomer hears a knock on her door and opens it, planning to give her next customer a seductive look, she must have been stunned to see her husband. Before she can say anything, he whispers, "Oh, Gomer, I love you more than you will ever know. Please come home with me."

Can you imagine? Such love and forgiveness are almost too hard to believe. It just doesn't make sense. Hosea has every right—according to Jewish law—to divorce his wife because of her serial unfaithfulness. This is one of those stories in the Bible that seems so random, so much a diversion. What is God up to here? I get the Lower Story: marry someone with a reputation for being promiscuous, and he or she will likely continue being promiscuous.

But what's the Upper Story? Is God saying we should marry prostitutes and try to turn them to God? I'm not sure this is a message I'm ready to support. Curiously, we never learn from the Bible if Hosea and Gomer lived happily ever after. They could have. But Gomer also could have continued sneaking out at night to earn some extra money on the streets. We just don't know, which begs the question: Why include this brief story in the Bible?

I think it's because God wanted to use Hosea's example to show us how far God himself is willing to go to reclaim those who have turned against him. Listen to what this prophet says to Israel, and see if you can catch the parallels:

> Hear the word of the LORD, you Israelites,
>   because the LORD has a charge to bring
>   against you who live in the land:
> "There is no faithfulness, no love,
>   no acknowledgment of God in the land.
> There is only cursing, lying and murder,
>   stealing and adultery."[8]

"Their deeds do not permit them
  to return to their God.
A spirit of prostitution is in their heart;
  they do not acknowledge the LORD."[9]

Return, Israel, to the LORD your God.
  Your sins have been your downfall![10]

The relationship of Hosea and Gomer mirrors God's relationship with Israel, and with us. Despite their covenant with God, Israel had been unfaithful. They had pledged their loyalty to God, but they snuck out at night to worship other gods. God not only knows this, but he catches them in the act. And what does he say?

Come home.

The ten northern tribes of Israel were heading in the wrong direction with their worship of other gods. Just as with the *Titanic*, which received warning messages from other ships, God sent numerous messengers to warn his people of the trouble that lay ahead. Why would he do this? Because he loved them and wanted them to survive and to share in the full blessing of his Upper Story.

He wants the very same thing for you and me. He sends us the same kind of messages today because he loves us and wants us to experience the fullness found in Christ. Will we say, like the *Titanic* operator did, "Shut up. Shut up. I am busy," or will we listen and make the necessary turn to avoid disaster?

Chapter

THE BEGINNING OF THE END (OF THE KINGDOM OF ISRAEL)

Come, all you who are thirsty,
come to the waters;
and you who have no money,
come, buy and eat!

ISAIAH 55:1

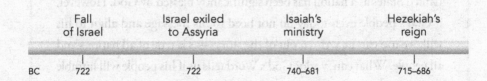

	Fall of Israel	Israel exiled to Assyria	Isaiah's ministry	Hezekiah's reign
BC	722	722	740–681	715–686

WHAT'S HAPPENING IN THE UPPER STORY

Absolutely nothing can stop God from keeping his promise to provide the way for all nations and all people to come back to him. God's plan is to use a new nation he formed from scratch to bring us the solution, namely Jesus. To fulfill this promise, God preserves the tribe of Judah because of his promise to David that the Messiah would come from his family. In 930 BC, God orchestrates the division of the twelve tribes of Israel, removing the ten tribes of the Kingdom of Israel from the two tribes of Judah. For 208 years, God sends prophets to warn both nations of their need to turn back to God alone, but they do not listen. So God uses the wicked nation of Assyria in 722 BC to conquer, deport, and assimilate the northern kingdom of Israel. They are lost, never to reassemble as a pure nation under God. God spares the southern kingdom from this disaster, not because they deserved it, but because of the unconditional promise God made to David.

ALIGNING OUR STORY TO GOD'S STORY

God is a very patient God. He longs for his people to return to him and experience the blessings of being aligned with his story. For 208 years, God warns and waits for the northern kingdom to change their ways. Eventually, based on God's justice, they are written out of the story. The United States as a nation has been significantly blessed by God. However, if God's people even today do not heed to his message and align to his will, we too can be written out of the story—as is true of all nations and all people. What can we do? God's Word tells us if his people will humble themselves and pray and seek his face, our nation can be healed.[1] Each of us can make a significant difference in the outcome of our nation's story.

One morning in January 2009, I woke up, got some coffee, and turned on the television. *The Today Show* was doing a special on George Washington the same week newly elected President Obama was taking the oath of office. The reporter explained that George Washington was offered the opportunity to become the first king of America, but he turned it down. The commentator pondered the question, "What if he had accepted?"

With the help of the Internet and a genealogy expert, the research staff traced all of George's living eight thousand descendants to see who would be sitting on the throne today. Climbing our first president's family tree took them to the city of San Antonio, Texas, where I live. The television camera panned into a local Burger King only to find Paul Washington asking for his order to be "king-sized." If George Washington had accepted the offer of monarchy, Paul would now be our ninth king of the United States.

The report concluded with images of Paul's son, Dick, and Dick's son, Connor, presumably Paul's successors to the throne. I about choked on my Cheerios because Dick and Connor attend Oak Hills Church, where I serve as pastor! In fact, Connor is good friends with my sons and has spent the night at my house many times. Not once has he ever mentioned this small detail of being related to George Washington.

Later when I chatted with the family about why their great-great-and-then-greater grandfather George declined the offer, they knew the answer. George Washington refused to become king because he wanted to avoid getting into the same situation that had brought the Pilgrims to the colonies in the first place. Perhaps it is best summed up by a motto set forth by the Committees of Correspondence just prior to the Revolutionary War: "No king but King Jesus."

As we pick up our story of the children of Israel, a nation whose kings have gotten them into a heap of trouble, you wonder whether holding to a motto like "No king but God" would have led to a vastly different outcome. This was certainly God's ideal plan that they rejected when they demanded to be like the other nations. Throughout 208 years under 39 kings, both the northern kingdom of Israel and the southern kingdom of Judah repeatedly turned their backs on God, and it was time for drastic action.

Through his prophets God warns, begs, and cajoles these two nations, relentlessly trying to convince them to turn from their wickedness so that they can enjoy a great relationship with him. This is all God has ever wanted. It's the overarching theme of the Upper Story: "I love you and want you to be a part of my perfect community, and all you have to do is put me first in your life." But in the Lower Story, both Israel and Judah couldn't resist worshiping all the gods of neighboring nations. And since they didn't worship the one true God, they also rejected his rules for living and had become a horribly inaccurate reflection of God's character.

The Bible reports that they even threw their own children into the fire as sacrifices to their pagan gods! They sold themselves to perform evil acts with others. They ignored *all* the commands God gave them. If he let them continue in their wicked ways, no one would ever see his true character and therefore be drawn to him. God patiently waited for them to come to their senses, but they ignored him. He gave them countless opportunities to bring their Lower Story into alignment with his Upper Story, but they were content to go about their lives as if he didn't even exist.

It was time for God to act, and he did so decisively. According to the Bible, he chose another nation—Assyria (roughly the equivalent of modern-day Syria)—to invade Israel, defeat it, and deport its citizens back to their own nation. Just like that, Israel—the northern kingdom—ceased to exist. Gone forever. History refers to the people who were deported to Assyria as "the lost tribes of Israel" because they simply do not exist as tribes, let alone as a nation. What most likely happened is that the Assyrians split them up and sent them to various cities, where they intermarried and eventually lost their cultural identities. These descendants of Abraham, who were given their own land and had once worshiped God and enjoyed his providence, were now permanently removed from his presence, escorted from the garden.

So now all that is left of God's special nation is tiny Judah to the south. Judah's king at the time was named Hezekiah, and he happened to be one of the good kings. As you recall, there was a total of thirty-nine kings in Israel and Judah during this 208-year period, and only five honored God. Hezekiah was one of these five good guys. He removed all the idols left over from his evil predecessor and pointed his citizens to the one true God. As a result of his faithfulness, God rewarded him and his kingdom with success. During Hezekiah's reign, Judah prospered. The remnant of God's special nation saw an increase in literacy and the production of great literary works. It also increased its military power.

Still, being so small, Judah was vulnerable to attack, and the Assyrians had just wiped out Israel. They are now on the border of Judah, eager to eliminate God's nation, but first the king of Assyria offers Hezekiah a chance to surrender. Hezekiah refuses.

Then the king tries to intimidate the citizens of Judah, warning them not to trust in Hezekiah's God, but they remain loyal to their king. When the saber rattling finally is over and attack seems imminent, Hezekiah turns to his true source of strength. He gets on his knees and prays, and the words of his prayer prove that he knows about God's Upper Story: "Deliver us from his [the king of Assyria's] hand, so that all the kingdoms of the earth may know that you alone, LORD, are God."[2]

Hezekiah gets it. He knows that the way he lives his life reflects God's character, so he honors God by being a fair and just king, leading his people to live the way God commands them to live. He knows that if his tiny kingdom survives an attack from the much larger Assyrian army, everyone will know that God is who he says he is and that the pagan gods of the Assyrians are powerless. He knows that none of this is about him, but about God. And because God is behind it, he knows that Judah will somehow survive the attack from the larger, more powerful Assyrian army.

As it turned out, there *was* no attack. The angel of the Lord entered the Assyrian camp just outside of Judah and killed 185,000 enemy soldiers. The king woke up in the morning and found his army almost completely wiped out—lying dead on the ground. The powerful, arrogant king of Assyria gathered what was left of his army and retreated to Nineveh and stayed there. It was a decisive victory that once again demonstrated God's love for his special nation.

You would think that after seeing what happened to Israel and seeing the miraculous way in which God spared them from a similar fate, Judah would never consider abandoning God and returning to idol worship. Then again, if you have been paying attention, you know that God's chosen nation seems to have a hard time living for him when everything is going great. Hezekiah died after faithfully serving God for twenty-nine years. His son Manasseh inherited the throne, and he turned out to be the exact opposite of his father.

Whereas Hezekiah removed idols, Manasseh reinstated them, even building altars devoted to foreign gods in the temple in Jerusalem—essentially thumbing his nose at God. He declared his allegiance to these foreign gods by publicly worshiping them—a not-so-subtle hint that everyone in Judah should do likewise. Instead of seeking guidance from God, he consulted with sorcerers and mediums, a practice prohibited by God. He even threw his son into the fire of one of the altars as a sacrifice to a pagan god. The Bible describes Judah under Manasseh as being more evil than the foreign nation that God had previously destroyed.[3]

Keep in mind that this was the remnant of the once powerful nation that God had chosen to help carry out his plan to create a perfect community in which everyone could enjoy his presence forever. More specifically, the promised Messiah—the King of kings—was to come from Judah. Yet the nation had turned its back on God and was plunging further and further into abominable practices that surpassed the evil of any other nation. God had to do something. He gave Manasseh a hint through a message from one of his prophets: "I am going to bring such disaster on Jerusalem and Judah that the ears of everyone who hears of it will tingle."[4]

When someone hears something like this, they might be led to reconsider their ways and get religious real fast. But despite all the warnings to Manasseh and his people, "they paid no attention."[5] Bad move. God raised up the Assyrian army to capture Manasseh in the most humiliating manner. They put a hook in his nose, bound his hands and feet with shackles, and led him away in plain sight of his subjects. Then they took him to Babylon and handed him over to become a prisoner in that pagan nation. Eventually, years after Manasseh's death, the Babylonians destroyed the capital city of Jerusalem and deported Judah's residents to Babylon.

Manasseh, the mighty king who thought he was too big for God (although he was only in middle school when he became king), sat in a dark and dirty prison cell. Accustomed to lavish banquets, he was lucky to be given stale bread and fetid water. The gods he worshiped were powerless to protect or rescue him. The God he repeatedly rejected finally took him out.

For all practical purposes, the nation that would be so pivotal to God's plan for all mankind was gone, which could only mean one thing: God broke an important promise he had made to King David some four hundred years before. How could the people of Judah be deported to Babylon when God promised they would be a nation—a nation from which the Messiah would come? How could anyone trust a God who breaks promises?

Enter another messenger—Isaiah, perhaps the best-known prophet in the Bible. Like all prophets, Isaiah's primary message is aimed at calling people back to God and away from wickedness. But he is probably better known to Christians for his prophecies about the Messiah. Although the Messiah will not arrive for another seven hundred years or so, Isaiah clearly knows what God is up to in the Upper Story.

God's messenger Isaiah reassures Judah that God will not allow them to remain captive in Babylon forever. After a period of time, he will bring them back home, not because they deserve it, but to keep his promise to David and to proceed with his plan to give everyone a chance to have a relationship with him. As Isaiah concludes his message from God to Judah, he reveals God's purpose for sparing his special nation:

"Then you [Israel] will know that I am the LORD;
    those who hope in me will not be disappointed . . .
Then all mankind will know
    that I, the LORD, am your Savior,
    your Redeemer, the Mighty One of Jacob."[6]

God *never* breaks a promise.

Judah's Lower Story—like many of our own Lower Stories—is a mess. But God specializes in turning our mess into his message to advance his grand

Upper Story. Nothing can thwart his relentless passion to provide a way for us to return to him. I wish I could report that my own story with God has been a consistent trajectory of growing closer to him. That from the time I entered into a relationship with God, I was like Hezekiah, the good king. But the truth is that there have been times when I have turned my focus away from him and onto other things to the point that they crowded God out. At first, the object of our affections may seem harmless, but it can quickly turn into a lifestyle of idol worship. This is what is insidious about the temptations we face when things are going well.

I can easily imagine Manasseh beginning his reign with every intention of being a great and godly king like his father. As he was anointed by the high priests of the temple, he may well have declared his faith in the one true God and meant it. But then his eye caught the exotic beauty of a golden statue. What harm could come from placing it alongside the altar in God's temple? One could argue that it actually made the temple more beautiful. Perhaps he reasoned that *all* gods are somehow cosmically connected to form a bountiful collection of deity—so why not worship all of them? Isn't declaring God as the *only* god a little arrogant and exclusive? Why can't we all just have our own gods and get along together?

Because God loves us so much that he can't allow it. He knows that in order for us to have a relationship with him, it must be pure. Anything less won't be a relationship at all. In the New Testament, believers are referred to as a "bride" for God's Son. What groom wants to stand at the altar and see his bride coming down the aisle with four or five other "grooms" by her side? God promises us residence in his perfect community forever, and all he asks is that we love *him*, and him only, and respond in humble obedience to the guidance he gives us.

But there is another dimension to this story that haunts me, and it has to do with the effect that disobedience has on *nations*. God clearly punished the bad kings for their wickedness, but he also punished both nations, Israel and Judah. He even allowed two pagan nations—Assyria and Babylon—to play crucial roles in punishing those nations that were especially chosen by God to carry out his divine plan for all mankind. I don't think I'm reading too much into this to suggest that God holds both individuals and nations accountable.

God waited patiently for 208 years before he finally decided he could not allow his nation to continue rejecting him and his ways. Will the day come when he runs out of patience with the United States and other nations in our world? The United States has been in existence for roughly this same fatal span of time. I don't have the answer, but the idea that this could happen ought to motivate all of us who love and trust God to pray for our nation—and not just pray, but seek to put Jesus on the throne of our lives so we can be the kind of husbands, wives, parents, neighbors, church members, and citizens who will do the right thing.

When those of us who believe in God live the way he calls us to live, our nation can be transformed—something God can accomplish through you and me, along with the descendants of George Washington—if we are willing to focus on the Upper Story. As for me and my house, "No king but King Jesus."

Chapter

THE KINGDOMS' FALL

The LORD is good to those whose hope is in him,
to the one who seeks him;
it is good to wait quietly
for the salvation of the LORD.

LAMENTATIONS 3:25–26

Manasseh		Josiah		Jehoiakim		Ezekiel's ministry	
	Amon		Jeremiah's ministry		Zedekiah		Jerusalem falls

BC	697–642	642–640	640–609	626–585	609–598	597–586	593–571	586

WHAT'S HAPPENING IN THE UPPER STORY

Of the thirty-nine kings of the divided kingdom of Israel, only five were good kings. Each one of the good kings came from the southern tribe of Judah. Yet overall, the kingdom of Judah is not markedly better than the northern kingdom of Israel, which God has now completely decimated. God would be justified in doing the same thing to Judah. However, there is a difference. He made an unconditional covenant with David, promising that the Messiah would come from David's family in the tribe of Judah. After 344 years of patiently sending prophets to warn them, God used another foreign nation to get Judah's attention. Babylon invaded and burned the city of Jerusalem, and it took captive the majority of the people. Babylon didn't overtake God's people of its own accord or as its own idea. God orchestrated it for his Upper Story purposes. This disciplinary action would not be permanent, as it had been for the northern kingdom of Israel when it was conquered by the Assyrians. It couldn't be. God keeps his promises. After seventy years—and hopefully a lesson learned—they would return home and continue their part in the grand story of God.

ALIGNING OUR STORY TO GOD'S STORY

Jeremiah was a prophet to the kingdom of Judah. Before Jeremiah was even born, God set him apart for this special assignment. Yet God warned him that the people would not listen to his message. We are reminded of two things: (1) God has a special assignment for each of us in the unfolding of his story, and (2) God doesn't call us to be successful, only faithful to the assignments he gives us.

*I*t has become an all-too-familiar story in my thirty years of ministry. A mom and dad have a child who strays from the truth. The son or daughter gets into all kinds of trouble—smoking, drinking, drugs, trouble with the law, lying, cheating, stealing . . . The parents, out of intense love, start with the confrontational approach. They sit down and have a straightforward talk about right and wrong and urge them to stop "or else." That doesn't work. They resort to other methods—counselors, punishments of various kinds, threats, bribes—anything they can think of to stop the destructive behavior. Nothing works. Finally, after hundreds of sleepless nights and emptied bank accounts have put a severe strain on their marriage, after they've used up all their favors from family and friends, they finally throw up their hands and declare, "There is no remedy." They are forced to send their child away—sometimes to a rehabilitation center, and sometimes they aren't sending them anywhere; they're just kicking them out and dropping all support to try to get their child's attention.

The children of Judah have put God in this exact position.

As we return to God's Upper Story, we find it moving quickly toward the end of a long journey that will culminate in his much-anticipated gift to the world, a Messiah who will change the way God relates to his people. It started in a garden with a perfect community—exactly what God wanted and the reason he came down to earth. To be with us. But as you recall, Adam and Eve chose to disobey the one rule they were given, and ever since then we've watched God patiently call his people back to him.

We've met some amazing people along the way who trusted God and played a special role in his story: Abraham, Sarah, Joseph, Moses, Ruth, David. We've also been introduced to some real villains: Pharaoh, Jezebel, Manasseh. In the Lower Story, their actions seem random and disconnected, but God uses them—the good and the bad—to orchestrate his Upper Story of calling us back into a relationship with him.

In the last chapter, we learned that Manasseh, the king of Judah, was captured and carried off to Babylon. This was the beginning of the end for the remnant of God's chosen nation. All that was left of the nation was its capital city of Jerusalem, and the succession of evil kings continued even as Nebuchadnezzar, the king of Babylon, captured another large group of Israelites and deported them to Babylon.

As he had done before, God continued to warn the people of what would happen if they didn't turn back to him. This time the warning came from a prophet named Ezekiel, who was in exile in Babylon, and it was graphically specific:

> I am about to bring a sword against you, and I will destroy your high places. Your altars will be demolished and your incense altars will be smashed; and I will slay your people in front of your idols. I will lay the dead bodies of the Israelites in front of their idols, and I will scatter your bones around your altars . . . and you will know that I am the LORD.[1]

You would think a message like that would bring the people of Judah to their senses, but they continued to ignore God and engage in evil practices. Time was running out for Judah. How long could they ignore God before he followed through on his threat to punish them if they didn't turn from their wickedness?

Have you ever made this kind of threat to your children: "If you do that one more time, I'm going to ____"? And then they do whatever it is you didn't want them to do, and again you threaten, "I mean it! *One* more time." Why didn't you punish them the first time they disobeyed? Because you really didn't want to. You hated the thought of following through on your threat, even though they clearly deserved to be punished and you gave them ample warning. Deep inside your heart, you harbored a wish that you would never have to punish your child. It broke your heart to think of her crying. All you ever wanted since he was a little baby was to enjoy him and give him a life that would allow him to thrive and reach his full potential.

That's how God looked at his nation. That's how he looks at us still. He loves us and wants to enjoy doing life together with us. If only we would allow him to.

So despite their total rejection of him, God gives the people he loves one final warning. With most of Judah in captivity in Babylon and Jerusalem about to be attacked, God calls another prophet: Jeremiah. In terms of the Lower Story, this has to be one of the worst times to represent God. The once proud and beautiful city of Jerusalem is now in chaos. All the wealthy people, artisans, merchants, and military have been deported, leaving only the poorest of the poor to contend with anarchy, famine, and violence.

They too have turned their backs on God, living only for themselves and their pagan idols. God wants Jeremiah to tell the people in this bleak and dangerous city of Jerusalem that they are a bunch of sinners and God's patience is running out, that if they don't turn back to him, their city will be destroyed. Oh, and one more thing. God tells Jeremiah that no one will listen to him.

Jeremiah tries to buy some time, and who can blame him? This isn't exactly one of the plum assignments in the Bible.

"I'm not a good public speaker," he protests.

"I'll tell you what to say," God answers.

"I'm too young," he continues. "I'm afraid."

"Don't worry; I'll be with you," God promises.

God's Upper Story is building to a climax, and God wants to give his chosen nation one final chance to avoid what is about to happen. He gives Jeremiah these words to pass along to the rebellious remnant of Judah who are living in Jerusalem:

> A lion has come out of his lair;
>> a destroyer of nations has set out.
> He has left his place
>> to lay waste your land.
> Your towns will lie in ruins
>> without inhabitant . . .
> "Go up and down the streets of Jerusalem,
>> look around and consider,
>> search through her squares.

If you can find but one person
    who deals honestly and seeks the truth,
    I will forgive this city . . ."
If you do not listen,
    I will weep in secret
    because of your pride;
my eyes will weep bitterly,
    overflowing with tears,
    because the LORD's flock will be taken captive . . .
All Judah will be carried into exile,
    carried completely away.[2]

It's almost as if God decides that if he sets the bar lower, he won't have to follow through with his discipline: "Just find me one honest person in the entire city. Just one decent citizen, and I'll forgive everything and we can resume our relationship." If you've ever thought of God as vengeful and full of wrath, remember this scene in his Upper Story. And remember the tears he will weep because his beloved nation will be removed from the land he gave them. This is the kind of God who wants to be with us and provide a way for us to live with him forever.

The people of Judah squandered their one last chance. It was time for God to make good on his promise. The Bible sums up this entire period in which God allowed his people to have their kings:

The LORD, the God of their ancestors, sent word to them through his messengers again and again, because he had pity on his people and on his dwelling place. But they mocked God's messengers, despised his words and scoffed at his prophets until the wrath of the LORD was aroused against his people and there was no remedy.[3]

When you get to the place where the God of the universe says "no remedy," you know it's over. And it was. Nebuchadnezzar, the king of Babylon, began his final assault on Jerusalem. Sensing what is about to happen, Judah's king, Zedekiah, asks Jeremiah to make a final plea to God, hoping "the LORD will perform wonders for us as in times past."[4] But Jeremiah gives God's message to him straight: "Too late. I've already handed you over to Nebuchadnezzar, and he will show you no mercy, pity, or compassion."

It wasn't pretty. Nebuchadnezzar's army broke through the walls of the city even as the king tried to flee. They chased him down and brought him before Nebuchadnezzar, who doled out a severe sentence. King Zedekiah's sons were killed in front of him. Then they gouged out his eyes, shackled him, and took him to Babylon. Nebuchadnezzar then set fire to the temple that Solomon had built to the glory of God. Soon the entire city was ablaze, just as Jeremiah warned them on behalf of God: "He will destroy it with fire."[5]

From our Lower Story perspective, the destruction of Jerusalem seems harsh and unnecessary. If you love your people so much, why treat them this way? Why put them through so much shame and devastation? But in the Upper Story, this is precisely why God had to act as he did: *he loves them so much*. If God continued to bless Judah while they were behaving in ways so contrary to his commands, it would send a confusing message about who God is and how community works with God.

God is trying to implant a vision that the kingdom to come, which will be made possible through faith in the Messiah, is going to be restored. It will be the restoration of the idea he had in the Garden of Eden—a life where there is no wickedness, no evil, no mistreating of people. And where there is an unashamed love of God. If he let Judah get away with their horrible behavior, who would ever want to live in God's community? His love for us is so great and his holiness so pure that he cannot compromise either.

Though Jerusalem fell, God continued to speak through his messengers Jeremiah and Ezekiel. Jeremiah stayed behind in Jerusalem to grieve its loss. The Bible says he wept bitterly for what had happened to the city and God's chosen nation; therefore, we refer to him as "the weeping prophet." His weeping over Jerusalem is recorded in the Bible's book of Lamentations; its opening lines give a haunting description of the once-royal city:

> How deserted lies the city,
> once so full of people!

> How like a widow is she,
>> who once was great among the nations!
> She who was queen among the provinces
>> has now become a slave.
> Bitterly she weeps at night,
>> tears are on her cheeks.
> Among all her lovers
>> there is no one to comfort her.
> All her friends have betrayed her;
>> they have become her enemies.[6]

Yet even in his sorrow, Jeremiah continues to call Judah back to God, foreshadowing the birth of a Messiah who would forever change the course of history. His hint at what God is planning for all mankind is echoed by Ezekiel: "I will cleanse you from all your impurities and from all your idols."[7]

God uses both prophets to repeat the singular message of his Upper Story: "I want to live with you and will make a way for you to come back to me." In my earlier years in ministry, it was not uncommon to end a church service with an invitation—an opportunity for people who had strayed from God to return to him. Often the congregation would sing a hymn designed to encourage those who might be resisting God's call on their lives, and one of my favorites began with these lines: "Softly and tenderly Jesus is calling."

The entire point of God's judgment of Judah was to get their attention and remind them of his promise. A King would come from their tribe, so they had to reflect the character of that King. Their banishment would be temporary, as God prepared them for this magnificent moment in history:

> "I will gather you from all the countries and bring you back into your
> own land. I will sprinkle clean water on you, and you will be clean; I will
> cleanse you from all your impurities and from all your idols. I will give
> you a new heart and put a new spirit in you . . . You will be my people,
> and I will be your God."[8]

Can you imagine how these words fell on the hearts of the people of Judah, now scattered throughout Babylon? Can you imagine how many people today long to hear God's tender invitation to come home? And what is amazing to me is that God uses us to reveal his heart and remind people that he is always waiting on them, eager to forgive them and restore their lives in ways they can't even imagine. If they will let him.

For some of the parents who have been forced to exile their children in the hope of restoring them to health and purpose, let me assure you that God's same actions toward Judah actually worked. Initially, Judah lashed out in horrific anger and hatred. But like God, the parents who wait the "seventy years" without giving in will likely find that the discipline is producing the good results they longed for. The child's rebellious spirit most likely will break, much like Judah's. The light finally came on in the head and heart of Judah. They came to understand the tough love was just that—resilient love for them. Judah's homecoming was an emotional event filled with the happiest tears one will ever see, like the tears and the joy that parents of a prodigal child will see when that child returns. This was God's plan for Judah. This is God's plan for us.

Chapter *18*

DANIEL IN EXILE

"For he is the living God
and he endures forever;
his kingdom will not be destroyed,
his dominion will never end.
He rescues and he saves;
he performs signs and wonders
in the heavens and on the earth."

DANIEL 6:26–27

Daniel exiled to Babylon	Daniel's ministry	Nebuchad-nezzar	Daniel and the lions' den	Babylon falls
BC 605	605–536	605–562	539	539

WHAT'S HAPPENING IN THE UPPER STORY

The southern kingdom of Judah is still enslaved by the pagan nation of Babylon. Jerusalem and the temple are turned to rubble. Many of the residents have been deported to Babylon, leaving a small and vulnerable remnant in Jerusalem like sitting ducks for the surrounding nations to take advantage of. From the Lower Story perspective, it looks like this was the initiative of the Babylonians. However, from the lens of the Upper Story, we see that God orchestrated the entire event. Judah is in a time-out of sorts. God is disciplining them for their persistent disobedience to his laws. Out of his deep love for them, God wants them to return to Jerusalem in seventy years with fresh passion and devotion. During this period, God speaks through another prophet named Daniel. These declarations about the future give hope and confidence to God's people that he will keep his unconditional promise to Abraham and David despite the people's disobedience and the struggle of their circumstances.

ALIGNING OUR STORY TO GOD'S STORY

Daniel and his three friends were deported to Babylon to be trained as leaders in the king's court. Not only did they outperform their contemporaries and rise in their positions, but they also maintained their pure devotion to God in a foreign land. As a result, even the kings of Babylon and Persia acknowledged and praised God. As Christians, we live in our own type of "Babylon" today. This world is not our home. We are citizens of heaven, the new kingdom to come. As the people of Judah looked forward to going back home to Jerusalem, we look forward to going home to the New Jerusalem. And as we wait, we should seek to work in excellence and integrity, walking in pure devotion to God regardless of the cost.

As I write this, our son, Austin, is a sophomore at Boerne Champion High School, a public school here in San Antonio. Every school morning, he gets up extra early on his own (sometimes he wakes me up!) and goes to campus and stands outside the school with a group of other kids who love God, and they pray. They pray for each other, for their leaders, and for their school. Sometimes other kids show up and tease them, even taunt them. But they don't back down. And they don't try to explain or defend themselves or act superior. They just quietly pray—even for the kids who try to ridicule them.

Will God honor them for taking a stand and putting him first in their lives? He already has. What started as a handful of kids has grown to a group of more than forty students praying for their school every morning.

As believers, we're all in exile. We used to sing these lyrics from an old gospel song: "This world is not my home, I'm just a passin' through." Like the people of God's exiled nation in Babylon, we're on our way to the new Jerusalem. Remember, God had promised Judah that he would not abandon them forever, that they would one day return to Jerusalem—and in our story, we are heading toward the time when they will return. God is getting them ready, and according to the Bible, he is also preparing a special place for you and me to live with him forever.

From slavery in Egypt, to wandering in the wilderness, to crossing over into their own land, to building a permanent temple to worship God, to having their great nation divided, and finally to being a small remnant—Israel's inglorious history appears to be over. Judah is in exile.

These are God's chosen people being forced to leave the land he gave them. Could anything be more tragic? One of the challenges for Babylon was what to do with all these new inhabitants. What does any nation do when they capture thousands of people and bring them into their country to live as prisoners? Few people realize this, but during World War II, more than four hundred thousand prisoners of war were held in approximately five hundred camps throughout

Germany. Though prisoners, they spent most of their days working in farmers' fields, helping with the harvest, stacking hay, and tending crops. They were even paid and received meals from the farmers, often developing strong friendships that continued after their release at the end of the war.

The Jewish exiles living in Babylon enjoyed the same kind of relationship with their captors. In fact, during this time, Babylon experienced a period of great prosperity and growth, and many of the new buildings and great pieces of art honoring Nebuchadnezzar were created by the exiles. The king was smart enough to recognize the talent of these new deportees and even handpicked the best and brightest to serve him as special advisers. This is where we meet a young man named Daniel and his three friends—Shadrach, Meshach, and Abednego.

Even if you haven't spent a lot of time in church or reading the Bible, I'm quite sure you've heard of these guys and know at least a little about their Lower Story experiences. You probably have heard the story of Daniel in the lions' den, and vaguely remember Shadrach, Meshach, and Abednego's trip to the fiery furnace. So I'm going to focus more on how they got into their predicaments and, more important, what all of this has to do with God's Upper Story. Because from a Lower Story perspective, Judah is toast. God's grand plan has hit a major barrier. It is awfully hard to build a perfect community when the people you plan to do it with are being held captive by a pagan king in a foreign country.

These four young men (most likely teenagers) are part of a larger group of exiles fortunate enough to be chosen by the king and groomed for future service in the royal palace. The training they are given is essentially the equivalent of a master's degree in Babylonian culture and language. For three years, they read the great literature of Babylon, studied its art, learned its customs, and discussed all these things with each other in their new language. It is safe to say that by the time they finish their three years of training, they are more Babylonian than the native population.

From the beginning of his training, Daniel is someone with a strong sense of right and wrong—what my son's teacher calls "a moral compass" for the classroom. Even though Dan has been selected for this exclusive training program, he isn't about to shift his allegiance entirely to the king. His first act of defiance comes at dinnertime. The king has provided the best wine and meat from his own pantry, but Daniel refuses to eat any of it and instead asks for only vegetables and water. He doesn't want to defile himself by eating from the king's table.

His resolve does not sit well with the official who brought him his food, and who could blame the guy for trying to get Daniel to change his mind? First, no one refuses anything from the king, let alone a prisoner given such a plush assignment. But what upsets the official most is the fact that Daniel is entrusted to his care, and if he eats only vegetables and water, he will shrivel and shrink from undernourishment—and the king will blame *him*. He begs Daniel to eat the royal food and drink the royal wine, but Daniel offers a compromise: "Allow us to try it for ten days and then compare us to the rest of the trainees who have been eating from the king's pantry."

About this time, I can almost see Shadrach, Meshach, and Abednego looking at each other, shoulders shrugged and palms up: "Did he just say *us*? No way. I was really looking forward to prime rib and a good Shiraz."

Begrudgingly or not, the three join Daniel in his little food experiment, eating nothing but vegetables and drinking nothing but water. When the official checks in on them ten days later, he is amazed to see that they look healthier and stronger than those who ate the king's rich food.

Is God a vegetarian?

I hope not, because I love to grill a good steak every now and then. Actually, there is more to the story that helps explain Daniel's deep-seated conviction. Daniel likely considered the food from the Babylonian king's table to be contaminated because the first portion of it would have been offered to idols. Likewise, a portion of wine was poured out on a pagan altar. Ceremonially unclean animals were used, such as pigs, which were neither slaughtered nor prepared according to the regulations of the law.[1]

While New Testament Christians are no longer under the law, the Bible does contain good advice about diets and foods to eat and to avoid that could benefit our unhealthy nation. However, the Upper Story point of this episode is that God takes care of those who honor him. Refusing to eat from the king's pantry because someone doesn't want to defile himself is a good way to get killed. Or at least kicked out of the elite training program. But Daniel refuses to back down, regardless of the cost. I believe God wants us to have that same courageous devotion to him. To be willing to take a stand, even if it comes with a high price tag.

Daniel's food strike is minor compared to the way his three buddies snub the king. After they all complete their three-year training period, the king selects these four to become his personal assistants—a high honor. In just about every category, they apparently serve him well. In fact, there is only one thing they refuse to do: worship the pagan gods of Babylon. To do so would dishonor God and break one of his guidelines for living well: *no other god but me.*

King Nebuchadnezzar decided to build a huge golden idol—ninety feet tall. When it is completed, he invites all the officials of his kingdom to a ceremony where it is introduced with this command: Bow down to it, or risk being thrown into a fiery furnace. Shadrach, Meshach, and Abednego refuse, which infuriates the king. But because they have served him so well, Nebuchadnezzar gives them another chance: Worship the god I made, or else we're going to see if any god can rescue you from that fire pit.

Such is their devotion to God that they reply, "If we are thrown into the blazing furnace, the God we serve is able to deliver us from it, and he will deliver us from Your Majesty's hand. But even if he does not, we want you to know, Your Majesty, that we will not serve your gods or worship the image of gold you have set up."[2]

Wow! It's one thing to take a stand for God if you're pretty sure he's got your back. But to do so knowing there is a good chance he will let you burn? In some countries around the world, Christians are under attack. I've heard amazing stories of modern-day martyrs who were given a chance to recant their faith in Christ to save their own lives, and I've often wondered, "What would I do in that situation?" What would *you* do if a gun was pointed at your head and you were told, "Deny that you are a Christian, and I will not pull this trigger"? I hope we would have the courage of Shadrach, Meshach, and Abednego.

Watch what happens as God steps in: Nebuchadnezzar has the three young men thrown into the fiery furnace, but "the fire had not harmed their bodies, nor was a hair of their heads singed."[3]

Whenever God does something big, it is for a higher purpose. True, he honors the devotion of these three guys, but he does something that has Upper Story written all over it. Nebuchadnezzar is so impressed with the power of their God that he makes it a capital offense to say anything against the one true God. God rescued Shadrach, Meshach, and Abednego for the same reason he asks us to live lives that reflect his character of honesty, compassion, and justice: *to bring others into his perfect community*. Everything God does is motivated by his deep love for people and desire to have a relationship with them.

Where is Daniel as this is going on? The Bible doesn't say, but it is not that he tried to avoid such a test, because later in his life he exhibits the same courageous devotion to God as his three friends did. By this time, he is serving a new king—Darius—and in the process, some of the king's officials have become jealous of Daniel. When they notice that Daniel never bows to the king's gods, they talk the king into issuing a familiar-sounding decree: Worship any other god than the king's, and you will be thrown into a den of hungry lions.

Like his three friends had done, Daniel refuses to obey the order. Even though it pains the king to follow through with his decree because he has come to truly love Daniel, he puts him in with the lions in the evening and then spends a sleepless night—such is his concern for Daniel. The next morning he awakes at dawn, rushes to the den, and is overjoyed to see that God has tamed the lions and Daniel is safe. And again, it is all for an Upper Story reason, because this Babylonian king issues yet another decree: "In every part of my kingdom people must fear and reverence the God of Daniel."[4]

In the Lower Story, Judah is in exile. God's special people are doing their best to make it as strangers in a strange land. Because of their skills and work ethic—and because Babylon is enjoying a period of prosperity—they have decent jobs and are able to care for their families. They get up. Go to work. Pick up their kids at school. Eat dinner together. Go to bed. And start all over the next day. Where once they were God's chosen people, now they are surrounded by pagans. They long for something better.

Sound familiar? I don't really believe in the "good old days," but do you ever find yourself longing for the days when our culture seemed less antagonistic toward people of faith? And do you ever wish God would come down and do something really big to prove he is God and therefore give you a little street cred?

The Upper Story of Daniel and his three friends gives us a clue as to how this can happen. When they put God above everything else—when they obeyed the first commandment—God went to work for them. I believe with all my heart that if we have this same level of commitment, we will see great things happen. Whenever people put God first, they never regret it. God always comes through. Maybe not in the way we expect him to or wish he would. But he always honors us when we put him above everything else.

In your work culture, it may be OK to pad your expense report. Everybody does it. No one gets caught. But when you turn in an honest and accurate expense report, you are putting God first because you are reflecting *his* values and character. He will honor this. Even if we are burned in the fire or eaten by lions, God promises that our testimony will work out for the good. Our courage may prod an army of others to trust him more boldly or even be the very occasion that causes a doubter to cross the line of faith into eternal life with God.

In your culture as a man, it may seem like you are just being "one of the guys" when you comment on a pretty waitress who leans over to pour you more coffee. But when you refuse to join in or even tactfully tell your buddies to clean it up, you are putting God first because he invented sex for men and women to enjoy in marriage. He will honor you for this.

In your culture as a woman, it may be OK to complain to your girlfriends about your husband, but when you catch yourself and refuse to do it, even though everyone else does, you are putting God first because his idea of marriage is built on respect. He will honor you for this.

In your culture as a student, it may be OK to pretend you don't know God in order to fit in with the crowd, but when you stand and pray with a small band of fellow believers before the school day begins, you are putting God first because he loves that attitude of dependence on him. He will honor you for this.

Because Daniel and his three friends took a stand, Babylonians who did not know their God turned to him. God still does great and mighty things to attract people to him. He uses people like you and me to do it. When we resist the pull of a similar alien land and live the way God wants us to, our friends, neighbors, colleagues, entire cities—maybe even nations—will turn to him.

With God, maybe exile isn't such a bad place to be after all.

Chapter 19

THE RETURN HOME

*"Give careful thought to your ways. You have planted
much, but harvested little. You eat, but never have
enough. You drink, but never have your fill. You
put on clothes, but are not warm. You earn wages,
only to put them in a purse with holes in it."*

HAGGAI 1:5–6

First return of exiles	Haggai and Zechariah	Opposition to temple building	Temple completed
538	520–480		516

BC

WHAT'S HAPPENING IN THE UPPER STORY

After seventy years exactly, just as the prophets foretold, the people of Judah made their way home from captivity. The loving discipline from the hand of God was designed to get their attention and send a consistent message to the surrounding nations that God's people's actions did not represent his character and plan. From the Lower Story, how fifty thousand people returned to rebuild the temple in Jerusalem makes no sense at all. King Cyrus of Persia blesses and funds the entire project for the spiritually and financially broke Israelites. From the Upper Story, there is no doubt as to how this all came about. Roughly 150 years earlier, Isaiah prophesies this very event. He even calls out Cyrus by name.[1] God moves in the hearts of kings and world leaders to reveal his identity and to work out his grand plan.

ALIGNING OUR STORY TO GOD'S STORY

When the Israelites returned to Jerusalem, their priority was to rebuild the temple, to place their focus where it needed to be—on the presence of God in their lives and on the will of God for their lives. They started out strong, but soon lost focus. Their priorities flip-flopped to rebuilding their houses first. Everything in their lives stopped working, and they were filled with frustration. Later, Jesus will tell us to "seek first his kingdom and his righteousness, and all these things will be given to you as well."[2] When we make first things first, God throws in the second things. When we make second things first, we lose all things. Align your life to God's Upper Story, and the Lower Story will go much smoother.

S ometimes life is all about pig slop.

The prodigal son can tell you about the pig slop. He smelled it, felt it, served it. He may have even tasted it. In one of Jesus' best-known stories, he described the pigpen experience of a stubborn-hearted son. The boy, born in privilege, demanded his inheritance before his father's death. He took the money to a first-century equivalent of Las Vegas to live large. Within a few days, he was on a first-name basis with the casino manager, the hostess and her friends, and a crowd of bystanders who loved to party, as long as they weren't paying.

Within a few more days, he was dead broke, looking for a job. He found one feeding pigs. The salary must have stunk as much as the swine did, because the boy was soon drooling over pig slop. He seriously considered taking a place at the trough and digging in. That's when he came to his senses and got back on track with his life. But it took some pig slop to get his attention.

The prodigal and the pigs. The Jews and the abandoned foundation of God's temple. What do these have in common? They both provide an answer to the question, "What does God do when we get off track?"

Here's the backstory. The children of Israel have passed the last seventy winters in Babylonian exile. Their city was razed; their beloved temple was ransacked. Except for the courage of Daniel and his three friends, the era would have been a shameful one. But after seven decades of darkness, a tunnel of sunlight pierces the clouds and surprises the people.

> In the first year of Cyrus king of Persia, in order to fulfill the word of the LORD spoken by Jeremiah, the LORD moved the heart of Cyrus king of Persia to make a proclamation throughout his realm and also to put it in writing:
>
> "This is what Cyrus king of Persia says:
>
> "'The LORD, the God of heaven, has given me all the kingdoms of the earth and he has appointed me to build a temple for him in Jerusalem

in Judah. Any of his people among you—may their God be with them, and let them go up to Jerusalem in Judah and build the temple of the Lord, the God of Israel, the God who is in Jerusalem. And in any locality where survivors may now be living, the people are to provide them with silver and gold, with goods and livestock, with freewill offerings for the temple of God in Jerusalem.'"[3]

What a remarkable turn of events! God turns the heart of Persia's king Cyrus toward the Jews and turns the Jews toward Jerusalem. And God prompts the king to give the exiles not only permission but also the resources with which to build the temple.

Now why would God do this? Why would he choose a pagan king to build his holy temple? Doesn't it seem a little odd that he didn't raise up a Jewish leader to take on this task? In the Lower Story, no—it doesn't make sense. Cyrus worshiped many different gods but didn't acknowledge the God of Israel. To go this route, God was, in one sense, using tainted resources to build his sacred dwelling place. It would be like having a mob boss who made a fortune through illegal means writing our church a check so we can build a new worship center.

But in the Upper Story, God is sovereign, meaning he and he alone determines what he does. And I think one of the reasons he chooses a pagan king to help build the temple is to send a message to his community: "I will use whatever it takes to finish my plan to build a perfect community where I can be with my people forever—even a king who doesn't know me."

But there is another reason God chooses Cyrus: it is part of his plan all along. Remember Isaiah? About one hundred years earlier, he laid out the whole story, prophesying the good, the bad, and the ugly that would happen to Israel. But the people wouldn't listen, which is why they missed the remarkable message having to do with Cyrus: God will raise him up and make him a strong leader, even though he does not believe in the one true God. Isaiah even calls Cyrus "the [Lord's] anointed,"[4] which is the same as calling him a messiah. And by now you know why God does these big, remarkable things in the world, which is exactly why he called on Cyrus to build his temple: "so that from the rising of the sun to the place of its setting, people may know there is none besides me."[5]

Cyrus's taking on the task of building God's temple is one of those big, remarkable things that attracted a lot of attention.

You may also wonder why God even needed a temple. Being all-powerful and capable of being everywhere present, he could just as easily do life with his people without all the trouble of building an elaborate temple. The temple is a physical place that reminds us that God wants to enter into our Lower Story to be with us. Physical presence brings great comfort. As I write this, my wife is recovering from surgery. For two days, I have been in the same room with her. The doctors and nurses are doing all the work. I'm just here in the room with her; I'm writing as she is sleeping. She says my presence helps. I know what she's talking about, because on several occasions, the tables were turned—I was the one in the bed. For the children of Israel, the temple was a physical place to remind them that God was with them.

Consider the location of the temple. Was it built high atop a steep mountain that no one could reach? Did God tell them to build it way out in the desert where no one could see it unless they made a long and difficult pilgrimage? No, it was smack-dab in the middle of the most populated city of ancient Israel— Jerusalem. Every time anyone walked past the temple, they were reminded that God wants to be right there with them. He wants to be in the neighborhood. The temple reminded them—and tells all of us—that God wants to be with his people.

But it also communicates a problem: our sin—our tendency to disobey God, despite our best intentions. Because of this sin, ordinary people could not enter the holiest place inside the temple, where God was present. Only a priest could be there, and then only after a blood sacrifice was offered. So for generations the temple stood as a reminder that the only way to have access to God was through a blood sacrifice offered by an intermediary.

Of course, from our perspective, we know what was going on. We know that through the temple, God was preparing the world for the coming of Jesus Christ, who gave himself as the final sacrifice for sin. Everyone can now have access directly to God through Jesus. The temple prepared the people. It was an educational tool, so that when Jesus came, the people could connect the dots more quickly. But now, after all the years in exile when they did not have this temple, God decided it was time to reconstruct it so he could move his plan along.

So in 538 BC, fifty thousand Jews, prompted by God and funded by Cyrus, made the nine-hundred-mile trek from Babylon to Jerusalem and got to work. God's big thing became their big thing, and they rolled up the sleeves of their robes and began building the temple.

One thing I've learned in my years as a pastor is that whenever you attempt something big for God, you can always count on opposition, and this is exactly what happened as the men began building the temple. Dissenters tried everything they could to block their efforts, but God's chosen people maintained their resolve. Day after day, despite interference from outsiders, they persevered, making God's priority their own. If you would have asked any of them why they were so focused on the task at hand, you might have gotten the Dan Aykroyd answer from the movie *The Blues Brothers*: "We're on a mission from God." Nothing would get in the way of that magnificent mission.

At least not for a few years. Then it started to happen. Little by little, they lost their focus. They began to turn less attention to the house of God and more attention to their own personal projects. Who knows why? Maybe stacking stones was too tiresome. Maybe the criticism was too irksome. Or more likely, they just started thinking about their own stuff—their own businesses, farms, enterprises, houses. One by one, they quit showing up at the work site. And then one day, no one came.

God's big thing had become a small thing to his people.

I can't prove this, but I can almost guarantee they never intended to abandon the project forever. I can almost hear their well-intentioned rationalizing: "We'll get back to it. Maybe next week. Or next month. Certainly before next year. But first I have to get the crops harvested. Then I have to finish putting the new roof on the house. Once I get caught up on things, I'll come back to it."

One week passed. One month passed. One year passed. Two years passed. Five years passed. Ten years passed. Fifteen years passed. For sixteen years, the temple project sat untouched! It turned into an abandoned construction site for sixteen years—enough time for the weeds and the grass to grow up over the footers of the foundation. Enough time for all the surrounding nations to look at the temple and think, "Well, they sure don't take their God very seriously." Enough time for a whole generation of children to grow up and look at the abandoned project and think, "Well, I guess our parents don't care much about that temple."

Meanwhile, as God's house languished, their own houses flourished. The prophet Haggai scornfully refers to their "paneled houses" as he tries to warn them about their self-centeredness.[6] These fortunate former exiles who returned to the land God had promised them now focused solely on their own interests, only to become more miserable as the days passed.

When we refuse to pay attention to God, he has a way of getting our attention. He puts a chill in the corner office. He puts a dent in the savings account. He permits a drought to descend on the farm. He sends a lonely wind through the big house. When our priorities become more important than God's, our lives are marked by futility.

We plant much, but we harvest little. We eat, but we never feel satisfied. We drink, but we never have our deepest thirst abated. And we earn our wages, only to see the money disappear. Do you ever feel as if you're making more money than ever before but you still don't have enough? Do you ever wonder why everything you thought would make you happy hasn't kicked in yet? When our focus shifts from God to ourselves, even our finest endeavors begin to collapse like tsunami-sucked-out sand castles.

I need to be very careful with this passage. I don't want to give you the impression that every tiny mishap is discipline meted out by an angry God. When you have to stop at a red light or you get a common cold, don't be quick to interpret this as God's judgment. The Bible reminds us that the sun rises on the evil and the good, and the rain falls on the righteous and the unrighteous.[7] Things happen, and we must not blame God for them.

But there are seasons of life that are so difficult, so challenging—one difficulty stacked on another for an extended period of time—that it just may be that God is trying to get our attention. There are seasons of God-ordained struggle—times of exhausted emptiness when nothing seems to work, nothing quenches our deepest thirsts, no achievement abates our restless hunger; times when we plant but never really harvest, when droughts turn our fields into dust and our retirements into pocket change; times when we are literally forced to our knees because nothing else seems to work. God allows times of difficulty to come so we will be sure to "give careful thought to [our] ways."[8]

In the Lower Story, we grind away at life and never seem to get what we are looking for. In the Upper Story, God is practically yelling at the top of his lungs, "Consider your ways. I have so much more for you, if only you would let me live with you." And he is not pleading with nations but with individuals, so this one isn't on Washington, D.C. God already has a nation, and he wants you to enjoy the benefits of citizenship, but first give careful thought to your ways.

Give careful thought to where your passions lie. Are you as eager to spend time with God in conversation as you are to hang out with your buddies in that man-cave you spent all last year building? Have you allowed the many good things in your life—your children, your career, your girlfriends—to squeeze God back into the corner of a basement closet? Many of us who love God have been blessed with great families, productive careers, and "paneled houses." All good things, but capable of gradually edging God out of our lives. Like the former exiles, we don't mean to deliberately ignore God. We'll get back to him soon. We just need to take care of these other things first.

I have yet to meet a follower of Christ who deliberately set out to ignore God, but I've seen many drift away from him because they allowed everything else—the kids, the job, the transfer, the demands, the stress, the struggle—to get in the way of the precious relationship he offers. The time comes when we no longer wake up thinking about God's temple. And with the passage of time comes the diminishing of passion. Tithing becomes tipping, prayers become rote quotes, and church attendance becomes an obligation. It's not that we forget God; it's just that we put him in a closet.

God's message to Israel through Haggai, and his message to you, is, "I won't stay in anyone's closet. I want to be there with you, wherever you are, whatever you're doing." He loves us too much to leave us to our own devices. So he pulls us aside for a Heart-to-heart chat. He asks us to give careful thought to our ways, wash the mud off the pigpen, and get his work accomplished. Amazingly, this is just what the Jews did. The Lord stirred up the leadership and the people got to work on the house of God. And they finished it. And God was once again living and dwelling among the people.

C. S. Lewis once wrote, "Put first things first and we get second things thrown in: put second things first and we lose both first and second things."[9] The prodigal son learned this, just as the children of Israel had to be reminded of this truth. He finally learned to put his father first and was given a seat at the table. As God's plan continues to unfold to bring his ultimate solution through Israel, let us heed the challenge in our own lives to make God's big thing our big thing.

Chapter

20

THE QUEEN OF BEAUTY AND COURAGE

_"And who knows but that you have come to your
royal position for such a time as this?"_

ESTHER 4:14

		Esther		Esther saves		Days
	Xerxes	becomes queen		the Jews		of Purim

BC   486–465   479

WHAT'S HAPPENING IN THE UPPER STORY

Judah has been back in Jerusalem for more than a hundred years. Yet a remnant has remained in Susa, the capital of the Persian Empire. This parenthetical story is contained in the book of Esther. The name of God is not mentioned once in this book, but his fingerprints are all over the story. Esther, a Jew, becomes queen around the same time that Haman, an Amalekite, is promoted to the position of leader over all the royal aides. Haman has it out for the Jews. Some suggest he is the offspring of the king of the Amalekites, the same nation that Saul failed to conquer five hundred years before. Haman convinces the king of Persia to sign an irrevocable edict to exterminate the Jews on one particular day. Haman rolls the dice, and it falls on Adar 13. Through Esther's courage, the tables are turned on Haman, and instead of killing Jews, Haman is executed. To this day, Jews celebrate the Feast of Purim, which can be translated "the Feast of the Dice." Solomon wrote years earlier, "We may throw the dice, but the LORD determines how they fall."[1] God's sovereign hand is not limited to Jerusalem, but reaches into Babylon and Persia and anywhere else his people live.

ALIGNING OUR STORY TO GOD'S STORY

From a Lower Story point of view, everything in Esther's story appears to be coincidence, luck, misfortune, or random events. Mordecai sees the Upper Story when he asks Queen Esther, "Who knows but that you have come to your royal position for such a time as this?" Many of the things happening to us in our Lower Story, whether lucky breaks or heartbreaks, are for a good Upper Story purpose. Watch for that purpose, and like Esther, be willing to take action with courage.

hile I don't know many Christians who admit to gambling, if most of us are honest, some moments in life feel like a day in Vegas. It's not just that fortunes can turn with a new shuffle, another roll, or a second spin; it's that life really can turn on a dime. One minute you're up, and the next you're penniless.

Sometimes it feels like your fate, your destiny is left to the roll of the dice. Sometimes you get lucky; sometimes you lose it all. But every now and then, there is a series of astounding events that work together to bring about either a colossal disaster or an amazing windfall. Some would call it coincidence; others would call it luck. Still others would say, "Someone is working behind the scenes, pulling strings, working out our destiny. This has God's fingerprints all over it."

If you can relate, then you're really going to connect with Esther. Her story is all about taking chances, and she knows what it means to "go big or go home."

The time is not the twenty-first century AD, but the fifth century BC. The city is not Las Vegas, but Susa, the capital city of the Persian Empire. The southern kingdom of Judah had been carried into exile a little more than a hundred years back—a move orchestrated by God as loving discipline toward the Israelites because of their repeated disobedience. According to God's plan, after seventy years the Jews finally had an opportunity to head back home. About fifty thousand of them did. The rest of them acclimated and became integrated into the Persian culture. They stayed.

So this explains the multicultural dynamics going on in our Lower Story here. Aside from her beauty, Esther didn't have a lot going for her. An orphan, she was raised by her cousin, Mordecai. And while most of God's people had returned to Jerusalem, she and Mordecai remained behind in the city of Susa. Living as a Jew in the heart of the Persian Empire wasn't particularly easy and carried with it risks of prejudice, even death. The king at the time, Xerxes, was considered the most powerful man in the world. He was known for his extravagance and recklessness, qualities clearly on display when we first meet him.

During the third year of his reign, Xerxes threw a huge party that lasted seven days and showcased his vast wealth to all the military and civic leaders from his kingdom, which stretched from India to the Mediterranean Sea. This event was an all-you-can-eat, all-you-can-drink gala held in the king's magnificent garden inside the royal palace.

After seven days of partying, Xerxes sends for his wife, Queen Vashti, to meet and greet the guests, but she refuses. Furious, the king consults with his legal experts to determine what he should do about her disrespectful behavior, and they tell him he should make an example out of her; if he didn't, wives all over Persia would think it was OK to stand up to their husbands. They then advise him to issue an irrevocable decree to banish her from the palace and find a new queen.

So long, Vashti.

And so Xerxes sends his aides throughout the entire kingdom to find women beautiful enough to suit his tastes. If you were a young and beautiful woman and one of the king's aides selected you as a royal candidate, you had no say in the matter but were carted off and handed over to a guy named Hegai, whose job it was to prepare you for the final selection process. Sort of Tyra Banks and Simon Cowell rolled into one fairy godmother type who could either make you or break you on your way to becoming Persia's Next Top Queen. Which is what happened to Esther. For whatever reason, she happened to be in the right place at the right time, captivating the king's aide with her beauty.

Her protective cousin, Mordecai, warns her not to reveal to anyone that she is a Jew, and he hangs out near the palace every day to try to find out how she is doing. As it turns out, she and the other candidates are doing quite well. The queen-in-training program was essentially twelve months in a beauty spa. Oil of myrrh facials. Deep tissue massage with aromatic lotions. Perfume and cosmetic treatments. Pilates and yoga. And nutritious meals formulated to enhance their physical beauty. Hegai is so smitten by Esther's beauty that he assigns her seven female attendants and gives her the best apartment in the palace.

After twelve months of pampering, it is time for the candidates to go before the king so he can choose his new queen. The instant Xerxes sees Esther—game over. He immediately selects her to be his queen, places the royal crown on her head, throws another huge party, and proclaims the day a holiday throughout his kingdom.

What a phenomenal Lower Story event! This is the kind of romance we find in *Cinderella* and *Camelot, My Fair Lady* and *Pretty Woman*. Only this one takes a decidedly Upper Story turn. Esther was in the right place at the right time for a reason that extends all the way to you and me. In the Lower Story, coincidences randomly cross our paths to our amusement and delight. In the Upper Story, there are no coincidences. It is no accident that a Jewish girl in exile finds herself wearing the queen's crown.

Shortly after Esther's coronation, Xerxes promotes one of his officials, Haman, to a position of prominence over all the other royal aides—a position that requires everyone at the king's gate to kneel before him. But Mordecai, who still visits the palace each day to check on Esther, refuses to kneel to Haman. The other officials notice and urge him to comply, but Mordecai refuses, telling them he is a Jew. When the aides report this to Haman, he decides it wouldn't be enough to just kill Mordecai—he asks and receives permission from the king to kill *every Jew* in Persia. Since the king didn't know his new queen was Jewish, he had no idea the dilemma he would eventually find himself in. Every Jew in the 127 provinces of Persia is targeted to be killed, but it has to be on one specific day.

To determine the date when Haman and his forces will go after the Jews, they literally roll the dice, and it lands on Adar 13 (equivalent to our February or March), a day roughly eleven months away. Lucky sevens for Haman; snake eyes for Israel. So a decree goes out, naming the date of the execution of every Jew in Persia, in essence placing every Jew on death row for eleven months, because once the king's seal was stamped on a decree, nothing could repeal it, not even the king.

When Mordecai sees the decree, he is so distressed that he publicly mourns in front of the palace. Day in and day out, he marches in front of the palace wearing sackcloth and ashes, the symbol of grief, to mourn the approaching day of annihilation. When Queen Esther's attendants tell her about her cousin, she sends them to him to find out why he is in such distress. Mordecai sees his opportunity. Only he knows that the queen is a Jew. He tells her about Haman's plot to kill every Jew in the kingdom and begs her to approach the king and beg for mercy for her people.

Remember Vashti? Esther did. As much as she wanted to go to bat for her people, she feared it would be hopeless. Approach the king without being summoned, and you mysteriously vanish. That's when Mordecai must have gotten a glimpse of the Upper Story. Why had they stayed behind in Babylon when all their Jewish friends returned to Jerusalem? Why did Vashti refuse to go to her king when she was summoned? Why was Esther among those chosen to become candidates for Xerxes's new queen? And why did Haman have to have it in for the Jews?

Mordecai's reply to Queen Esther reveals, through a question, why all of these random events occurred: "Who knows but that you have come to your royal position for such a time as this?"

What would *you* do if you had to risk everything to accomplish the one reason you were placed on this earth?

Esther weighs Mordecai's sobering question and replies, "Go, gather together all the Jews who are in Susa, and fast for me. Do not eat or drink for three days, night or day. I and my attendants will fast as you do. When this is done, I will go to the king, even though it is against the law. And if I perish, I perish."[2]

After three days, she approaches the king. What should have been certain death is greeted with yet another "coincidence" as the king tells her she can request anything—up to half his kingdom—and it will be hers. What luck! She requests a dinner that very evening with the king and Haman, a dinner at which she simply asks the king if he and Haman will join her for another dinner the next night. At that dinner, she exposes Haman's plan to destroy her and her people, revealing for the first time that she is a Jew.[3]

The king is so upset that he storms out of the room, but Haman remains behind to beg for Esther's mercy. And in yet another case of bad luck, Haman stumbles and falls against Esther just as the king walks back into the room. He sees his beloved queen under Haman and orders him put to death for attempted rape. He also appoints Mordecai to Haman's vacated position, another "lucky" development in God's Upper Story. Remember, the king's decree to kill every Jew cannot, by law, be revoked. But Mordecai now has the power to be granted a request of the king, so he asks Xerxes to give the Jews permission to at least defend themselves.

On Adar 13, non-Jewish people from all 127 provinces attacked the Jews. Their motivation for doing such a horrific thing was the permission granted in the original decree to take all of the possessions of the Jews you killed— legalized looting. It was a bloodbath, but one carried out at the hands of the Jews, who took out 75,810 of their assailants on that day, including ten sons of Haman. The next day, they celebrated—a tradition that continues to this day. It's called the Feast of Purim, from the word *pur*, which means "lot" or "dice." It is celebrated every year on March 10 as a reminder that God's Upper Story is not ruled by chance but by his sovereign power. His reign is not limited to Jerusalem but reaches into Babylon and Persia and anywhere else his people live.

What if your greatest fear, your heaviest burden, has been given to you "for such a time as this"?

Esther could have told her cousin to mind his own business: "Leave me alone. It's comfortable in the palace. Being a queen has its privileges. Let God take care of our people. Only a fool would risk all that I have." And who would have blamed her? Look what happened to the last queen who refused to obey the palace rules!

You may never be in a position where obeying God is a matter of life and death. I hope you never are. The worst thing that could happen to most of us for taking a stand for God is a little ridicule. People may think we're fanatics if we walk in a March for Life. Our neighbors may be offended if we hold a "Backyard Bible School" for one week in the summer. Our colleagues at work may call us "Bible thumpers" if we pull out our compact New Testament and read it in the break room. Other parents may not like it when we go to a school board meeting and politely share our concerns about intelligent design being left out of the science curriculum.

You may even think it's crazy to wake up in the middle of the night burdened about a friend at work who is going through a divorce. You have this wild idea that if you could just talk to him and his wife, perhaps you could help them find a way to save their marriage. You're not a marriage counselor, but you just can't shake the feeling that you could do something that may make a difference in their relationship. Then the second-guessing begins. Maybe you'll just make things worse. It's probably too late and beyond repair. You don't really know his wife very well.

I believe God still speaks to us in a quiet whisper, offering us the blessed privilege of "saving his people" through wild and crazy acts of loving obedience. Imagine the places we could go and the things we could do to reflect God's love for his children. Imagine what may happen in our families, neighborhoods, cities, nations, and world if we adopt Esther's commitment as our own: "I will go to the king . . . And if I perish, I perish."[4]

Esther was willing to take her chances because she knew who controlled the dice. Listen to the wise words of Solomon: "We may throw the dice, but the LORD determines how they fall."[5] Are you willing to make the same bet?

Chapter 21

REBUILDING THE WALLS

"I will send my messenger, who will prepare the way
before me. Then suddenly the Lord you are seeking
will come to his temple; the messenger of the covenant,
whom you desire, will come," says the LORD Almighty.

MALACHI 3:1

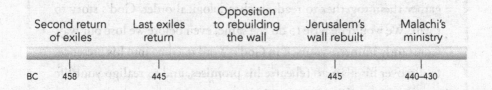

Second return of exiles	Last exiles return	Opposition to rebuilding the wall	Jerusalem's wall rebuilt	Malachi's ministry
BC 458	445		445	440–430

WHAT'S HAPPENING IN THE UPPER STORY

The primary role of Israel in the telling of God's Upper Story is coming to fruition. The Old Testament comes to end, and we turn the page to the next movement in this divine, epic drama. The prophet Malachi closes this part of the story by telling us that the next prophet will introduce the world to the long-awaited Messiah from the tribe of Judah. The prophet's name is John the Baptist. To wrap up this chapter of the story, the children of Israel have returned from captivity to their homeland. They have rebuilt the temple for God's presence to dwell, and they will rebuild the wall around Jerusalem to protect themselves from surrounding enemies. The most important building project of all is the rebuilding of their lives with God. At the people's request, Ezra stands up in the presence of all Israel and reads God's story from the beginning. This reminded the children of Israel that God has been writing this epic for a long time and has always kept his promise. Their best decision is to simply align their collective Lower Stories to his Upper Story!

ALIGNING OUR STORY TO GOD'S STORY

Every time Israel lost their way, their good and godly leaders would gather them together to read, in chronological order, God's story to them. We would be wise to do the same, even before we lose our way. Constantly immerse yourself in God's Word to come into his presence, to discover his plan, to rehearse his promises, and to realign your life to your part in this amazing adventure!

The Old Testament comes to an end with three building projects. There is the rebuilding of the temple under the leadership of Zerubbabel—God once again has a place to stay with his people. Sacrifices are once again being made for their sins. Second, there is the rebuilding of the wall around the city of Jerusalem under Nehemiah's leadership. The people now have protection from the many folks who had been bullying them on and off through the years.

But the most important rebuilding project is the rebuilding of the lives of God's people. As evidence of the heart makeovers they are experiencing, they initiate an event that is not Zerubbabel's idea, nor Nehemiah's idea, nor even Ezra the priest's idea. It is the people's idea. They want to initiate a restoration with God, just as it should be.

They all gather together at the Water Gate—thousands of them, all the men, women, and children. They tell Ezra to bring out the Book of the Law of Moses.[1] It has been 140 years since they heard anyone read God's word to them. They are truly hungry, spiritually famished. They have been through so much. They have been rightfully disciplined by God and are finally ready to listen. Scripture tells us they are sitting on the edge of their seats.

Ezra intends to read the entire Book of the Law, which, you may recall, is what Joshua did after the sin of Achan.[2] This spiritual exercise serves to refocus, re-center, remind Israel of what is truly important. It aids in the rebuilding program of a life aligned with God's Upper Story.

Similarly, this has been our first goal as we've gone through the Story, that God would refocus, re-center, remind, and rebuild our lives on what is foundational—his Upper Story.

Then Ezra begins to read from the sacred book. For several hours—daybreak until noon—he reads, and as he shares God's laws with the people, they begin to weep and mourn. The more he reads the louder their wailing. As they listen to God's instructions for living well in community with him and each other, they are heartbroken over their failure to obey. Unlike the old revival preachers,

Ezra doesn't need to tell them they are sinners. The very words God had given to Moses convict them, and they are overwhelmed with a spirit of repentance.

Nehemiah, who is standing next to Ezra, sees this moving display of grief and shouts to the crowd, "Don't cry! This is a day to celebrate and have a party. Go and eat your best food and drink your best wine. Whatever you do, don't be sad. Let God's joy be your strength."[3]

Nehemiah remembered that God not only gave the law to help his people live well but also made a way for them to atone for their sins when they broke the law. He knew that the community God envisioned was one characterized by joy and contentment, not tears.

Nehemiah knew that everything God's people had experienced was part of a plan to build a perfect nation and include as many people in it as possible. Once the people who had been weeping understood this, they "went away to eat and drink, to send portions of food and to celebrate with great joy."[4] What a perfect picture of what God wants for us. *Enjoy the best blessings of life. Share them with others. And celebrate!*

God's people finally seem to get it! They lift their hands to the heavens and shout, "Amen! Amen!"—a Hebrew word that literally means "so be it." What a different attitude from the days of the kings!

The same emotion comes on people today as they finally understand what the Bible is all about. The Bible does not consist of ancient, unrelated paintings. No, it is a beautiful mural all joined together to tell of God's great love for us and the extent to which he will go to get us back. When our souls finally get this message, it is so wonderfully overwhelming that tears of joy spring to our eyes.

Levites, those who serve in the temple, form small groups throughout the large crowd, making sure the people understand what is being read. The Bible is sometimes hard to understand. We need others to help us—to make sure we all get God's message to us.

That has been our second goal of The Story experience—to equip the whole church, the whole family of God, in a way that allows us to share in the experience together so we can help each other understand it.

But it doesn't stop there. As the people hear the Law, they find things they aren't doing. They don't want to be those who "merely listen to the word";

they want to be those who "do what it says."[5] They discover that the next event coming up on the Jewish calendar that God asked them to observe is the Festival of Tabernacles. They get after it—so much so that we are told, "From the days of Joshua . . . until that day, the Israelites had not celebrated it like this. And their joy was very great."[6] Obeying God's word, aligning our lives to his plan, brings joy to our lives like nothing else.

You may have missed this—I certainly did when I first read the Bible. At the end of the Old Testament, it seems that the people have finally learned something about who is in charge. There is no mention of reinstating their king. This royal figure was never God's perfect idea, but he allowed it. While there were a few good kings, for the most part, they led the people astray. At last, the people no longer ask for a king. "Been there, done that; got the royal T-shirt."

The last person to speak before the Old Testament comes to a close is Malachi. He tells us that the next prophet who is going to speak for God is going to introduce us to the One we have been waiting for, the One who will provide the once-and-for-all solution for getting us back to God.[7] He is going to introduce us to the Messiah. Who is this messenger he talks about? When we turn to the pages of the New Testament, we learn that he is talking about John the Baptist. Matthew tells us, "In those days John the Baptist came, preaching in the wilderness of Judea and saying, 'Repent, for the kingdom of heaven has come near.' This is he who was spoken of through the prophet Isaiah."[8] Isaiah had foretold the role of John the Baptist, and now Malachi restates it.[9] Malachi foretells that the next time God speaks—which will be four hundred years later—it will be through the lips of John the Baptist, the one who would prepare the way for Christ to come.

When I read these passages, I'm reminded of Christmastime and Easter—and the seasons in the church calendar called Advent and Lent. In both of these seasons, we are called to prepare our hearts for the arrival of Jesus Christ, first in the incarnation of the Christ child in the manger and then in his resurrection from the tomb. As we will explore in greater detail in the New Testament, preparing the way for Christ to return is always in season.

I hope you have enjoyed our journey through the Old Testament—a thirty-nine-volume library filled with stories of adventure, love, heartbreak, triumph, power, disappointment, struggle, war, and peace. You must remember, however, that it isn't just a collection of unrelated accounts and historical records. Each story we have encountered has contributed to the unfolding of the one Story of God.

In fact, as many events and people have revealed, every single story of God's people and the nation of Israel points to the first coming of Jesus Christ, the Messiah. Now as we move into the New Testament, it is finally time for us to meet this One we have been waiting for—our Savior. Like the children of Israel, we too must prepare the way for the Lord. We must prepare our hearts to receive this One who gives us back our intended life and destiny with God.

Are you ready to meet him? Then, along with the Israelites, who proclaimed it thousands of years ago, we say, "Amen! Amen! So be it!"

Movement Three

THE STORY
OF JESUS

Matthew–John

*J*esus left the Upper Story to come down into our Lower
Story to be with us and to provide the way for us to be
made right with God. Through faith in Christ's work on the
cross, we can now overturn the curse of sin brought on by
Adam's choice and have an intimate, life-giving relationship
with God.

Chapter 22

THE BIRTH
OF THE KING

*"My soul glorifies the Lord
and my spirit rejoices in God my Savior,
for he has been mindful
of the humble state of his servant."*

LUKE 1:46–48

Jesus is born	Flight to Egypt	Jesus visits the temple
6/5 BC	5/4 BC	AD 7/8

WHAT'S HAPPENING IN THE UPPER STORY

More than two thousand years have passed since God made the promise to Abraham, more than a thousand years since he promised David that the solution to overturn Adam's fateful curse would come from his family. Every story of Israel has pointed to this day. Three hundred fifty-three Old Testament prophecies will be fulfilled to give us confidence that Jesus is the promised Messiah, including that Jesus would be born in Bethlehem.[1] God orchestrated Caesar Augustus's decree for an empire-wide census to move Mary and Joseph to Bethlehem in time for the delivery. From the Lower Story, the conception of Jesus appears to be a scandal. Yet from the Upper Story, this is the *solution* to our scandal. The sin disease is passed down through the seed of humanity. Jesus is not born of man, but born of God. He is the second man to walk on earth without sin in his nature. The first was Adam, who failed to remain sinless. Jesus, the second Adam, stayed sinless throughout his life on earth. He is our second chance.

ALIGNING OUR STORY TO GOD'S STORY

From the Lower Story, Mary and Joseph are just a number in the census. To the world, they are poor and irrelevant. But they matter to God. They are from the tribe of Judah, and they are chosen by God to bring Jesus into the world. When approached by an angel, Mary simply said, "Yes, be born in me!" We are in the same position as Mary and Joseph. God wants to live in us. Take down the "no vacancy" sign and say the same thing Mary did: "Yes, be born in me. Make my heart your home."

For most children, the longest night of the year is Christmas Eve. Once they are tucked in bed, sleep comes slowly. The excitement and the anticipation for the next morning are almost unbearable. For just this one night of the year, time seems to stand still.

For Mom and Dad, Christmas Eve is the shortest night of the year. Mom still has presents to wrap, and Dad has to put together that elaborate "big gift" that requires "easy assembly." But they have to wait until the kids are asleep so that an "accidental" trip downstairs doesn't spoil the surprise. If everything goes well, they might crawl into bed about 3:00 a.m., only to be awakened two hours later to screams of "Is it time yet?"

I don't know anyone who likes to wait. If you're in a hurry at the grocery store, then please don't get in line behind me, because I seem to put a slow-motion freeze on any line I'm in. The cashier will stop and call for a price check at least three times, and then when it's time for the nice elderly woman in front of me to pay, she reaches into her purse and pulls out a big envelope of coupons and starts looking for the ones to cash in for her groceries. When it's finally my turn, the cash register runs out of tape and the checkout person can't find a new roll. You mean it happens to you too?

If you're a woman and you've been pregnant, very likely this is the one question that turns you into a ninja inside: *How much longer do you have?* Those last few weeks just drag by, don't they? It's almost like it's your fault if the baby doesn't arrive when everyone thinks it should. But the real fun starts when you get past your due date—and still no baby. Nine months is a long time to wait for a baby.

So is four hundred years.

This is how long God's people had to wait after the temple had been rebuilt. Except they weren't waiting for a baby; they were looking for a king who would "reign on David's throne and over his kingdom."[2]

Instead, they got a scandal.

At least this is what it looked like in the Lower Story. A young couple—Joseph and Mary—are engaged to be married. Then Mary gives Joseph the news: "I'm pregnant." Put yourself in his shoes. You fall in love with a beautiful young woman who is still a teenager. You propose to her, and she accepts. You have been taught that sex is a gift reserved for marriage, so you honor the love of your life by not sleeping with her. And then she tells you she is pregnant.

Most guys would be furious. They would accuse her of messing around with someone. But Joseph is decent about it. He doesn't want to add to Mary's problems by getting mad at her, and he decides the best thing to do is to quietly end the relationship and move on with his life.

What he couldn't have known was that God sees things differently in the Upper Story. What was a scandal to Joseph was a solution to God. Remember, God's Upper Story has one major theme: "I want to give you a way to come back to me so we can do life together." And Joseph has a major role to play in this plan. God cannot let him get away, so he sends one of his angels to give him a glimpse of the Upper Story. In a dream, the angel tells him, "Joseph son of David, do not be afraid to take Mary home as your wife, because what is conceived in her is from the Holy Spirit. She will give birth to a son, and you are to give him the name Jesus, because he will save his people from their sins."[3]

When the angel reminded him that he wasn't just any Israelite but one from the line of David, Joseph knew why that was such an important fact. He had probably heard the prophecies read hundreds of times in the temple: the long-awaited Messiah would come from the tribe of Judah—David's tribe. *His* tribe!

And the part about the baby in his fiancée's womb being conceived by the Holy Spirit? Naturally, Joseph would have been relieved to learn that Mary had been as true to him as he was to her, but that wasn't something God thought up to help Joseph and Mary save face. Remember when we learned in the story of Cain and Abel that the sin nature is transmitted to all of Adam and Eve's offspring through the seed of mankind—that because of Adam and Eve's choice to disobey God, sin is literally in our DNA?

This is why starting over with Noah's family didn't work. While Noah was truly a righteous man and really tried hard to do what was right, even he was a carrier of the virus. It is also why, no matter how hard you and I try to be good, we cannot succeed on our own. Sooner or later, sin wins out over our good intentions, separating us from God.

The promised Messiah who would provide each of us a way back to God to live with him forever in his perfect community had to be free of this virus. Mary's child could not be given to her by any man—even a godly man like Joseph. The baby in Mary's womb had been placed there by the very Spirit of God. What appeared to be scandalous in the Lower Story was in essence the great "good news" of the Upper Story.

In what has to be the first recorded sonogram, the angel tells Joseph "it's a boy" and his name is Jesus—a form of the name Joshua, which means "the LORD saves." And then, just to make sure Joseph really gets what is going on, the angel connects the dots for him: "He will save his people from their sins."[4]

The Good News was about to arrive. God's people had been waiting for more than two thousand years—ever since God promised Abraham that he would be the father of a great nation. The Bible tells us, "All this took place to fulfill what the Lord had said through the prophet: 'The virgin will conceive and give birth to a son, and they will call him Immanuel' (which means 'God with us')."[5] What was happening to Mary was foretold by the prophet Isaiah seven hundred years earlier. Everything in the life and history of Israel had been pointing to Jesus' arrival—everything!

The baby growing inside of Mary's womb was God himself. God's own Son was leaving the Upper Story to come down to not only be *with* us but also be *one* of us. To walk with us, talk with us, live with us. We refer to this as the *incarnation*, which literally means "in the flesh." Through Jesus, God came down and took up flesh to be among us. To be our representative—the ultimate avatar. He came to do for us what we could not do for ourselves: take away our sin that keeps us from God.

And what about Mary? Historians tell us she was just a teenager (it was common for young women at that time to be married in their teens). She loved Joseph and kept herself pure for him, and then she suddenly discovered she was pregnant. Confused and frightened, she must have wondered how this could have happened. And she knew what a scandal it was and that Joseph would probably leave her. What would she do as a single teenage mom?

In her Lower Story, her life is falling apart. But as we have learned through every story up to this point, God's Upper Story is all about turning our chaos and confusion—even our mistakes—into something beautiful. This is no unplanned pregnancy, but the miraculous unfolding of God's ultimate plan to provide a way for anyone to live in his perfect community forever.

Joseph—ever the stand-up guy—awakens from his dream and goes straight to Mary to reassure her that everything is going to be all right. That he isn't angry with her and knows she has not slept with anyone else. He tells her all about the dream and that she will soon give birth to the Son of God. He reaffirms his desire to be her husband, and soon after, they are married.

You know the rest of the story. Nearly everyone does. Even though businesses try to avoid the word *Christmas* as they welcome us into their stores with "Happy Holidays." Even though municipalities do their best to replace manger scenes with Frosty, Santa, and Rudolph. Just about everyone can tell you what happened next in the Lower Story.

Mary and Joseph travel to Bethlehem, the town of their ancestors, so they can be counted in the census that Caesar Augustus, the emperor of Rome, has ordered.[6] As they arrive in Bethlehem, Mary goes into labor. Mention the phrase "no room in the inn," and just about anyone can tell you how Joseph tried to find a nice place for Mary to have her baby, but all the "inns" were full—all they could find was a cave-like area behind one of the inns. Apparently, the best we could do for the arrival of God to our world was the barnyard suite at the Manger Motel. In the Lower Story, this is not what we expected. In fact, it is just plain wrong.

I'm not the only one who thinks this way. An elementary school was preparing to put on a great Christmas pageant for parents. All the important parts were given to the brightest students. The smartest girl was chosen to be Mary; the smartest boy played Joseph. The next smartest group played the three kings, the angels, and the shepherds.

There was only one part no one wanted: the innkeeper. Who wanted to be the bad guy who turned Mary and Joseph away? They gave the part to a boy who was a little slower than the others but who had a big heart.

As the day for the big pageant approached, the boy playing the innkeeper began to worry. He couldn't imagine telling Mary and Joseph there was no room in the inn. What was he going to do?

Finally, it was curtain time. Parents, relatives, and friends packed the auditorium. They proudly watched the story unfold as their children skillfully carried out their important roles. Meanwhile, the innkeeper grew more and more anxious. The pressure mounted as Mary and Joseph approached. He didn't know what to do, but somehow he caught a brief glimpse of the Upper Story.

When Mary and Joseph knocked, the scruffy little innkeeper threw open the door and shouted with a big smile, "Come on in. I've been expecting you." With that, the crowd cheered and clapped and the play came to an end.

Maybe this is more in line with what God had in mind. To fulfill the prophecy, Jesus has to be born in Bethlehem in humble circumstances. Caesar Augustus thinks he himself is in charge of the world, but he isn't. God knew what he was doing, even using something as benign as a census to bring about his Upper Story plan.

For the children of Israel, the wait is over. In a stable surrounded by farm animals, Jesus is born. The heavens rejoice as angels announce his birth. Shepherds race to the humble manger to worship the newborn King. In the City of David. A Savior. The Messiah. The Lord.

Exactly according to plan. Not to save face for Mary and Joseph, but to save a nation.

To save you and me.

Chapter

23

JESUS' MINISTRY BEGINS

*As soon as Jesus was baptized, he went up out of the
water. At that moment heaven was opened, and he saw
the Spirit of God descending like a dove and alighting
on him. And a voice from heaven said, "This is my
Son, whom I love; with him I am well pleased."*

MATTHEW 3:16–17

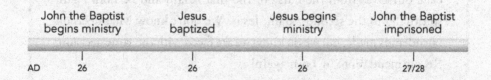

John the Baptist begins ministry	Jesus baptized	Jesus begins ministry	John the Baptist imprisoned
AD 26	26	26	27/28

WHAT'S HAPPENING IN THE UPPER STORY

The Old Testament ends with Malachi's prophecy that the next prophet would introduce the long-awaited Messiah from Judah. But no one anticipated another four hundred years would go by until John the Baptist would walk out of the wilderness with this important announcement: "Look, the Lamb of God, who takes away the sin of the world!"[1] John is making the connection that the Passover lamb that saved the firstborn sons of Israel from the angel of death in the book of Exodus was really a symbol foreshadowing Jesus. For the Jews, this connection and the profound claim to Jesus' identity are undeniable. But just as God promised Abraham, the blessing has been expanded to include all nations, starting with the Samaritans. The Samaritan woman's decision to believe in Jesus is one of the earliest fulfillments of this ancient promise.[2] God always keeps his promise—even today. Salvation is available to "whoever believes in him."[3]

ALIGNING OUR STORY TO GOD'S STORY

Jesus told Nicodemus that in order to remove the curse of Adam and inherit eternal life with God, he needed to be "born again."[4] What does this mean? All humanity carries Adam's sin virus that keeps us separated from God. The only solution is for us to disassociate ourselves from the curse of the first Adam and be born again spiritually to the second Adam, Jesus. We don't know what decision Nicodemus made, but we do know we are faced with the same decision. Recommendation: be born again!

*I*f you've ever spent time walking around the downtown areas of big cities, you've probably seen them—street preachers. Loud, determined, over-zealous, they definitely refuse to hide their light under a bushel. They are hard-core messengers of the gospel who sometimes carry signs that read "Repent!" or "Prepare to meet thy God." As a preacher, I'm serious about helping people experience God's forgiveness, but these guys are on message 24/7 in front of the toughest crowds possible.

I suspect this is what a lot of people thought about John the Baptist. Like today's street preachers, John was a bit "out there"—a scruffy, eccentric hippie dude who lived off the land by eating bugs and honey and wearing wild clothes made out of camel's hair. And yes, he slogged through the wilderness with this message for anyone who would listen: "Repent!"

In the Lower Story, he appears as just another strange guy who thought he spoke for God, and he might have been easy to ignore except for the fact that his message had a familiar ring to it. When the Jewish leaders asked him who he was, he replied, "I am the voice of one calling in the wilderness, 'Make straight the way for the Lord.'"[5] This is exactly what the prophets Isaiah and Malachi said he would say, and any devout Jew would know that something big was going on here. Something *really* big.

Maybe a little weird by Lower Story standards, but in the Upper Story, John has a divine purpose. He is about to introduce us to God's solution for restoring us into a relationship with him—a way for us to live in his perfect community forever—though he approaches his assignment a bit reluctantly. It is one thing to be a street preacher, but to actually baptize the Messiah? As he tells Jesus, "I need to be baptized by you."[6] Not the other way around.

But Jesus insists. So John, the shaggy guy in camel's hair with a wild look in his eyes, baptizes Jesus, the long-promised Messiah. And at that moment, heaven opens up and the Spirit of God descends on him like a dove. Then a voice from heaven declares, "This is my Son, whom I love; with him I am well pleased."[7] This is one of the few times in the entire Story that Father, Son, and

Holy Spirit—the Trinity—appears at the same time. John the Baptist, eccentric as he is, finds himself in the middle of a historic event. The first to reveal the identity of Jesus is God himself.

After I trained in seminary to be a minister, I needed to be ordained—consecrated or set apart by a formal religious body for service to God. It's not only a spiritual requirement for ministry but a legal one as well. For me, and for any minister, this solemn event marks the official beginning of a life devoted solely to serving others on behalf of God. John's baptism of Jesus has this effect, as it marks the beginning of Jesus' ministry.

And though he only ministers for about three years, what a ministry he has!

Right after the baptism, the Spirit of God leads Jesus into the wilderness, where for forty days and nights he goes without food. We don't talk much about fasting, but it is a discipline that forces us to depend totally on God. Jesus is hungry and vulnerable to the temptations of Satan, but with each temptation Jesus responds by quoting Scripture.

If you've ever wondered why memorizing Scripture is vitally important, the experience of Jesus in the wilderness makes a pretty good case. Knowing God's word protects us from the temptations we face every day. But Jesus has an added advantage in the battle against evil. He is sinless. Without blemish. Though he came to live with us as a human being, he is also God, incapable of sinning.

Early in his ministry, Jesus once again crosses paths with John the Baptist, who shouts when he sees him, "Look, the Lamb of God, who takes away the sin of the world!"[8] No Jewish person could have missed the significance of that statement. In the Old Testament, only the blood of a young, unblemished, innocent lamb could be used as a sacrifice to atone for sin.

In those days, a man would bring the lamb to the priest, who placed his hand on the head of the innocent animal, officially transferring all the man's sin and guilt to the lamb. The priest would then slice the throat of the lamb, catching its blood in a bowl that was placed on the altar for the forgiveness of sins. John was announcing to the world that Jesus is the ultimate lamb—the Lamb of God—the final sacrifice for our sins.

Most of us know that Jesus ultimately sacrificed his life on our behalf, but those who heard John's outrageous claim had no idea what would happen in three years. All they have is the word of a rather unconventional preacher. For all they know, he is just another nutcase, and who would have blamed them for thinking this? But over the next few years, Jesus' ministry would validate John's claims.

For example, soon after his baptism, Jesus attends a wedding in the town of Cana. His mother, Mary, is there as well. About halfway through the festivities, the hosts run out of wine. Mary, obviously aware of her son's true identity, begs him to do something to spare the hosts the disgrace of not having enough wine for their guests. Jesus asks the servants of the house to fill six large stone jars with water. Then he tells them to draw some for the master of the house to drink.[9]

Not only is the water transformed into wine; it is better than any wine previously served that day. The guests think the bridegroom has cleverly saved the best for last. But the servants and others who know what happened realize that this man whom John called the Messiah is indeed special.

In fact, it isn't long before others begin seeing the way Jesus reaches out to others. After he selects twelve men as his disciples, he begins teaching and healing people wherever he goes. Israel is not a large nation, and soon word of his powers spreads quickly throughout the region. Some conclude he is the Messiah; others—usually the religious leaders—are troubled by his claims.

At one point, while Jesus is in Jerusalem, he receives an unexpected visit in the middle of the night from a Pharisee named Nicodemus. Pharisees were Jewish leaders who not only interpreted the religious laws but also were quick to judge anyone who violated those laws. Today we describe people like this as "legalistic"—more concerned about rules than a relationship with God. So it is not surprising that most Pharisees were deeply troubled by Jesus and his ministry because he didn't fit into their rule books. But Nicodemus is particularly drawn to him, recognizing that anyone who performs these kinds of miracles must come from God.

During their conversation, Jesus reveals God's plan for restoring us into a relationship with him when he tells Nicodemus that in order to be a part of the divine community, we must be "born again." He then offers one of the clearest declarations of who he is and why he came down to be with us: "For God so loved the world that he gave his one and only Son, that whoever believes in him shall not perish but have eternal life."[10]

This statement—likely the most memorized verse in the Bible—describes in the simplest terms the intersection between our Lower Story and God's Upper Story. We live "down here," in all the ordinary messiness of life that is limited by what we can see and experience firsthand, including what appears to be the final stop—death. But Jesus, who was "up there," came down to defeat death for us so that we can live eternally with him. We don't have to slaughter and sacrifice animals—that was a temporary fix. We don't have to try harder to be good, because that will never work due to our inherent sinfulness. All we have to do is believe.

For a Pharisee, this is a tough message to swallow. They—as well as a lot of us—have been led to believe it's all about following the rules. This is a false picture of God that has caused many people—perhaps even you—to stay as far away from God as possible. They have this image of a stern old guy waving a long list of impossible rules, keeping track of all the times they have broken them so he can bust their chops. But Jesus says, "Just believe."

We don't know how Nicodemus responded to Jesus' conversation at that time, but we do know that after Jesus died, Nicodemus helped a believer in Jesus, a man named Joseph of Arimathea, bury Jesus. My theory? I believe Nicodemus threw away his rule book and followed Jesus.

He isn't the only one to be transformed by Jesus' simple message.

On his way back to Galilee, Jesus decides to go through Samaria. Most Jews looked down on the people who lived there and went out of their way to avoid them. Not Jesus. Around noon, he comes to a well and sits down to rest when he notices a woman coming to draw water. When he asks her if she would draw some for him to drink, she is surprised and a little fearful. She knows he is a Jew, and she is a Samaritan. According to Jewish sources, "the Samaritans are descendants of the colonists whom the Assyrians planted in the northern kingdom and who intermarried with the Israelite population that the Assyrians had left in the land" after they overtook them in 722 BC.[11]

In other words, the Samaritan woman knows her place. But Jesus, whom she has never met before, engages her in conversation, even to the point of telling her he knows she's had five husbands and is now living with a man she is not married to. He explains what it means to worship God in spirit and in truth, but she tries to brush him off: "'I know that Messiah' (called Christ) 'is coming. When he comes, he will explain everything to us.'"[12]

Imagine her surprise when Jesus responds, "I, the one speaking to you—I am he."[13] She runs back into her town and reports what has just happened to her, and many Samaritans that day become followers of Jesus, fulfilling more prophecy. This good news, as promised first to Abraham, is not just for Israel. God wants to give everyone a chance to come back to him.

Wherever Jesus went, crowds came out to see him and he healed people with a variety of infirmities—blindness, disfigurement, disease. He even brought back to life a man who had died. Every time he performed a miracle, it further validated that he was who he said he was: the promised Messiah.

But it also fueled the hatred of those who wanted to kill him. On one occasion, Jesus heals a man with leprosy and then tells the man his sins are forgiven. The legalistic religious leaders overhear him and are outraged: "He's blaspheming! Who can forgive sins but God alone?"[14] They just didn't get it. He *was* God, but they refused to accept this truth and continued their efforts to get rid of him.

We began this chapter with John, and it is fitting that we end with him. Never one to back down from the authorities, he finally lands in jail because of his preaching. Knowing he is about to be executed for his bold proclamation that Jesus is the Messiah, he sends word to Jesus, asking this question: "Are you the one who is to come, or should we expect someone else?"[15] A little understandable self-doubt, perhaps, but he has to be sure. He needs to be certain he has the right guy.

Jesus sends back the reassuring answer that he is indeed who he says he is. This is all John needs to hear. It is really all any of us needs to hear. A short time later, John is beheaded, but he dies knowing that his unconventional life as a "street preacher" was not in vain.

The Lower Story is all about doing. We go to work. We come home. We try to be good moms and dads. We set goals and make resolutions. We try to do all the right things, hoping our good efforts will be rewarded. The Upper

Story is all about believing. Believing that Jesus is who he says he is. That he is the only solution to our biggest problem—separation from God.

Say what you want about street preachers. They may be unconventional. Their methods may take you out of your comfort zone. But like John the Baptist, they know they serve the One who takes away the sin of the world.

There's nothing crazy about that!

Chapter 24

NO ORDINARY MAN

"I am the vine; you are the branches. If you remain in me and I in you, you will bear much fruit; apart from me you can do nothing."

JOHN 15:5

Jesus begins ministry	Jesus gives Sermon on the Mount	Jesus sends disciples	John the Baptist dies	Jesus feeds 5,000 people	Jesus as the bread of life
AD 26	28	28	28/29	29	29

WHAT'S HAPPENING IN THE UPPER STORY

The ministry of Jesus is in full motion. His every move is inspired by his Father to advance the Upper Story, giving all people the opportunity to reverse the decision of the first Adam and to provide the way back into the garden. The kingdom of God is the primary focus of Jesus' ministry. His teachings give people a vision for the life God intended for us all to live from the very beginning. The healing ministry of Jesus not only shows mercy to the recipients but also authenticates the identity of Jesus. He is no ordinary man; he is the Savior of the world!

ALIGNING OUR STORY TO GOD'S STORY

Jesus cast a vision for the eternal kingdom to come where we will live in perfect harmony with God and other believers. His teachings encourage us not to settle for a Lower Story kingdom that doesn't last. Some pursue this temporal paradise and ignore God's offer altogether. They do so at their own peril. Don't be discouraged by your Lower Story circumstances. Lift up your head and rise above it. If you are a believer, this is not how your story ends.

*H*ave you ever met someone and known almost immediately that he or she was somebody special?

I'm talking about someone you meet for the first time who has an extraordinary personality—a commanding presence that draws you to them magnetically.

This is the effect Jesus had on people when he entered their towns or homes. It became clear early in his ministry that, even though he was the only child of a humble carpenter from Nazareth, he was special. And one of the qualities that stood out and attracted attention was the way he taught people about God.

For the most part, the faithful Jewish people were accustomed to going to the temple and listening to their rabbis read from the Book of the Law. Imagine going to church every Sunday and having your pastor open his Bible to the Old Testament book of Leviticus and begin reading the detailed instructions on what you can eat and what you can wear and what kind of haircut you can get.

But when Jesus taught, he told stories, or parables—stories that communicated truth in ways that the reading of the law could never match. For example, Jesus wanted his followers to understand that to be part of God's nation, they had to live differently than those who belonged only to an earthly nation—in this case, one governed by Caesar. Since he was teaching people who lived in an "agri-culture," he told a story about farmers:

"Listen! A farmer went out to sow his seed. As he was scattering the seed, some fell along the path, and the birds came and ate it up. Some fell on rocky places, where it did not have much soil. It sprang up quickly, because the soil was shallow. But when the sun came up, the plants were scorched, and they withered because they had no root. Other seed fell among thorns, which grew up and choked the plants, so that they did not bear grain. Still other seed fell on good soil. It came up, grew and produced a crop, some multiplying thirty, some sixty, some a hundred times. "

Then Jesus said, "Whoever has ears to hear, let them hear."[1]

If you are not a farmer, this little parable may seem confusing or cryptic. What does *this* have to do with how I live my life? Thanks to Kroger, I don't do gardens—at least not a big enough garden to feed my family. But to the rural people of Israel, this parable connected. They knew full well the challenge of growing their wheat and barley in the dusty, rocky countryside. And so if you visit the area today, you can look across the fields and see lush plots of the best fruits and vegetables growing in the valleys. Good soil makes all the difference.

Jesus is telling his hearers that if they want to grow in their faith—if they want to be nourished as members of God's nation—the seed of God's word needs to fall on a tilled and soft heart so it can grow deep and produce fruit on the branches of our lives externally.

But because Jesus shared this truth as a story that met people where they lived, he got their attention. They knew this was no ordinary teacher.

But Jesus also used a more direct style. In his only recorded sermon in the Bible—the Sermon on the Mount—Jesus literally turned the world upside down for his "congregation."

Imagine the scene. Jesus has just performed a miracle of healing. Word of this miracle has spread quickly, and crowds of people gather to see this incredible teacher and perhaps learn from him. Jesus stands up to speak, and a hush falls over the throng of people sitting on the side of a large hill that formed a natural amphitheater near the Sea of Galilee:

Blessed are the poor in spirit . . .

Blessed are those who mourn . . .

Blessed are the meek . . .

Blessed are those who hunger and thirst for righteousness . . .

Blessed are the merciful . . .

Blessed are the pure in heart . . .

Blessed are the peacemakers . . .

Blessed are those who are persecuted because of righteousness . . .[2]

The word *blessed* can be loosely translated as "happy," and in the Lower Story, being poor or meek is never associated with being happy or blessed. No one wants to mourn or be persecuted, and purity is for prudes.

But Jesus is trying to demonstrate what life is like in the Upper Story. He wants to give them, and us, a vision of how God's kingdom is different—how character is more important than possessions and circumstances. The kingdom of God he describes will be a new garden—a restored version of the garden we learned about in the beginning of this Story—where God will once again come down and dwell with all who believe in him.

These "blessings," which we call the Beatitudes, were just the introduction, but it was enough for everyone to realize there was something extraordinary about this man Jesus. He challenged contemporary religious practices of the day: "When you pray, do not be like the hypocrites, for they love to pray standing in the synagogues and on the street corners to be seen by others." He attacked materialism: "Do not store up for yourselves treasures on earth . . . But store up for yourselves treasures in heaven." He warned against the seductive power of money: "You cannot serve both God and money." He even coached them about anxiety: "Can any one of you by worrying add a single hour to your life? . . . Do not worry about tomorrow, for tomorrow will worry about itself. Each day has enough trouble of its own."[3]

This entire sermon is Upper Story wisdom to help them live better in their Lower Story lives. Not just for their sakes, but for the sake of the kingdom of God to which they belonged. Jesus wants his followers to live in such a way that others are drawn to them, just as they were drawn to him: "Let your light shine before others, that they may see your good deeds and glorify your Father in heaven."[4]

Naturally, someone with such an unconventional message who also had the ability to perform miracles attracted a lot of attention. Sometimes the crowds pressed in so heavily that it was difficult for Jesus to move. On one such occasion, a woman who had struggled with a chronic medical condition thought if she could just brush against him in the crowd, she would be healed. She hopes to sneak away unnoticed, but as soon as she touches him, much to her dismay, Jesus turns and asks, "Who touched my clothes?" His followers try to convince him that in such a large crowd, a lot of people are touching him, but he persists until the woman finally confesses what she has done. Jesus responds compassionately: "Your faith has healed you."[5]

What do you do with someone like this? Someone who doesn't fit your image of a religious leader? Sooner or later, all those who were initially drawn to Jesus had to make a choice. Either he is the promised Messiah, or he is not. Once, after feeding a crowd of five thousand people with only five loaves of bread and two fish, some of the people followed him to a neighboring town to learn more about this unusual teacher. They wanted to know what they could do to serve God, and Jesus told them, "Believe in the one he has sent."[6] In other words, "Go all in and believe that I am the Messiah." He then told them that he alone was the source of fulfillment, and he added something that caught them off guard:

> "Unless you eat the flesh of the Son of Man and drink his blood, you have no life in you. Whoever eats my flesh and drinks my blood has eternal life . . . Whoever eats my flesh and drinks my blood remains in me, and I in them . . . Your ancestors ate manna and died, but whoever feeds on this bread will live forever."[7]

If there was any question about Jesus being different, this pretty much settled it. Jesus put it all out there, calling his followers to so identify with him that it was as if they had partaken of his body. To literally become one with him. It was his way of saying something not everyone wanted to hear back then, and many still do not want to hear it today: "I am the only way."

The Bible tells us that some of his followers turned away from him after hearing this challenge. He was asking too much of them. They wanted Jesus *and* their own way. They wanted ordinary bread, not the Bread of Life. Sound familiar? How many times did we learn that God's followers wanted to worship God *and* the other gods of the surrounding nations? How many times do *we* want God alongside the idols of wealth, status, power, and fame?

Jesus was no ordinary teacher. He was the kind of person everyone noticed when he walked into a room. His ministry was validated by remarkable teaching and miraculous interventions. But he demands our singular devotion. At some point, after observing all that he did, we have to make our own choice. We have to decide if he is the one we really want to follow.

One time, the disciples of Jesus were spending the night on a boat in the middle of the lake when a storm woke them up. They couldn't make their way back to shore because of the high waves, and shortly before the sun came up, they saw Jesus walking toward them on the water. Peter wasn't so sure it was Jesus, so he shouted out, "Lord, if it's you . . . tell me to come to you on the water."[8] Jesus replied, "Come," and Peter got out of the boat and began walking—until he looked down at the water and began sinking.

Jesus reached out to save him and then chided him for doubting.

As Jesus and Peter climbed into the boat, Jesus' disciples worshiped him and made this profound declaration: "Truly you are the Son of God."[9]

It is not enough to think of Jesus as just a great man. In the Lower Story, we may meet many great men and women—celebrities, politicians, actors, professional athletes. If we want to rise above the day-to-day circumstances of our lives, however, we must be prepared to meet someone who redefines the word *extraordinary*. We have to make the same commitment Jesus asks of all his followers.

Believe in the one the Father has sent.

Chapter

25

JESUS,
THE SON OF GOD

*"I am the way and the truth and the life. No one
comes to the Father except through me. If you really
know me, you will know my Father as well. From
now on, you do know him and have seen him."*

JOHN 14:6–7

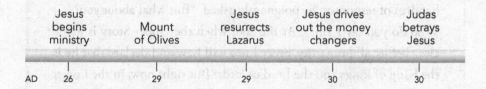

Jesus begins ministry	Mount of Olives	Jesus resurrects Lazarus	Jesus drives out the money changers	Judas betrays Jesus
AD 26	29	29	30	30

WHAT'S HAPPENING IN THE UPPER STORY

The Messiah has come! But he's not recognized by everyone. In the Lower Story, he looked like a poor man from Galilee to some. To others, because of his teachings, he appeared to be a prophet. Those closer to him rightfully identified him as "the Anointed One," but thought he was going to reestablish the throne of David on this earth—an easy mistake to make if you weren't paying careful attention. Those most threatened by Jesus labeled him as a blasphemer, an imposter. Jesus even said, "Before Abraham was born, I am!"[1] From the Lower Story, he is the offspring of Abraham, but from the Upper Story, he is the creator of Abraham. He is God. He made his true identity known by riding into Jerusalem on a donkey at just the right time. This fulfilled the prophecy of Zechariah regarding the coming Messiah. The people recognized it and shouted, "Blessed is the coming kingdom of our father David!"[2] They didn't realize what kind of king he came to be—a suffering king—and what kind of kingdom he came to rule—an eternal kingdom.

ALIGNING OUR STORY TO GOD'S STORY

Jesus asked the disciples, "Who do people say I am?" After they gave a handful of responses, he poignantly asked, "But what about you? . . . Who do you say I am?"[3] At the end, when the Upper Story is made clear before all humanity, every knee will bow and declare that he is the King of kings and the Lord of lords. But right now, in the Lower Story, we all must answer this question. Your eternal life depends on your declaration that Jesus is the Son of God, who came to take away the sins of the world![4] He is the way, the truth, and the life![5]

When I was a young boy, we had a black-and-white television set. A few of my friends had color TV sets (their families must have had more money—something I didn't realize at the time). It wasn't until much later in life that I knew the uniforms worn by the Boston Celtics were green. I always thought they were, well, gray.

Game shows were all the rage back then—not during the day but during prime time—and one of my favorites was *What's My Line?* Contestants with unusual occupations or extraordinary accomplishments were interviewed by celebrity panelists. Only questions that could be answered with a yes or no were allowed. After a few minutes of questioning, the panelists tried to guess the contestant's occupation:

"Are you a professional athlete?"

"Yes."

"Do you play football?"

"No."

"Do you play baseball?"

"Yes."

"Are you a pitcher?"

"Yes."

"Did you win thirty-one games last season?"

"Yes."

"Are you Denny McLain?"

"Yes!" (Cue audience applause, cheers, music, flashing lights in shades of gray.)

I guess you had to be there (and if you don't know who Denny McLain is, don't tell me—I already feel old enough!). We thought the show was pretty cool, though.

As we continue to follow Jesus during his brief time on earth, we enter a part of his story that could be titled *What's My Line?* He is the unknown guest with the unusual occupation, and the panelists are his disciples, the religious leaders, and ordinary people from Galilee to Jerusalem. Of course, it's more than a game. The entire Story is all about returning to God, and we can only do this if we know the true identity of this man named Jesus.

The people who met Jesus knew he was no ordinary man. But the question on everyone's mind was this: "Who is he really?" And it is one of the most important questions any of us can ask. It is one thing to be mesmerized by all of Jesus' teachings, but his primary occupation is not that of a teacher. People were impressed by all of the miraculous healings he performed, but his primary occupation is not that of a physician or even a miracle worker. You can even be inspired by how he lived his life and loved people, but his primary occupation is not that of an all-around good guy. All of these things are important and add to the evidence of his true occupation. But he is more than even the sum of all these wonderful attributes.

Probably the people closest to Jesus were his hand-chosen followers, the disciples. These twelve men traveled with him wherever he went, and they came from all walks of life. They were his entourage, if you will, and if anyone was going to know who Jesus really was, it would have to be them. So when Jesus asks his disciples if they know who he really is, it's not surprising that Peter quickly answers, "You are the Messiah."[6]

Right answer. Wrong set of expectations about what this means.

Jesus warns Peter and his buddies to keep this a secret for now and then goes on to explain that the Messiah will have to "suffer many things and be rejected by the elders, the chief priests and the teachers of the law, and that he must be killed and after three days rise again."[7]

Peter can't believe his ears. He pictured the Messiah as the great "anointed one" who had come to earth to rescue the faithful. According to the Bible, Peter rebukes Jesus for saying all these things about being rejected and killed. When you hear the word *rebuke*, you think of a good scolding, but I'm guessing he was so incredulous that he said something like, "No way! Quit talking that nonsense. You are the Messiah!"

Jesus had his work cut out for him in helping people redefine their expectations about him as Savior. At first, he really gets in Peter's face, chastising him for thinking of the Messiah only from his Lower Story perspective, but then he uses this incident as an opportunity to teach Peter and the crowd that had gathered the true cost of discipleship from the Upper Story point of view:

"Whoever wants to be my disciple must deny themselves and take up their cross and follow me. For whoever wants to save their life will lose it, but whoever loses their life for me and for the gospel will save it. What good is it for someone to gain the whole world, yet forfeit their soul?"[8]

In helping his followers learn exactly who he is, Jesus is also explaining what it takes to be one of his followers. It is the same Upper Story message we have seen from the very beginning of the story: either you're "all in," or you're out. The disciples not only know who Jesus is, but now they know who *they* have to be if they want to be his followers.

In another scene from this story, religious leaders and ordinary citizens are also wrestling with the important question of who Jesus is. At the time, Jesus happens to be in Jerusalem during a popular religious holiday called the Festival of Tabernacles.

Remember the Festival of Tabernacles in our story of Judah returning home from captivity in Babylon? After Ezra read the entire Book of the Law to them, they recognized that there were practices that they were not observing, and one was the Festival of Tabernacles—an observance commemorating the time when they lived in "booths" or temporary tents in the wilderness and God provided for them in miraculous ways. So during this weeklong festival, Jewish people built tents on their property and lived in them for the week. They also grabbed palm branches and waved them, much like Americans wave sparklers on the Fourth of July.

When Jesus was in Jerusalem during the Festival of Tabernacles, people began to play *What's My Line?* with him. Some said, "He's a good man." Others said, "No, he deceives people." About halfway through the festival, Jesus began to teach, creating even more speculation: "How did this man get such learning without having been taught?"[9] Great question, one that led to conclusions such as these: "Surely this man is the Prophet." Others said, "He is the Messiah."[10]

Still others asked, "How can the Messiah come from Galilee? Does not

Scripture say that the Messiah will come from David's descendants and from Bethlehem, the town where David lived?"[11] Whoever asked this question wasn't paying attention. If he'd had access to Google, he could have done a quick search and learned that Jesus was indeed from the lineage of David and was born in Bethlehem. One thing we have learned for sure: God always pays attention to the details.

Jesus then starts dropping clues about his identity. He declares, "I am the light of the world."[12] The Jewish people would know that only God himself is the source of light, so this is a major hint. Later Jesus says, "You are from below; I am from above. You are of this world; I am not of this world,"[13] which we may translate, "I am from the Upper Story; you are from the Lower Story." He was telling his hearers that he resided in heaven, which they knew was where God resided.

Someone asked sarcastically, "Are you greater than our father Abraham?" They were getting a little tired of Jesus' claims and tried to put him in his place. Knowing how the Jewish people revered Abraham and knew their history, Jesus made a statement that may seem curious to us but was heavy with meaning for them: "Very truly I tell you . . . before Abraham was born, I am!"[14]

Remember back in the Old Testament when God commissioned Moses to go to Pharaoh and take the Israelites out of Egypt? Moses wonders what he should say to the Israelites who question his calling. God replies, "This is what you are to say to the Israelites: 'I AM has sent me to you.'"[15] These Jewish skeptics knew exactly what he was saying, and it angered them that he considered himself to be God. Even though many people had chosen to follow him because of his teachings, this group began to throw stones at him, but he quickly escaped.

In the Lower Story, we are confronted by a man—a historical figure. The fact that Jesus lived on earth and left behind many great teachings cannot be disputed. But his claim to be the Son of God requires those who are confronted by him to make a choice. Either he is who he says he is, or he is a liar, or, as C. S. Lewis famously explained, he is a lunatic. Essentially, these are our three options: Lord, liar, or lunatic. In the Upper Story, the stage is being set for a dramatic event that will have eternal implications. A divine mission put in place back in the garden is about to be completed.

Fast-forward to the Passover festival, a grand celebration commemorating the day that the angel of the Lord passed over the homes whose doorposts had been sprinkled with the blood of a lamb, sparing the firstborn boys in those homes. Before Jesus went to Jerusalem for this celebration, he instructed his disciples to bring him a donkey. They thought it was a curious request, but they ran off and soon returned with the donkey. Evidently, they were unfamiliar with the words of the prophet Zechariah of the Old Testament; otherwise they would have caught this clue that Jesus was giving them:

> "Rejoice greatly, Daughter Zion!
> Shout, Daughter Jerusalem!
> See, your king comes to you,
> righteous and victorious,
> lowly and riding on a donkey,
> on a colt, the foal of a donkey."[16]

The common people of Jerusalem must have known, however, for when Jesus rides into the city on that donkey, they greet him as if he is, well, the Messiah! They scatter palm branches on the ground to make a path for his entry. They also wave palms as he passes in front of them. According to Jewish culture, the palm branch is a symbol of victory, the equivalent of a ticker-tape parade. As the man who was born in a humble stable rides into Jerusalem on a small donkey, the crowds lining the street shout exactly as the prophet Zechariah said they would:

> "Hosanna!
> Blessed is he who comes in the name of the Lord!
> Blessed is the coming kingdom of our father David!
> Hosanna in the highest heaven!"[17]

God's people had been told that the Messiah—the Anointed One—would come. That a new king from the lineage of David would reign over them. This parade through their city must have felt like Inauguration Day. Finally they would have their king who would restore Israel to greatness—maybe even lead them to attack and conquer Rome. This was the day they had waited for for so long, the day when their oppression would end and they would finally be free.

What they couldn't have known was that God had something even greater in mind. Yes, they would soon have a way to overcome any oppression. Yes, once God's divine mission was completed, they would experience freedom as no one had ever known. If they could just hold on a little while longer and keep believing in this King, even when he didn't seem very regal.

It is one thing to believe that Jesus is the Messiah when everyone is cheering him on as he rides into town. But what will happen when things don't go the way they hope they will go? The Jewish people knew what it was to abandon God when he didn't fit their idea of who God was. Which is why it is so important that they know who Jesus is.

In the Lower Story, Jesus is a remarkable man in history whose teachings continue to this day to provide a foundation for moral and ethical behavior. He was a good man who had a special place in his heart for the poor and oppressed. He is easy to like. But if we are to find our place in the Upper Story, he has to be more than just a good guy. Everything he did during his brief stay on earth was to convince mankind that he was the only solution to our separation from God. That he was God himself, living among us and willing to die for us.

It was more than just his line.

It's who he *is*.

Chapter 26

THE HOUR
OF DARKNESS

*Then one of the Twelve—the one called Judas Iscariot—
went to the chief priests and asked, "What are you
willing to give me if I deliver him over to you?" So they
counted out for him thirty pieces of silver. From then on
Judas watched for an opportunity to hand him over.*

MATTHEW 26:14–16

The Lord's Supper	Jesus washes disciples' feet	Jesus comforts disciples	Jesus arrested	Peter denies Jesus	Jesus crucified

AD 30

WHAT'S HAPPENING IN THE UPPER STORY

From the Lower Story, it appears Jesus is lost. One of his disciples rats him out for thirty pieces of silver. His most trusted disciple, who promised to never leave him, betrays him in his hour of need. The Jews demand that he be crucified instead of the guilty criminal named Barabbas. The Romans nail Jesus to a cross between two thieves. When Jesus yells, "It is finished," no doubt those standing by thought, *You're absolutely right. You* are *finished.* But this is not what Jesus means. *He* is not finished, but the Upper Story work he came to do is now complete. The plan that was set in motion back in the Garden of Eden is done; God's promise to Abraham and David is now fulfilled. All the prophecies from the Old Testament are fulfilled, and salvation is available to all nations. Jesus, the Son of God, has died for the sins of the world, once and for all.

ALIGNING OUR STORY TO GOD'S STORY

The Upper Story has been centered on providing the way for all people to come back into a relationship with him. We could not make this happen in and of ourselves because of our sin nature. God the Father has provided the only way for us. He sent his Son to do for us what we could not do for ourselves. The sinless Son of God, the second person of the Trinity, took on flesh and died on the cross. To align ourselves with God's story and find our way back into the garden, we must acknowledge our sin before Jesus and invite God to forgive us. Have you done that yet?

I'm not much into politics. I treasure the privilege of being able to vote, and like most people, I pay attention to candidates' positions on issues that are important to me. But I don't spend a lot of time studying the ins and outs of what goes on in Washington or in my state capital. Except on election night.

All the drama of waiting to see who wins captivates me. But what I find even more fascinating is the reaction from those who support the losing candidate. Such huge disappointment—often tears. In just a few hours, the mood goes from high hope and anticipation to absolute devastation. After all that work, expense, and excitement, it's over. It all comes down to that moment, which didn't turn out like they believed it would.

This must have been how the people in Jerusalem felt just a few days after they welcomed Jesus with palm branches and shouts of praise. They thought they had found their God-sent king who would establish his all-powerful kingdom on earth. But it didn't work out that way.

Every story in the life of Israel pointed to the coming of Jesus. The God of the Upper Story created the entire Lower Story so that he could come down and be with us. This is all he wanted. Within the vastness of the universe and beyond, he created a beautiful garden. After he created the first two people, Adam and Eve, he came down to begin life with them. A wonderful life of being with his people that was meant to extend all the way through history to you and to me. But because they chose *their* plan instead of God's, Adam and Eve were escorted from the garden. Sin—essentially selfishness and a disregard for God and others—became mankind's inheritance.

God never wanted to be separated from his people, so he promised to provide a way to get us back. To reunite with his people in a perfect community. He put a plan in place—a plan that has been unfolding throughout history. It appeared to the Jewish people who lined the streets of Jerusalem waving palm branches that this plan had culminated in a triumphal entry by Jesus. But what next? What is Jesus, the Son of God, going to do to provide a pathway back to God?

He is going to die. Not fight the Romans. Not set up a power base from which to rule as David or Solomon did. Not create the kind of kingdom they expected him to create.

It begins with the betrayal of Jesus by Judas, one of the twelve disciples. For a mere thirty pieces of silver, he tells the Jewish authorities where they can find Jesus. They arrest him and the disciples scatter, leaving Jesus on his own. Even Peter, his right-hand man, refuses to acknowledge that he even *knows* Jesus. Three times.

Jesus' captors take him to Caiaphas, the high priest. They stage a kind of "kangaroo court," complete with well-rehearsed "witnesses" making false charges against him. It is clear they want to find enough evidence to sentence him to death. But Jesus—the Lamb of God—refuses to defend himself against the trumped-up charges. Innocent and blameless, he allows them to frame him. It is part of the plan. It has to happen this way.

At one point, the high priest asks Jesus if he is the Messiah. Jesus responds by saying from now on he will be sitting at the right hand of God in heaven.[1] That's all it takes. The high priest charges him with blasphemy as the Jewish teachers and elders begin hitting him and spitting in his face.

It is the beginning of the end.

In order to kill him legally, they need the approval of Pilate, the governor appointed by Rome to oversee and work with the Jewish leaders. Pilate has no interest in this matter. He is only trying to save his own political skin and surmises that the best way to do this is to let the Jewish leaders decide. But just for good measure, he has Jesus flogged—carrying out a brutal Roman custom in which the accused is tied to a post and beaten with a whip that has sharp objects on the end. It was called a "cat-o'-nine-tails," and it literally rips the flesh to the bone.

Once the sadistic Roman soldiers get started, they quickly escalate their cruelty. One soldier makes a crown out of thorny vines—the crown of thorns—and jams it onto Jesus' head, piercing the skull. Another places a purple robe on him to mock his claim to royalty. They then bring him out to the Jewish leaders and ask what they want to do with Jesus as the crowd repeatedly screams out, "Crucify him!"

Crucifixion was a gruesome form of capital punishment reserved for the vilest criminals. It was designed to ensure a slow and painful death. The accused is nailed to a wooden cross, the cross is raised and set into a hole in the ground, and then everyone waits. Sometimes several minutes. Sometimes several hours. Sometimes several days. Relief comes only in the final breath.

To further mock Jesus, they crucify him between two common criminals. And while he is dying on the cross between these men, the Roman soldiers and Jewish leaders continue to hurl insults at him. When he begs for a drink of water, they put wine vinegar on a rag and offer it to him. As he hangs dying on that cross, the soldiers play a game of chance to see who will win the right to take his clothes.

After a few hours of tortuous pain and brutal suffering, Jesus dies. To his followers, it is now over. *Maybe he wasn't the Messiah after all*, they must have thought to themselves. *How can he possibly save us if he is dead and gone? Was this whole thing just a farce?*

To those who once lined the streets to welcome their Messiah, this must have seemed like a nightmare—a cruel act of a capricious God who may not even exist. They had heard the amazing message that all they needed to do was believe. In simple faith, despite the criticism coming from their religious leaders, they did just that. They believed.

And now he was gone. In the Lower Story, this was a disaster—a colossal failure. In the Upper Story, it is the beginning of a major victory that had been planned from the beginning of time. How do we know? Consider the clues.

All of this happened during Passover week. In ancient Israel, it was the blood of a lamb that saved them. Jesus was first introduced by John the Baptist as the Lamb of God. The shedding of his blood was necessary for our salvation, and God had carefully selected the exact time for this to happen. Jesus was even more precise when he said to his disciples in Gethsemane, "Look, the hour has come."[2]

Then there was Judas, who couldn't have known that his role in the Story had been planned by God and predicted by the prophet Jeremiah six hundred years earlier. Jesus even predicted his betrayal in the presence of his disciples when he said, "One of you is going to betray me," and then identified Judas.[3] This was no random act to get a little extra silver, but a critical step in God's plan to bring us back to him.

When Jesus was in Gethsemane the night before his death, he prayed to the

Father, "If it is possible, may this cup be taken from me. Yet not as I will, but as you will."[4] In the Lower Story, Jesus knew what tomorrow would bring. Pain and humiliation. A torturous physical death. But the bigger deal, the climax of God's Upper Story, would occur when he was hanging on the cross and all the sins of mankind were transferred to him.

Despite his longing for some other way than the head-on collision with the cross, Jesus aligned his life to the Upper Story. Later that evening when Judas and a band of soldiers came to arrest Jesus, Jesus said to Peter, "Put your sword away! Shall I not drink the cup the Father has given me?"[5] God had answered. There was no other way to provide the pathway for us to come back to God.

Everything about these final days had been planned and foretold. When Jesus refused to defend himself before Pilate, he was following the plan that was prophesied by Isaiah: "He was oppressed and afflicted, yet he did not open his mouth."[6] When a Roman soldier rammed a spear into Jesus' side as he hung on the cross, this man was following the plan that had been recorded several hundreds of years ago: "He was pierced for our transgressions."[7] And who would have thought that Peter, the stalwart and loyal disciple, would deny that he knew Jesus? Only Jesus, who predicted that it would happen. Nothing that unfolded took Jesus by surprise. It was all being orchestrated by the Author of the Upper Story.

When Jesus finally died, the religious leaders declared, "He is finished." But from the cross, Jesus cried out as he took his last breath, "*It* is finished."[8]

From the Lower Story, defeat; but from the Upper Story, victory. Jesus knew he had accomplished his mission on earth. As God's Lamb, he had been slain—the ultimate sacrifice to pay for everyone's sins, including yours and mine. Not just for the Jewish people, but for Gentiles too; slave and free, men and women, everyone.

I have a friend who raises sheep as a hobby. He got into it when his kids were young, but even now that they've left the nest, he still has sheep. He told me that raising sheep has helped him better understand why Jesus is referred to as the Lamb of God. Any other animal would fight back when cornered, but if a predator attacks a lamb, the meek little animal humbly awaits his demise. Jesus couldn't fight back because it wasn't part of the plan. He could not run away and escape his cruel punishment, because if he did, we would never be able to get back to God.

God had to do something about the problem of sin. It kept him away from the people he loved. He had to give his Son the characteristics of a lamb so that he would accept the punishment that should have gone to those who deserved it. The shedding of blood on ancient altars was only a temporary fix. The only way to demolish the barrier between God and mankind was to provide an acceptable sacrifice for all our sins, and Jesus became the blameless Lamb whose blood cleanses us and makes us brand-new. To illustrate the destroying of the barrier, the moment Jesus died, the thick curtain in the temple that separated us from the Most Holy Place, the dwelling place of God, was torn in two.[9]

The writer of Hebrews said it best:

> Therefore, brothers and sisters, since we have confidence to enter the Most Holy Place by the blood of Jesus, by a new and living way opened for us through the curtain, that is, his body, and since we have a great priest over the house of God, let us draw near to God with a sincere heart and with the full assurance that faith brings, having our hearts sprinkled to cleanse us from a guilty conscience and having our bodies washed with pure water.[10]

Of course, at the time, the loyal followers of Jesus had no idea what had just happened. The man they thought was the Messiah had just died. One of his followers, Joseph of Arimathea, received permission from Pilate to retrieve the body of Jesus and prepare it for burial. In one of those "rest of the story" moments, another person helped Joseph bury Jesus. He brought with him seventy-five pounds of myrrh and aloe—rich spices and lotion that would be applied to Jesus' body between layers of fine linen, according to Jewish custom.[11] And who was this man who lovingly prepared Jesus for the tomb?

His name was Nicodemus, the man who visited Jesus late at night to ask Jesus what it meant to be born again. I think he got it. But if he still had any doubts, they would soon be erased.

In three days.

Chapter

THE RESURRECTION

"You are looking for Jesus the Nazarene,
who was crucified. He has risen! He is not
here. See the place where they laid him."

MARK 16:6

| | Jesus | | Jesus appears to Mary Magdalene |
| Jesus buried | resurrected | | and the disciples |

AD   30

WHAT'S HAPPENING IN THE UPPER STORY

From the Lower Story perspective, death seems so final. From the Upper Story, it is only the beginning. Jesus came to represent us by taking on a perishable body. He was not born by human seed, but by the Holy Spirit; therefore he did not inherit the sin virus. During his thirty-three years among us, he resisted every temptation. Unlike Adam, Jesus was sinless. He was successful. "The wages of sin is death,"[1] but because Jesus wasn't a sinner, death could not keep him in the grave. His perishable body did die when he was crucified on the cross. Yet three days later, he rose from the dead with a new, imperishable body. He conquered death once and for all. When he walked incognito with the two men on the road to Emmaus, he shared the Upper Story in chronological order, pointing out that this was God's plan all along.[2] God has kept his promise, and the way back to him has been opened for all people from all nations!

ALIGNING OUR STORY TO GOD'S STORY

Jesus has provided the way back to God through the forgiveness of our sins. "If you declare with your mouth, 'Jesus is Lord,' and believe in your heart that God raised him from the dead, you will be saved."[3] Yes, the imperishable body you received from the first Adam must die but, like Jesus, you too will be raised from the dead with a new imperishable body when Jesus returns to earth. This is your hope. This is your destiny in Christ. "The gift of God is eternal life in Christ Jesus our Lord."[4] Have you made your declaration?

Have you ever stood at the graveside of someone you loved? I have many times, and it always underscores the reality that for the deceased, life as we know it is over. As I stand by the grave of a friend, I may recall memories of that person—the good times we shared or the tough times we faced together. But I am always left with the empty feeling that he is gone, and there is nothing I can do to bring him back. Even if he belongs to God, filling me with the hope that I will see him again in the kingdom that is to come, I can't shake the feeling that our relationship is over. The followers of Jesus certainly knew this feeling.

You would think that killing Jesus would have been enough for the religious leaders who felt threatened by him. That having him arrested, tried on false charges, and then hung on a cross would put an end to their concerns about this small movement of people who believed Jesus was the long-awaited Messiah. No, they were still worried about political insurrection from this small band of rabble-rousers. They worried that these very followers would stage a resurrection—by stealing the corpse of their leader—just to keep the memory of Jesus and his teachings alive.

The devious teachers of the law were convinced that Jesus would never rise from the grave as he said he would—but what if his zealous followers broke into the grave and removed his body? It would certainly *look* like Jesus escaped the grip of death, which would only fuel the fervor of his followers and very likely create an unstoppable movement. Jesus had already stirred up too much trouble; they weren't about to let him continue to cause problems from the grave.

To make sure no one tampered with the tomb containing his body, the people who convinced Pilate to have Jesus crucified asked him to provide a sentry to guard the tomb. Pilate agreed, and he added the extra measure of ordering the stone door to the tomb to be sealed so that if anyone tampered with the grave, they would have proof—the final blow to this whole nonsense about Jesus being the Messiah.

As much as they wanted to believe that Jesus would return, his followers were running low on hope. They had just experienced the saddest day of their lives, watching someone who identified himself as God's Son die along with two common criminals. On numerous occasions, Jesus had given them a glimpse of the Upper Story by telling them he would die but then rise again after three days. But they were stuck in their Lower Story, where death was final. Many of them probably felt a little foolish for believing all that nonsense about the Messiah. Maybe their religious teachers were right. Maybe Jesus really was a poser. The ancient prophet said the Messiah would be a "Mighty God, Everlasting Father."[5] Not a humble man in a robe and sandals who couldn't save himself, let alone others.

The day after he was crucified was the Jewish Sabbath—a day when people went to the temple and then stayed in their homes. But the following day, two women—both named Mary—went to the tomb to pay their final respects. As they make their way to the tomb, both Marys carry the same burden of grief in knowing that Jesus is gone. Forever. So you can imagine their shock when they get to the tomb and the stone has been rolled away! Their immediate thought is that the body of Jesus has been stolen. You would think that, recalling all the times Jesus had told them he would die and then be raised, they would have jumped for joy. But that was expecting a lot after everything they had been through the previous two days.

Thankfully, an angel sitting next to the tomb tells them what happened. When the angel had first appeared, the Roman soldiers guarding the tomb passed out. The stone had been rolled away, and Jesus was not in the tomb. "He is not here," said the angel. "He has risen, just as he said . . . Go quickly and tell his disciples."[6]

Even after hearing this good news, Mary Magdalene cannot quite get her arms around what is happening. She sits by the tomb crying when a man approaches her. In her grief, she doesn't recognize it is Jesus. He asks her why she is crying, and she explains that someone has taken the body of Jesus from the tomb. Thinking the man may be a caretaker for the burial grounds, she adds, "Sir, if you have carried him away, tell me where you have put him, and I will get him."[7]

Jesus then simply speaks her name, and in that instant, she knows it is him.

She is overjoyed and naturally reaches out to embrace him, but he tells her to go share with the disciples what she has just discovered.

Ah, the disciples. The closest friends Jesus had on earth—a group of men who knew him better than anyone. And yet. On the same day that Jesus appeared to Mary Magdalene, two disciples were walking to Emmaus, about seven miles from Jerusalem. Like Mary, they were both devastated and confused by the series of events that had happened over the past few days and were unpacking what they had seen and heard.

Jesus approaches them, but like Mary, they don't recognize him, even when he asks them what they've been talking about. So they explain how they had known this guy named Jesus and how they believed he was a great prophet and had hoped he was the Messiah but now he was gone. Can't you just imagine Jesus chuckling and thinking, *What does it take for these guys to get it?*

As it turns out, he challenges them with a quick history lesson so that they can see that everything that happened had been prophesied hundreds of years before. He told them the one Upper Story of God. Once they realize they are speaking to Jesus, they race back to Jerusalem to tell the rest of the disciples: "It is true! The Lord has risen."[8] Even as they celebrate this great news, Jesus appears in front of all of them and continues to teach them how his mission on earth is coming to an end and how they are going to carry it on after he returns to heaven.

Unfortunately, one disciple—Thomas—isn't there as Jesus explains all of this. He shows up after Jesus leaves, and even though his friends proceed to tell him all about their meeting with Jesus, his response gives him the unenviable title we use to this day to describe someone who is slow to believe things: *Doubting Thomas.* "Unless I see the nail marks in his hands and put my finger where the nails were, and put my hand into his side, I will not believe."[9] It isn't until a week later, when Jesus appears to Thomas and invites him to examine his wounds, that he finally declares, "My Lord and my God!"[10]

The time was rapidly approaching when Jesus would leave his human experiences in the Lower Story and return to his Father, the author of the Upper Story. Apparently, everything was in place to finally provide a way for anyone to get back to God, but the mission now would be shared, beginning with a handful of men and women. Ordinary people from all walks of life.

Jesus accompanied his disciples into the mountains for one last retreat to give them both their mission and a promise. While his message was directed to his disciples, it speaks clearly to anyone who has decided to follow Jesus, and it has come to be called the Great Commission. God wants as many people to come back to him as possible, and his primary way to get them back is through you and me:

> "All authority in heaven and on earth has been given to me. Therefore go and make disciples of all nations, baptizing them in the name of the Father and of the Son and of the Holy Spirit, and teaching them to obey everything I have commanded you. And surely I am with you always, to the very end of the age."[11]

His enemies thought they had finished Jesus off. But despite their great pains to discredit him and keep him in the tomb, he returned, just as he said he would—just as the prophets said he would. His own victory over death gives everyone the same opportunity to live forever with God, which has been the plan from the beginning. Jesus' mission on earth has been completed. Now it was up to a small group of men and women who believed.

Only one question remains: How can Jesus be with us, as he promised, if he is returning to heaven?

Movement Four

THE STORY OF
THE CHURCH

Acts–Jude

*E*veryone who comes into a relationship with God, through faith in Christ, belongs to the community that God is building, the church. The church is commissioned to be the presence of Christ in the Lower Story—telling his story by the way we live and the words we speak. The church points people to the second coming of Christ when he will return to restore God's original vision.

Chapter

28

NEW BEGINNINGS

*"All this I have spoken while still with you. But the
Advocate, the Holy Spirit, whom the Father will send in
my name, will teach you all things and will remind you of
everything I have said to you. Peace I leave with you; my
peace I give you. I do not give to you as the world gives.
Do not let your hearts be troubled and do not be afraid."*

JOHN 14:25–27

Jesus' ascension	Coming of the Holy Spirit at Pentecost	Paul believed in Jesus as the promised Messiah	James martyred, Peter imprisoned	Paul's 1st missionary journey
AD 30		35	44	46–48

WHAT'S HAPPENING IN THE UPPER STORY

God created a community through the nation of Israel to reveal his plan and point all people to the first coming of Jesus. Now God is creating a new community called "the church" to reveal his plan and to point all people to the second coming of Christ. Our job is to spread the good news all over the world that Christ has prepared the way back into relationship with God. All believers form the body of Christ, and collectively, we extend the presence and purpose of Jesus on earth. Just as Jesus was, we are sustained and empowered by the Holy Spirit to fulfill God's Upper Story plan here on earth. With sin no longer separating us from God, the Spirit, who previously existed behind the thick curtain in the temple, now takes up residence in us, his new temple. He's on the move again, just like the tabernacle in the desert. He is with us always.

ALIGNING OUR STORY TO GOD'S STORY

This is where we intersect with God's Upper Story. This is where we find our role in the grand epic. The instructions in this part of God's Word provides us with our road map and marching orders. God promises to use the community of believers to accomplish this part of his plan, just as he promised to use Israel to accomplish an earlier part. He has given us everything we need to be successful—his Word and his Spirit. The Holy Spirit give us the power, not to do our will, but *God's* will. Before God's Spirit came to Peter, Peter disowned Jesus three times in the hours before Jesus' crucifixion. But then Peter boldly aligned his life with God's story through the power of the Spirit within him. Align your life to God's will and experience his unlimited power.

*I*n the early nineteenth century, a Baptist preacher predicted that Jesus would return sometime between March 21, 1843, and March 21, 1844. Even though he gave Jesus a full year to decide when to return, by March 22, 1844, even *he* had to admit he was wrong—and he subsequently changed the date to October 22, 1844.

In 1910, astronomers correctly noted that Halley's Comet would appear, leading many church leaders to believe this would coincide with the return of Jesus. Astronomical events seem to precipitate similar predictions. In 1919, six of the planets in the earth's solar system were to be aligned in an unusual way, clearly a sign of Jesus' return, right? Maybe not.

Several years ago, a pastor predicted that Jesus would return on June 28, 1981. So his congregation sold all their possessions and waited for that day in vain. Who needs furniture if you are going to heaven? Then in 1988, a former NASA engineer wrote a little pamphlet proving that Jesus would return in that same year. It sold 4.5 million copies. And as the year 2000 approached, many popular and respected church leaders predicted Jesus would return as the new millennium began. By some estimates, there have been more than two hundred specific predictions of when Jesus would return, and they have all been wrong.

It would be easy to dismiss those who try to set a date for the return of Jesus as crazy extremists, or at least as seriously misguided souls, but for the most part, they have been strikingly ordinary and, above all, sincere. In fact, this desire to know the exact date of Jesus' return dates back to one of the last meetings Jesus had with his followers.

Jesus knew he was about to return home to heaven, and he wanted to reassure his disciples that they wouldn't be left on their own for long. As he explained what would happen in his absence, the disciples thought he was referring to the time when he would come back to earth to restore his kingdom—what we often refer to as his second coming. Jesus' answer explains why all those well-intentioned date setters were wrong—why none of us can predict when

Jesus will return: "It is not for you to know the times or dates the Father has set by his own authority."[1] As a matter of fact, even Jesus doesn't know when he will return, and if he isn't concerned about setting a date, why should we be?

What is more important to Jesus is the mission he gives his followers, and he knows how difficult it will be for them to carry it out on their own. So he shares the rest of the plan with his disciples. They had gathered in a large room to get away from the crowds, and Jesus tells them about the Holy Spirit: "You will receive power when the Holy Spirit comes on you; and you will be my witnesses in Jerusalem, and in all Judea and Samaria, and to the ends of the earth."[2]

During his ministry on earth, Jesus had taught the gospel or "good news," which essentially described the way to return to an authentic and personal relationship with God. But his teaching ministry is now about to end, so it is up to his followers to take over by being a "witness" to this wonderful news.

In the early years of my own ministry, "witnessing" was an active verb—a major one. It was something you got out there and did. Entire campaigns were devised to get church folks out in their neighborhoods, going door-to-door to tell others about Jesus. Nothing wrong with this, except for an occasional door being slammed in your face. But Jesus said we would *be* witnesses, not *do* witnessing. Being a witness is all-encompassing. It's what we do 24/7; it's who we are.

Certainly it includes telling others about Jesus. But it is also expressed in how we live—in how we treat others. The kind of witness Jesus talks about would come to expression in lives that reflect the values of God's perfect community—something that may be easy to do on a Sunday morning, but a lot harder to put into action during the week, when the Lower Story realities of life crowd out our Upper Story intentions.

Which is why we need the power that Jesus promised. The Holy Spirit, the third person of the Godhead, is coming down into our Lower Story just as Jesus is returning to his place in his Father's Upper Story. The Spirit is going to enter the lives of all who believe in Jesus, giving us the courage and guidance to accomplish our mission as witnesses. The force of our message will be our changed lives—the people we are becoming in our new relationship with God.

This news, both heard with ears and seen with eyes, will draw people to Jesus Christ, and the Holy Spirit is right there with us every step of the way.

Jesus even gives his followers a road map so they will know this good news is for everyone, not just for the Jewish people who had a head start because they knew and worshiped the one true God. He instructs them to start in Jerusalem and then move out to the broader region of Judea. From there they will go out into the next region, and then just keep going until *everyone* on the planet has had the opportunity to learn about Jesus and join the perfect community he is preparing.

After a pep talk like this, they were either ready to break down the door and get going or scared to death. Most likely, a little of both. As far as they were concerned, this whole thing about God's kingdom was now on them. So they did as Jesus ordered and waited in Jerusalem for the Holy Spirit. In the meantime, Jesus left, just as he said he would, and for a short time, the disciples were alone.

Then it happened. Jerusalem was once again packed with people who had come to celebrate the holiday of Pentecost, which occurred fifty days after Passover. The disciples are gathered in a room, and the Holy Spirit comes on them like fire spreading on dry tinder. Immediately they are filled with a newfound courage and boldness to carry out the mission Jesus had given them.

They fling open the doors of their now musty holding place and enter the streets of Jerusalem, which are swarming with people. Peter begins to tell anyone who will listen that this Jesus of Nazareth is the Messiah they have been looking for, and most important, that they can enter into a relationship with him and therefore be with God forever. No more sacrifices and burnt offerings. No more intricate rules. All they need to do is repent, believe, and be baptized. Their sins will be forgiven and they will be saved from the punishment they deserve because of those sins. By the time Peter stops talking, three thousand new followers are added to their number.

The bride of Christ, his church, is born. And we're not talking about a three-thousand-member megachurch. These Spirit-infused followers of Jesus met in homes all over Jerusalem. Historians tell us that each house church likely had about thirty people gathering together. If this is true, there were more than one hundred churches honeycombed throughout the city.

What did these new followers of Jesus do when they met? Like busy bees, they did a lot:

> They devoted themselves to the apostles' teaching and to fellowship, to the breaking of bread and to prayer. Everyone was filled with awe at the many wonders and signs performed by the apostles. All the believers were together and had everything in common. They sold property and possessions to give to anyone who had need. Every day they continued to meet together in the temple courts. They broke bread in their homes and ate together with glad and sincere hearts, praising God and enjoying the favor of all the people.[3]

Now that's what I call doing church! They devoted themselves to belonging, to fellowship. The first church service was experienced over the evening meal of the day—over dinner. It was here that they not only had a great feast but also ate bread and drank from the cup to remember the death of Jesus and all that it had done to change the outcome of their lives.

They were a family. They prayed together and studied the Word of God together. They took care of their neighbors, selling their possessions so they could meet the needs of each other and the people around them. Their offer of care was different. It was unconditional. When they helped someone, they didn't expect anything in return. God had already given them everything in Jesus Christ. They were merely paying it forward.

These new disciples were the coolest, most compelling people around, full of joy for what Jesus had done for them, and when others saw what was going on, they wanted to be part of it. These little churches grew daily with new people who wanted to be saved from their sins so they could enjoy the same fellowship they saw in those house churches. Who wouldn't want to be a part of such a family, such a movement of God?

This part of the story is so exciting because here is where our lives intersect with the Upper Story. Those of us who have accepted the gift of salvation in Jesus Christ not only have been forgiven, but have also received the Holy Spirit to empower us to live this new and better life. We have become a part of this new community. Everything these early followers experienced is available to us today. This new beginning that started with a handful of ordinary people continues to this day.

Nothing can stop it. Not even the gates of hell will prevail against the church!

Jesus doesn't leave us to carry out his mission alone. He gave us the Holy Spirit to guide and empower us to be witnesses of Jesus' transforming power in our lives. He also gave us the wonderful promise that he will return again someday. More on that later—but I won't be able to give you the exact date when this will happen. And that's OK, because it doesn't really matter.

Our mission isn't to know when Jesus will return. Instead, we are to live as if it will happen tomorrow. And just to make sure we know how to live in this new Spirit-filled community, God has given us a remarkable guide. While this person started out with the same name as a notorious king we learned about in the Old Testament, you know him better as Paul.

Chapter

PAUL'S MISSION

I always thank my God for you because of his grace given you in Christ Jesus. For in him you have been enriched in every way—with all kinds of speech and with all knowledge— God thus confirming our testimony about Christ among you.

1 CORINTHIANS 1:4–6

Paul's 1st missionary journey	Jerusalem Council	Paul's 2nd missionary journey	Paul's 3rd missionary journey
AD 46–48	49–50	50–52	53–57

WHAT'S HAPPENING IN THE UPPER STORY

God told Abraham that "all peoples on earth will be blessed through you."[1] This promise was fulfilled in Jesus, Abraham's offspring, and now it's time for God to make good on that promise. He selects Paul to be the primary catalyst. God gives him the direct call to take the message of Jesus Christ to the Gentiles (everyone other than the Jews). Paul responds to that call and is responsible for planting many Gentile churches, strengthening numerous others, and writing thirteen of the twenty-seven books of the New Testament. He is the fulfillment of Isaiah's prophecy: "I have made you a light for the Gentiles, that you may bring salvation to the ends of the earth."[2] He taught that not only do we enter a relationship by God's grace, but we continue to walk in that grace and not under law. Paul knew that God now lives inside believers, empowering them to live a Christian life. Yield to the Spirit's presence in you, and you will be changed for the good.

ALIGNING OUR STORY TO GOD'S STORY

Jesus said the church would spread from Jerusalem to Judea and Samaria and then to the ends of the earth.[3] Before Paul came to faith in Christ, he persecuted the church and caused it to spread to Judea and Samaria.[4] After Paul comes to faith, he is given the mission to take the good news to the Gentiles and establish churches at the ends of the earth. God uses everyone—protagonists and antagonists alike—to accomplish his Upper Story plan. God used Paul in both roles to further his plan. He will use our story to advance his story too. The difference? Protagonists who are willing to align their lives with God's story receive the blessings that come from working not against God, but with him.

I love action movies, especially ones with heroes who have to discover who they really are and how much power they have. Whether it's Superman realizing he is just a little bit stronger than the other guys in the gym or Spider-Man accepting the great responsibility that comes with his amazing Spidey powers or Jason Bourne discovering who he used to be before government agents messed him up—they all have to embrace who they are really meant to be.

Similarly, I love conversion stories, which may be the Christian equivalent to the stories of these superheroes discovering their powers. Stories of how people have gone from not knowing Jesus to inviting him to enter their lives. If I were to spend much time with you, I would probably have to ask you at some point, "What's your story?" To me, these are the *best* stories ever. They are real and true and better than any comic book hero's adventure or covert agent's secret mission.

A lot of people think that people in my line of work believed in Jesus from the minute they were born. And while it is true that a lot of ministers were blessed with faithful parents who took them to Sunday school and taught them to love Jesus, this is not my story. My parents were good, solid, salt-of-the-earth people who professed no belief in Jesus, as far as I could tell. They loved me and equipped me for many areas of my life; however, I had to encounter Jesus on my own and receive his radical, life-changing experience directly.

The neat thing about conversion stories is that they are all as unique as an individual's fingerprints. Some people have a difficult time identifying a specific time when they first believed because they grew up in church. Others recall a parent or Sunday school teacher asking them if they wanted to invite Jesus into their lives. Still others can point to a dramatic event—a serious illness, a tragic accident, the loss of a relationship—that woke them up to God's invitation. What all these stories have in common is how accepting Jesus changed their lives, because when you decide to follow Jesus, you also accept his mission. You are just so grateful to experience God's love that you want to share it with others.

Few people in history have had as dramatic a conversion or as powerful an impact on the Christian faith as a young Jewish man who experienced a radical 180-degree turn in his life. Saul was a zealous Jew who took it upon himself to try to stop the spread of this new movement begun by Jesus. When one of Jesus' followers, Stephen, was stoned to death for teaching about Jesus, it was Saul who gave the crowd his approval to kill him. From that point on, "Saul began to destroy the church."[5] Like a bounty hunter, he roamed the land, "breathing out murderous threats against the Lord's disciples."[6]

On one of his "missions" to track down the followers of Jesus, he experienced a major roadblock, literally, in the form of a high-voltage smackdown. A bolt of lightning knocked him to the ground, blinding him as a voice cried out, "Saul, Saul, why do you persecute me?"[7]

It was Jesus, who gave him a new name—Paul—and a new mission, which he would carry out with the same zeal as he had his previous mission. Talk about discovering your secret identity! In fact, he was so effective in teaching about Jesus that he became the target of unbelievers who wanted to kill him. A supreme irony not lost on Paul himself. Over the course of his mission, he would be beaten many times, thrown into prison, and eventually killed for his extreme commitment to spreading the good news about Jesus.

To support himself and his new mission, Paul made tents, which has given us the concept of the "tentmaker" missionary.[8] Today, hundreds of people volunteer to go to other countries to spread the Good News of Jesus, supporting themselves as carpenters, teachers, nurses, and other workers.

Paul responded to God's call to continue the job of taking the message of salvation to "the ends of the earth," where mostly Gentiles lived. Not only is this the commission that Jesus gave the church, but it is included in the promise that God made to Abraham all the way back at the beginning of this Story. He tells Abraham that it will be through his offspring that all nations will be blessed.[9] Jesus is this offspring, and Paul is the deliverer of the promise to the nations beyond Israel. No wonder, then, that Paul is often referred to as "the apostle to the Gentiles."

Paul lived in Antioch, and from there he set off on three long journeys over the course of approximately eight to ten years. Travel in those days wasn't quite the same as clicking on Travelocity and catching a sweet deal on an upcoming flight. Even short journeys posed a significant physical challenge. You either walked, rode a camel or donkey, or sailed the treacherous waters of the Mediterranean Sea in a primitive sailing ship. Paul did all three, and then some. As with Peter before him, his energy came from the presence of the Holy Spirit in his life.

On his very first trip, he established a pattern of going to the Jewish synagogue in each town he visited and making his pitch. For example, when he was in Pisidian Antioch, he was given the opportunity to speak without an appointment. He explained the good news simply and in a way his hearers would understand:

"The people of Jerusalem and their rulers did not recognize Jesus, yet in condemning him they fulfilled the words of the prophets that are read every Sabbath. Though they found no proper ground for a death sentence, they asked Pilate to have him executed. When they had carried out all that was written about him, they took him down from the cross and laid him in a tomb. But God raised him from the dead, and for many days he was seen by those who had traveled with him from Galilee to Jerusalem. They are now his witnesses to our people.

"We tell you the good news: What God promised our ancestors he has fulfilled for us, their children, by raising up Jesus . . .

"Therefore, my friends, I want you to know that through Jesus the forgiveness of sins is proclaimed to you. Through him everyone who believes is set free from every sin, a justification you were not able to obtain under the law of Moses."[10]

Essentially, he was connecting the dots for the Jewish people so that they could see that their own scriptures—the Old Testament—pointed to Jesus Christ. Everything that happened to Jesus was foretold in those ancient texts, including everything that would be done to him on the cross.

Then Paul simply invited his hearers to believe their own prophecies and accept the gift of salvation that Jesus offered.

The people of Pisidian Antioch invited Paul to come back on the next

Sabbath and speak again. Word got out, and on that day, nearly the entire population of the city gathered in the synagogue. But the local religious leaders got jealous and started to make trouble for Paul and his traveling companions, which is when he decided to take his message on the road. Paul explained to the people of this city:

> "We had to speak the word of God to you first. Since you reject it and do
> not consider yourselves worthy of eternal life, we now turn to the Gentiles.
> For this is what the Lord has commanded us:
>
> > "'I have made you a light for the Gentiles,
> >   that you may bring salvation to the ends of the earth.'"[11]

More than seven hundred years earlier, the prophet Isaiah knew the plan and how it would reach beyond Israel:

> I will also make you a light for the Gentiles,
>   that my salvation may reach to the ends of the earth.[12]

Taking the good news to his Jewish countrymen was one thing; trying to sell this message to Gentiles—non-Jewish people—would be much more difficult. The Gentiles didn't have the same religious background. They didn't know the ancient stories from the Old Testament. They didn't know Abraham from Moses. They didn't worship Yahweh and weren't looking for a Messiah.

We often face the same challenge, whether we realize it or not. Over the years, I've noticed that Christians sometimes assume everyone knows about their religious traditions. So we try to share the good news by using language no one really understands but us and talking about unfamiliar concepts that must make us look like we just arrived from another planet. Nothing can end a conversation quicker than the words *animal sacrifice* and *substitutionary atonement*. This is where Paul can teach us a few things about good communication.

When Paul arrived in Athens, he might as well have been Superman arriving on earth from his native planet Krypton. The citizens of this great city know nothing of the Law, the Prophets, or the Psalms. They are known for their great intellect and ability to reason. Not particularly religious, they at least tried to hedge their bets by erecting a statue on an altar bearing this inscription: "TO AN UNKNOWN GOD."[13] Paul brilliantly and eloquently builds a rational case for believing, beginning all the way back at the story of creation and leading to the resurrection of Jesus. He doesn't start with the story of Abraham or Moses, like other teachers before him who ministered to Israel. He starts with creation, where all of humanity finds common ground, to make his point.

Some reject his message, but many others are intrigued and want to learn more. By adjusting his message to meet the needs and interests of his audience, Paul is at least given a fair hearing, and even convinces many to believe.

During Paul's travels, the church grew rapidly as many Jews and Gentiles came to faith in Jesus Christ. It was literally changing the spiritual climate of the region. In the city of Ephesus, for example, a number of people came to faith in Jesus—people who previously practiced sorcery—and they gathered their pagan scrolls and burned them publicly.[14] The calculated value—fifty thousand drachmas—would translate to about four million dollars today!

In the Lower Story, Paul was a devout Jew who thought he was justified in trying to stop the spread of this nonsense about Jesus. But in the Upper Story, God had a different plan. It was the same plan he had been working on from the first days in the garden: *bring my people back to me*. And he knew that Paul would play an important role in that plan.

By God's grace and the strength of the Holy Spirit, Paul did just that. He planted numerous churches in highly Gentile-populated cities. He wrote many letters (thirteen are contained in our Bibles) to help strengthen the churches throughout the world. And he provided us with an example of how to share the good news with people who may not be immediately inclined to accept it.

I guess that's why I like superhero movies and conversion stories. Conversion, after all, is *change*, and it is the change in a person's life that I find so exciting. Paul underwent an amazing change, and as a result, thousands of other people also were changed.

Have you allowed God to reveal who you really are?

Chapter

30

PAUL'S FINAL DAYS

*And we know that in all things God works
for the good of those who love him, who have
been called according to his purpose.*

ROMANS 8:28

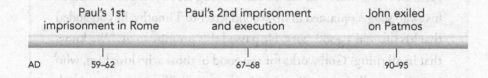

Paul's 1st imprisonment in Rome	Paul's 2nd imprisonment and execution	John exiled on Patmos
59–62	67–68	90–95

AD

WHAT'S HAPPENING IN THE UPPER STORY

The church is in full motion, achieving the next chapter in God's grand story of redemption. God's original plan in the garden centered on community—God and mankind together, just as God is three persons and yet one being. Adam and Eve were made in the image of God as a community—two persons and yet one unit. But that community was broken when sin entered their lives. The church is the restoration of that communal expression. Paul and the other New Testament writers taught that we are the unified body of Christ. We each have a part, a purpose, and a spiritual gift that joins us with other believers to extend the presence and purpose of Christ on earth. We are many people, yet one being—the body of Christ. Sin has been removed for all who embrace the vision of God and is no longer a barrier to living in God's actual presence. The church is the restored people who will enter back into the garden with God. Paul calls us to start living now as we will live then—in conformity to the image of Christ.

ALIGNING OUR STORY TO GOD'S STORY

We are first introduced to Paul as Saul. He approved the killing of the first Christian martyr, Stephen. At the end of Paul's life, the tables turn, and he is martyred for his unswerving and courageous faith. In his swan song, contained in his second letter to Timothy, he concluded that his life told a good story. He passed this promise to us: "We know that in all things God works for the good of those who love him, who have been called according to his purpose."[1] When we align with God's Upper Story, he promises to write a good story with our lives.

Does anyone write letters anymore? I'm not talking about business memos or quick notes on Post-its, but personal, handwritten letters to someone you care about. In this age of e-mail and texting and tweeting, receiving an old-fashioned letter seems about as common as finding a message in a bottle.

I love it when I get a letter in the mail, though. It doesn't happen often, but every now and then, among the bills, junk mail, and the flyer for the new fitness center down the street, I find a hand-addressed envelope with a letter inside. Often it is from an older person, someone who views Facebook as a nice way to see pictures of their grandkids but not the proper way to correspond about meaningful topics. I can't tell you how my heart sort of jumps when I see a letter like that addressed to me. I feel amazingly special!

A friend of mine told me how, when his daughter was in college, he regularly mailed her letters. Today she is a married woman with young kids and is at the front end of a legal career—smack-dab in the middle of a generation that grew up in the digital age of e-mail rather than snail mail. When her dad quit sending her letters, she called him and pleaded, "Daddy, please keep sending me real mail."

Real mail. I like that.

It is just this kind of real mail that has helped us as followers of Jesus learn how to live in a way that reflects God's values. As Paul traveled throughout parts of Asia, southern Europe, and the Middle East, he wrote letters to the new believers he left behind. Many of these believers—especially the Gentiles—had no clue about God and how he wanted them to live. Paul knew that if they simply professed a belief in Jesus but did not live according to his values, none of their friends and neighbors would be particularly motivated to join them in adopting their new belief system.

The way we live is often our most convincing message, and these new believers had to change the way they lived to conform to God's standards. This isn't always an easy thing to do. Like a sculptor who envisions a beautiful statue inside a slab of marble, we must view our lives as works of art in progress that require some chiseling.

The goal for us as followers of Christ is to let the Master Artist chisel away anything in our lives that doesn't look like Christ. Paul put it this way: "Follow God's example, therefore, as dearly loved children and walk in the way of love, just as Christ loved us and gave himself up for us as a fragrant offering and sacrifice to God."[2] We want to grow more like Jesus out of our passionate response to the amazing height and depth of the love that God has for us. Enough to send his only Son to die for us. Enough to work through the countless details and millions of threads that knit our Lower Story to his Upper Story to form one seamless Divine Epic.

In at least one way, Paul's time in prison was a blessing because it gave him time to write. Once, when he was under house arrest in Rome, he wrote four letters we now appropriately call the "Prison Epistles" (*epistle* is an old-fashioned word for "letter"). One, called Philippians because it was written to the believers in the city of Philippi, offers practical guidance about attitude and behavior and includes nuggets such as these:

- Conduct yourselves in a manner worthy of the gospel of Christ.
- Do nothing out of selfish ambition or vain conceit. Rather, in humility value others above yourselves.
- In your relationships with one another, have the same mindset as Christ Jesus.
- Do everything without grumbling or arguing.
- Shine among them like stars in the sky.
- Rejoice in the Lord always.
- Let your gentleness be evident to all.[3]

How could anyone in jail write from such a positive perspective? Paul could, because he had been chiseled to look like Christ Jesus. In Christ, our circumstances do not dictate our joy; our relationship with and hope in Christ do. In fact, it is often how we live when our circumstances are at their worst that either attracts or repels others.

In another letter to the believers in the city of Ephesus, Paul warns against the kinds of behaviors that don't reflect the values of God's community: falsehood, bitterness, anger, slander, sexual immorality, greed, foolish talk, drunkenness.[4] He knows that if followers of Jesus live just like those who do not know Jesus, no one will want to become a part of God's community. To help these new believers understand, he talks about taking on a new attitude, much like you would put on a new set of clothes: "You were taught . . . to put off your old self, which is being corrupted by its deceitful desires . . . and put on the new self, created to be like God in true righteousness and holiness."[5]

In the same letter, he addresses a problem that plagued the early church and continues to create problems for us today: getting along with each other. In Paul's day, the rifts were between Jewish believers and Gentile believers. Today in our denominations and other groupings of believers, sometimes we don't play nice together. Here is what Paul has to say:

> Christ himself gave the apostles, the prophets, the evangelists, the pastors and teachers, to equip his people for works of service, so that the body of Christ may be built up until we all reach unity in the faith and in the knowledge of the Son of God and become mature, attaining to the whole measure of the fullness of Christ.
>
> Then we will no longer be infants, tossed back and forth by the waves, and blown here and there by every wind of teaching and by the cunning and craftiness of people in their deceitful scheming. Instead, speaking the truth in love, we will grow to become in every respect the mature body of him who is the head, that is, Christ. From him the whole body, joined and held together by every supporting ligament, grows and builds itself up in love, as each part does its work.[6]

We are all part of the same body—the body of Christ. We are to come together as one, in complete unity. We are to value each other and use our unique gifts, like a body uses its different parts, to accomplish God's Upper Story purposes.

All too soon, Paul's mission on earth came to an end. One of the great tragedies of the early church is that so many of its pioneers were killed because of their beliefs. Most of the remaining eleven disciples were martyred for teaching others about Jesus. According to tradition, Peter was crucified upside down. During his third and final visit to Rome, Paul was arrested and thrown into a wet, dark dungeon. He knew he wasn't going to make it out; it was time to pass the baton to the next generation to run the race set before them. So he began to write more letters.

Two of these letters went to Timothy, a young man who had accompanied Paul on his first missionary journey and was like a son to him. In these short letters, we can sense Paul's urgent desire to make sure that Timothy remains strong in the faith. He urges Timothy to "fight the good fight" of contending for the faith, just as Paul himself has "fought the good fight . . . finished the race . . . kept the faith."[7] As the memory of Jesus faded, many false teachers appeared on the scene to try to start their own movements, and Paul knew Timothy would be challenged.

Though Timothy was extremely talented, he also seems to have been timid and prone to back down from leading because of his youthfulness. So Paul encourages him from his prison cell: "For the Spirit God gave us does not make us timid, but gives us power, love and self-discipline."[8]

Perhaps Paul was also thinking of what awaited Timothy, for he would certainly pay dearly for continuing to teach the good news, as his mentor had. So Paul tries to prepare Timothy for what may happen to him:

> You, however, know all about . . . the persecutions I endured. Yet the Lord rescued me from all of them. In fact, everyone who wants to live a godly life in Christ Jesus will be persecuted, while evildoers and imposters will go from bad to worse, deceiving and being deceived.[9]

From a Lower Story perspective, following Jesus can be risky. Not everyone wants what you're selling, and even today, people who follow Jesus face persecution, imprisonment, and even death. Paul persevered because he knew what awaited him in the Upper Story. In one of the most moving passages of this letter, he offers us this beautiful explanation of why we should never let anything keep us from serving God:

For I am already being poured out like a drink offering, and the time for my departure is near. I have fought the good fight, I have finished the race, I have kept the faith. Now there is in store for me the crown of righteousness, which the Lord, the righteous Judge, will award to me on that day—and not only to me, but also to all who have longed for his appearing.[10]

According to historians, it wasn't long after he finished this letter that Paul was beheaded.

Apparently, Paul's letters to Timothy gave him all the encouragement he needed. Not only did he carry on Paul's mission by sharing the good news with others; he got thrown in jail for doing it. We don't know for sure if Paul knew about the experiences of his young partner in ministry, but if he did, I'm sure it brought a smile to his face as he sat in the dungeon awaiting his execution. If Timothy went to prison, it meant that he had stood up for his faith. Timothy was going to be just fine. God had raised up the next generation to carry the torch of Jesus' great love with great boldness.

He always does.

As we will see in the next chapter, even though we are near the end of the Story as it is told to us in the Bible, that doesn't mean the story is over. God isn't done yet. He needs to add more chapters to his Upper Story of calling people back to him. You. Me. All of us who have embraced the gospel of Jesus Christ and have become a part of this new community called the church. While the purpose of the community of Israel was to point people to the first coming of the Messiah, our purpose is to point people to the second coming of Jesus.

Therefore, we need to be like the church of Ephesus. We need to be one. We need to be united in the common mission of Christ. We need to individually and collectively live out our role in God's Upper Story plan.

And we need to be like Timothy—standing firm in our beliefs despite the efforts of others to discredit us and our message. Like the mentor Paul, we need to be able to say, "I am not ashamed of the gospel,"[11] and boldly live according to God's values, always prepared to explain the gospel when people ask us why we are different.

Most of all, we need to grow. We need day by day to become more like Jesus. We need to let God chisel away anything in our lives that doesn't look like Jesus until others will be able to see him in us and decide to follow him too.

Aren't you glad that Paul wrote *real* mail?

Movement Five

THE STORY OF
A NEW GARDEN

Revelation

One day, God will create a new earth and a new garden and once again come down to be with us. All who place their faith in Christ in this life will be eternal residents in the life to come.

Chapter
31

THE END OF TIME

"These words are trustworthy and true. The Lord,
the God who inspires the prophets, sent his angel to show
his servants the things that must soon take place."

REVELATION 22:6

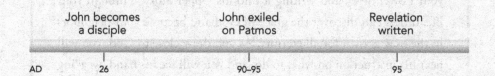

John becomes a disciple		John exiled on Patmos		Revelation written
AD 26		90–95		95

WHAT'S HAPPENING IN THE UPPER STORY

God's story doesn't make a line, but a circle. And now we're nearly all the way back to where we began. The last two chapters of the Bible read almost identically to the first two chapters of the Bible. God is creating a new heaven and a new earth. The tree of life is at the center of the garden. A community of people will be there with new bodies that are not infected with sin. The tree of the knowledge of good and evil that gave Adam and Eve the choice to reject God's vision is not there. God has come down to live among us and take a walk with us in the "cool of the day."[1] This is not really the ending of the story, but a new beginning. God has restored what was lost in the first beginning through Christ. The next major event that will set this last movement into action is Christ's return. Let our prayer be the same one that John ended the Bible with after he saw what is to come: "Come, Lord Jesus!"[2]

ALIGNING OUR STORY TO GOD'S STORY

The events described in Revelation are still to come. You know what that means? You are a character in God's story; you have a role to play. The same God who called and empowered ordinary people to do extraordinary things during Bible times is doing the same today. He is taking your Lower Story and writing it into his Upper Story. Through your life, others can discover the grace of God and become your neighbors in the new garden for all eternity. As you draw close to God, you will hear his instruction on what to do, and you will see his hand, weaving the details of your life to move his story forward. Nothing will bring greater fulfillment than knowing you have a purpose in God. Live every day with the expectation that this could be the day your Savior returns.

Have you ever read a book or listened to a story that you didn't want to end? A story that was just so good that you wanted it to keep going and going and going? We are about to finish the last page of God's story as collated in the Bible. As we know by now, however, his Upper Story doesn't end there. It just keeps going and going and going. *Forever.*

The final book in the Bible is called Revelation, because it reveals how life on earth as we know it will end. But it could just as easily have been called "The New Beginning," because it is all about what life in God's perfect community will be like. This book may mark the end of the Bible, but it's really the beginning of a brand-new adventure.

We received this book from the disciple John—the same John who wrote the gospel of John and the letters of 1, 2, and 3 John. He was one of Jesus' original disciples, known as the "disciple whom Jesus loved." At the Lord's Supper, John sat next to Jesus, and he is the one who was so excited about the empty tomb that he outran Peter to be the first to arrive.[3]

When he wrote this book, John probably couldn't run quite so fast anymore; he was an old man. Historians tell us that he is the only apostle who was not killed for professing his faith in Jesus Christ. Instead, he was banished to an island called Patmos to spend his remaining days, completely isolated and surrounded by water, like being on the set of a spiritual *Cast Away*. The religious and political leaders thought his ability to do further damage would be controlled if they kept him far from everyone. Wow, did they ever miscalculate!

It is on this island that God visits the beloved John and gives him a clear vision of what is yet to come, including the best picture we have of what the kingdom of God is going to be like. This final book of the Bible has sparked great hope in believers throughout the ages. It keeps us going in the darkest of times. Regardless of how difficult life may be at the moment, we have, through Jesus' sacrifice, this wonderful place to look forward to. We know we will "retire" someday to his perfect community.

If this new community sounds a little familiar, it is by design. Not mine, but God's, for when we read this final part of the Story, we find ourselves right back where we started. Genesis 1 and 2 are remarkably similar to Revelation 21–22, with several noticeable differences.

For example, John writes, "Then I saw 'a new heaven and a new earth,' for the first heaven and the first earth had passed away, and there was no longer any sea."[4] Remember how the story began? "In the beginning God created the heavens and the earth."[5] Our future home will be a whole new earth—one that is not groaning or dying anymore because of the curse of sin.

John continues describing the glimpse into the future that God gives him: "I saw the Holy City, the new Jerusalem, coming down out of heaven from God, prepared as a bride beautifully dressed for her husband."[6] While he was still on earth, Jesus alluded to this city when he said, "I am going there to prepare a place for you."[7] So we will have a brand-new place to live on a brand-new earth, but this is not enough for God. Do you remember why he created us in the first place? Do you remember the one major theme of the Upper Story? Maybe what John describes next will refresh your memory: "And I heard a loud voice from the throne saying, 'Look! God's dwelling place is now among the people, and he will dwell with them. They will be his people, and God himself will be with them and be their God.'"[8]

I knew an old preacher who would be preaching away and stop suddenly, exclaiming, "If you were looking for a good place to say amen, you just missed it." This verse is one of those places. Wow! God is coming down again into the Lower Story to be *with* us, just as he was with Adam and Eve. He is going to do life with us in wonderful ways that we can't even begin to imagine! Not in a tabernacle with a curtained room to separate him from us, but right there with us, as in the original garden. Walking with us. Talking with us. This is all he has ever wanted. This alone should be enough to make us yearn to be there with him, but there is more.

In this community that God has been building, there will be no tears. No need for them, because there will be no death, no pain, no sadness. This is all Lower Story stuff. God has been eager to wipe away all those tears we have shed in our Lower Story lives. One of the first things I want to do when I get there is to stand next to my mom. She died of cancer, and I can't tell you how much I cried as she suffered and then cried more tears out of loneliness after she left us. God will take that same finger depicted in Michelangelo's painting as giving life to Adam and wipe the final tear from my eyes as my mother greets me in a perfectly restored body!

Remember the garden at the beginning of the story? God is reconstructing it for us—with a few minor changes to make it even better:

> Then the angel showed me the river of the water of life, as clear as crystal, flowing from the throne of God and of the Lamb down the middle of the great street of the city. On each side of the river stood the tree of life, bearing twelve crops of fruit, yielding its fruit every month. And the leaves of the tree are for the healing of the nations. No longer will there be any curse. The throne of God and of the Lamb will be in the city, and his servants will serve him. They will see his face, and his name will be on their foreheads. There will be no more night. They will not need the light of a lamp or the light of the sun, for the Lord God will give them light. And they will reign for ever and ever.[9]

There is that tree of life again. It was in the Garden of Eden the last time we saw it. It was the tree that bore fruit to eternal life. Adam and Eve—and consequently all mankind—were banished from that garden, but now we have unguarded access to it again. And there is not just one tree, but two trees along a crystal-clear, life-giving river. These trees bear fruit not once a year, but once a month. Everything about this new community is about abundant, eternal life.

One tree, however, is missing from this reconstructed garden—the tree of the knowledge of good and evil. It is the tree that God placed in the first garden for Adam and Eve so they could choose whether or not to embrace God's vision of life. Why isn't it in this new garden? Because it isn't needed. You have already made the life-giving choice when you accepted Jesus Christ's offer of forgiveness.

Most important of all, when we return to this garden, we will see the face of our Lord God. We will see the intense love in his eyes that went to such a great extent to get us back. It will overwhelm us every day for eternity and will compel us to worship him. We will join with the angels as we sing:

301

"'Holy, holy, holy
is the Lord God Almighty,'
who was, and is, and is to come."[10]

We are finally home. The ultimate home we have always yearned for, a place of rest and joy and peace and comfort and life and love. A home of wholeness, of completion with our Creator, our Abba Father who loves us so relentlessly, so fiercely that there is nothing he won't do to save us.

God knows what our Lower Story lives are like. Some days are good; some are not so good. We do our best as men and women, husbands and wives, parents and children, bosses and employees, and in the many other roles we play. But things don't always turn out the way we hoped they would. And no matter how hard we try to do the right things, to be good, we never seem to be good enough—to others and to ourselves. In fact, no matter how hard we try, we aren't even capable of measuring up. Our best efforts are like filthy rags before the shimmering holiness of God. But it's not up to us to make it happen. God provided another way through his beloved Son, Jesus.

This is why God is writing an Upper Story that is infinitely more magnificent (not to mention complicated—can you imagine keeping track of every character who has ever lived?) than any one Lower Story chapter by itself. His continuous theme tells us how much he loves us and how he has provided the way for us to come home to live with him in a perfect community. It shows us how to get back to our heart's true home—the new Jerusalem. No matter how many times his people turned away from him, he kept calling them back until he finally gave his precious Son as the ultimate sacrifice for our disobedience.

If you are a follower of Jesus Christ, no matter how difficult your life has become, no matter how dark your pathway, no matter how intense your weariness, take courage. Your Lower Story doesn't end there. Because you believe in Jesus, your story has just begun, and it will be a phenomenal one. Plus, you have a guaranteed role in the Upper Story, where you will live forever with God.

If you haven't yet responded to the call to follow Jesus, you could miss out on all that God has for you, both here on earth and especially in his perfect community called heaven. If you've hung with me this far, you know that no amount of trying will work. You know that neither I nor anyone else can give you a list of rules that will get you back to God.

Aren't you tired of trying so hard, especially because you know deep down that it will never work? Don't you want to come home, to rest your weary heart? The only thing God asks of you is that you open your hands and accept his gift of forgiveness for your sins. This simple act of faith reserves a place for you in this eternal home. Wouldn't you like to come home? You can do so right now.

In simple faith, bow your head and pray this prayer to God:

Dear God, I know I have inherited a sin nature from Adam. I act out of this nature in many selfish ways that make me unfit for your perfect community. I know now there is nothing in myself that I can do to change this. It is often hard for me to grasp, but I know you want to be in a relationship with me. The extent you have gone to provide the way to you overwhelms me. You sent your one and only Son, who died on the cross for my sins. By faith I humbly accept your offer of forgiveness. Today by your grace I am embracing your vision of life that brings us back together forever. I will align the remaining days of my life on earth with your Upper Story plan in the power of your Holy Spirit, which is coming into my life right now. In Jesus' name, Amen.

Welcome to the family of God! Make sure you tell someone, maybe the person you've sensed has been praying for you to make this eternal decision. If you are not already connected to a church, by all means, make that your next priority. This is the most tangible way you can connect your story to God's story. God is using the church, as he did Israel, to advance his Upper Story. He has a unique role for you to play that will change lives for eternity. Take the cannonball plunge, and go all in!

God came down in the beginning because he wanted to do life with us. He returned again in the form of a baby, according to his Father's plan, to make a way once and for all for *anyone* to live forever with him. He is coming again to establish a new community for all of us who have received his forgiveness. And in response, we echo the words with which John ends the Bible—the words that continue the Story:

Come, Lord Jesus.[11]

Conclusion

YOUR PART
IN THE STORY

*L*et's go back to the breathtaking Sistine Chapel in Rome. You now know the backstory of the three hundred characters that Michelangelo painted on the ceiling and how they fit together to tell the one love story of God. You know how each played a part in the unfolding of God's Upper Story plan to get us back.

You look up, and over in the corner, much to your surprise, you see the back of a man who looks like Michelangelo. He is painting a scene on a blank spot on the ceiling. As you hone in on the painting in progress, you quickly recognize that it is a rendering of our current day. As you look a little more closely, the scenery seems all too familiar. It includes all the places and faces of *your* world. Adrenaline kicks in and rushes through your entire body as soon as the reality dawns on you—this artist is painting a portrait of you!

You are a part of the grand Story of God. You know how the story ends, but there are still things to be done, things to be said. How will the artist depict *your* life on the ceiling, in the middle of all the folks we've read about?

Will the portrait show that, unlike Adam and Eve, you chose to eat from the tree of life and not the tree of the knowledge of good and evil?

Will it depict you as a person who trusts in God, even against overwhelming odds, like Abraham and Sarah did?

305

Will you be drawn as a person like Joseph, who forgave people who hurt you in the Lower Story because you understood and embraced the bigger plan of God?

Will the portrait show that you placed the blood of the lamb above the doorposts of your life, like Moses and the Hebrew people did in Egypt?

Will the painting display that your body is a tabernacle for the dwelling of God, like the tent was for Israel in the wilderness?

Will it show that you backed down from the giants in your life or that you faced them, like Joshua did?

Will it creatively portray your body as a jar of clay containing the light of Jesus Christ, as in the story of Gideon?

Will it show you inviting foreigners, refugees, outsiders, and outcasts into your life, as Boaz did with Ruth?

Will it depict you as one who wants to be like everyone else, as with Saul, or a person after God's own heart, like David was?

Will it draw a time in your life when you did wrong but then, with a heart of true repentance, came clean with God and the people you offended, like David did?

Will the drawing show a life of full-out worship to God, or will it be forced to pen a portrait of compromise, as with Solomon?

Will it show a house united with your family and with God or a house divided against God and family, as we saw in the lives of Rehoboam and Jeroboam?

Will you be portrayed as one who did evil in the eyes of the Lord, as thirty-two of the kings of Israel and Judah did, or will you be remembered as one who followed the Lord boldly, as young King Josiah did?

Will your painting depict you as one who proclaimed the message of God not only with your words but also with your life, as the prophet Hosea did?

Will you be drawn as a person who fights with swords of anger and revenge or with knee pads on in prayer, like King Hezekiah did?

Will the portrait maker render you as one who knew the call of God on your life and walked in faithfulness in the face of obstacles, like Jeremiah did?

Will you be drawn with the resolve of Daniel not to defile yourself by the diet of your culture but to present yourself as fully devoted to God?

Will your painting show you as one who put God's big thing as your big thing, like Judah did after they returned from exile?

Will the portrait of your life be filled with the courage of Esther?

Will your eyes contain the tears of one who deeply loves God's Word, like Ezra and the people of Judah?

Will the scene be of Christmastime, as you celebrate the birth of Jesus into the world like the angels did—singing, "Glory to God in the highest heaven."

Will you be portrayed as one "born again," like Nicodemus was?

Will the portrait have you carrying a banner proclaiming your heart's declaration that Jesus is the Son of God, the Messiah, the Light of the world, the great I AM, as the disciples declared?

Will the drawing of your story have your hand placed on the head of Jesus, transferring all your guilt and shame to him as he hangs on the cross?

Will the scene include you, standing by the empty tomb with hands raised to the heavens, celebrating the resurrection of Jesus, as Mary and John did?

Will you be drawn as one member of several in your community who devoted their lives to being the presence of Jesus on earth, as those in the early church did?

Will the artist choose a scene out of your life in which you were spreading the good news of Jesus to a neighbor or stranger far away, like Paul did?

Will the portrait capture you passing on your faith to the next generation, like Paul did with Timothy?

Will the painting have you praying to the heavens, "Come, Lord Jesus!" because you are as passionate for Jesus to return as John was?

The decisions you make today provide the content that the artist will use to create your portrait in the mural of God's story. I encourage you to love God and align your life to his Upper Story plan. If you do this, God promises that all the events in your life will turn out for the good.

But the most important picture of all is the painting of you and God taking a walk in the cool of the day in the garden to come. If this painting is drawn of you, then it means you have truly captured God's Big Idea—he wants to be with you!

ACKNOWLEDGMENTS

I want to acknowledge just some of the people who have helped shape my life and ministry and the content of this book.

To Ray and Mary Graham for caring enough to invite a young boy and his sister to their church's summer Vacation Bible School in 1974. This is where I first heard and received the message of Jesus.

To my father-in-law, Al Bitonti, who from the time I was fifteen years old drew me into the Bible by the force of his undeniably Christlike character.

To my professors in undergraduate and graduate studies, who showed me the ropes of biblical languages and hermeneutics and increased my hunger to correctly handle Scripture—particularly Dr. Tom Bulick, Dr. Ron Walker, Dr. Darrell Bock, Dr. Elliot Johnson, and Dr. Howard Hendricks.

To the congregation of Pantego Bible Church, who let me cut my teeth on teaching the Bible to them as their pastor at the age of twenty-eight. A crown awaits you in heaven for your patience and continual encouragement. What a wonderful sixteen years we had together!

To the congregation of Willow Creek Community Church, who gave me the opportunity to first teach *The Story* at the New Community gathering on Wednesday nights. Your genuine craving for the pure Word gave me the inspiration to press forward. Three years wasn't quite long enough.

To the late Dallas Willard for offering me the daunting task of rewriting a masterpiece—*Renovation of the Heart*—for students. This labor of love caused me to drink deeply from the well of Scripture. I haven't been the same since.

To the late George Gallup Jr. and the entire team that worked on the development of *The Christian Life Profile* tool. The meetings in Dallas and Princeton were more valuable than a formal degree in spiritual formation.

To the congregation of Oak Hills Church. What a crazy thing to take the senior minister role from beloved Max Lucado after his twenty years as senior minister of Oak Hills. You have taken us in and embraced our family. Our journey through *The Story* during our first year together will go down as one of the highlights of my ministry. Let's make more memories in the days to come. To my Village Green and Cordillera Ranch neighbors. Acts 17:26 tells us that God planned for us to live in the same neighborhood at the same time. God has been so good to the Frazees for placing you in our lives. May we continue to be Jesus to each other and to the neighbors we are called to love as ourselves.

To Mike Reilly and Bob Buford. I shake my head in disbelief at all the ways you have encouraged me and my family. You have cultivated and fertilized my work through many seasons. I hope you are pleased with the fruit it has produced.

To Max Lucado. Your belief and participation in the Story project have been key. I'll never forget how the wheels of your golf game came off the day we talked about this whole idea. I watched with my own eyes as you put on the wheels of your amazingly creative mind. They spun out of control as we pondered the possibilities of such a project and its value to the church. More than that, you have become my friend and partner. Thank you for everything.

To Nancy Zack, my assistant and lifesaver. I would get nothing done and never be in the right place without you. Thanks for moving to San Antonio.

To our four children—Jennifer, David, Stephen, and Austin. Not a day goes by that I don't thank God for placing you at the heart of my story. You bring your mom and me and your God great joy. I find intense purpose and passion helping you as your stories as adults unfold.

To Desmond and Gretchen. It is so great to have you in the Frazee clan. I'm grateful to be a part of your story and will do everything I can to encourage you as much as my father-in-law (I like "father-in-grace" better) has encouraged me.

To my grandchildren, Ava and Crew Rand. Your very presence wrecks me. I so long for you to understand the heart of God's love for you. You just might be his favorites! I will do my best to help you and show you. Promise.

To Rozanne, my dear wife of thirty-five years and counting. You are my Rachel, my Ruth, my Esther. Your unwavering belief and support all these years overwhelm me. You are my best friend; the two have truly become one. As we enter this next chapter, I'm excited to support you as you have supported me. You have a lot to say.

To the entire Story Team at HarperCollins Christian Publishing. You have embraced the vision behind the Story project in ways I could not have fathomed. This project would not be where it is at today without the capable leadership of Beth Murphy and Shelley Leith. A special thanks to Estee Zandee and Dirk Buursma for holding my hand and coaching me on this second edition.

To Michael Seaton and his team for filming the thirty-one video segments that complement this book. I must hold the record for the number of shoots in one sitting.

Finally, to Jesus Christ. This whole story begins, pivots, and ends with you. You are the central character of this story and of my life. I am eternally grateful—literally!

NOTES

INTRODUCTION: THE ART GALLERY AND THE MURAL

1. Matthew 10:39 MSG.
2. Matthew 6:9–10 (*The Story*, p. 341).
3. Matthew 6:11–13 (*The Story*, p. 341).
4. Matthew 26:39 (*The Story*, p. 372).
5. Ibid.

CHAPTER 1: CREATION: THE BEGINNING OF LIFE AS WE KNOW IT

1. Genesis 1:2 (*The Story*, p. 1).
2. See "An Overview of the Solar System," *Nine Planets*: http://nineplanets.org/overview.html (accessed March 4, 2011).
3. Genesis 1:26–27 (*The Story*, pp. 2–3).
4. Genesis 2:16–17, paraphrased.
5. Genesis 3:6.
6. Genesis 4:7 is the first time evil actions are referred to as sin.
7. Genesis 3:22–24 (*The Story*, pp. 6–7).
8. Genesis 6:5 (*The Story*, p. 8).
9. Psalm 139:5.

CHAPTER 2: GOD BUILDS A NATION

1. Genesis 12:4 (*The Story*, p. 13).
2. Genesis 22:2 (*The Story*, p. 19).
3. 2 Chronicles 3:1.

311

CHAPTER 3: JOSEPH: FROM SLAVE TO DEPUTY PHARAOH

1. Genesis 37:4.
2. Genesis 37:28.
3. Genesis 39:2 (*The Story*, p. 31).
4. Genesis 39:6 (*The Story*, p. 31).
5. Genesis 39:7 (*The Story*, p. 31).
6. Genesis 39:9 (*The Story*, p. 31).
7. Genesis 39:20–21 (*The Story*, p. 32).
8. Genesis 46:29 (*The Story*, p. 40).
9. Genesis 45:4–8 (*The Story*, p. 39).
10. Genesis 50:20, paraphrased.
11. Romans 8:28 (*The Story*, p. 435).

CHAPTER 4: DELIVERANCE

1. Exodus 1:8: "Then a new king, to whom Joseph meant nothing, came to power in Egypt" (*The Story*, p. 43).
2. Genesis 15:13.
3. Exodus 4:10, 13 (*The Story*, pp. 46–47).
4. Exodus 4:20.
5. Isaiah 55:8–11.
6. Exodus 3:12.
7. Romans 9:17–18.

CHAPTER 5: NEW COMMANDS AND A NEW COVENANT

1. Matthew 22:37, 39.
2. Exodus 25:8 (*The Story*, p. 63).
3. Exodus 26:1–14.
4. Exodus 40:34 (*The Story*, p. 70).

CHAPTER 6: WANDERING

1. Numbers 10:11 (*The Story*, p. 71).
2. Numbers 11:1 (*The Story*, p. 71).
3. Numbers 11:5–6 (*The Story*, p. 72).
4. Numbers 11:20 (*The Story*, p. 73).
5. Numbers 12:6–8 (*The Story*, p. 74).
6. Numbers 13:27, paraphrased.
7. Howard F. Vos, *Nelson's New Illustrated Bible Manners and Customs* (Nashville: Nelson, 1999), 114.
8. Numbers 14:11.
9. Deuteronomy 30:19–20 (*The Story*, p. 87).

CHAPTER 7: THE BATTLE BEGINS

1. Quoted in Steve Israel, ed., *Charge! History's Greatest Military Speeches* (Annapolis, MD: Naval Institute Press, 2013), 203.
2. Numbers 13:31 (*The Story*, p. 75).
3. Numbers 14:7–9.
4. Joshua 1:6, 7, 9 (*The Story*, pp. 87, 89–90).
5. Joshua 1:7–8 (*The Story*, p. 89).
6. Joshua 1:5 (*The Story*, p. 89).
7. Joshua 1:16 (*The Story*, p. 90).
8. Joshua 6:16 (*The Story*, p. 93).
9. Deuteronomy 9:5, emphasis added (*The Story*, p. 86).
10. Genesis 15:16.
11. Deuteronomy 12:31.

CHAPTER 8: A FEW GOOD MEN . . . AND WOMEN

1. 1 John 1:9.
2. Judges 6:15.
3. Judges 7:1–8.
4. Judges 6:5 (*The Story*, p. 107).
5. Judges 7:20, paraphrased.
6. Judges 8:33–34 (*The Story*, p. 112).

CHAPTER 9: THE FAITH OF A FOREIGN WOMAN

1. Ruth 1:16–17 (*The Story*, p. 122).
2. Ruth 1:21 (*The Story*, p. 122).
3. Ruth 3:9 (*The Story*, p. 125).
4. Matthew 1:5 (*The Story*, p. 318).
5. Joshua 2 (*The Story*, pp. 90–91).
6. Ruth 4:14 (*The Story*, p. 127).

CHAPTER 10: STANDING TALL, FALLING HARD

1. 1 Samuel 8:3 (*The Story*, p. 135).
2. 1 Samuel 8:5 (*The Story*, p. 135).
3. 1 Samuel 8:20 (*The Story*, p. 136).
4. 1 Samuel 9:2 (*The Story*, p. 136).
5. Exodus 17:14.
6. 1 Samuel 15:22.
7. 1 Samuel 15:29.

CHAPTER 11: FROM SHEPHERD TO KING

1. 1 Samuel 16:12, (*The Story*, p. 146).
2. 1 Samuel 16:11 (*The Story*, p. 146).
3. 1 Samuel 16:12 (*The Story*, p. 146).
4. Acts 13:22.
5. Deuteronomy 6:4–5 (*The Story*, p. 85).
6. Deuteronomy 30:11, 15–18 (*The Story*, pp. 86–87).
7. 1 Samuel 17:45 (*The Story*, p. 149).

CHAPTER 12: THE TRIALS OF A KING

1. 2 Samuel 6:14 (*The Story*, p. 157).
2. Psalm 34:14.
3. 2 Samuel 12:13 (*The Story*, p. 163).
4. Psalm 51:1–2 (*The Story*, pp. 163–64).
5. 1 John 1:9.

CHAPTER 13: THE KING WHO HAD IT ALL

1. 1 Kings 11:9–13.
2. 1 Kings 1:34.
3. 1 Kings 1:52.
4. Proverbs 1:3 (*The Story*, p. 179).
5. Proverbs 20:19 (*The Story*, p. 181).
6. Proverbs 21:5 (*The Story*, p. 182).
7. Proverbs 21:6 (*The Story*, p. 182).
8. Proverbs 20:21 (*The Story*, p. 181).
9. Proverbs 20:4 (*The Story*, p. 181).
10. 1 Kings 10:9 (*The Story*, p. 190).
11. 1 Kings 10:23 (*The Story*, p. 191).
12. 1 Kings 11:4 (*The Story*, p. 192).

CHAPTER 14: A KINGDOM TORN IN TWO

1. 1 Kings 12:24.
2. 1 Kings 12:24 (*The Story*, p. 195).
3. Matthew 16:18.

CHAPTER 15: GOD'S MESSENGERS

1. Carole Bos, "ICE WARNINGS IGNORED," *AwesomeStories.com*, March 1, 2004, www.awesomestories.com/asset/view/ICE-WARNINGS-IGNORED -Fatal-Voyage-The-Titanic (accessed September 9, 2016).
2. 1 Kings 16:2; see also 1 Kings 15:34; 16:19, 26; 22:52.

3. Genesis 6:7; 9:11.
4. 1 Kings 16:30 (*The Story*, p. 202).
5. 1 Kings 18:22–24 (*The Story*, p. 204).
6. 1 Kings 18:29 (*The Story*, p. 204).
7. 1 Kings 18:39 (*The Story*, p. 205).
8. Hosea 4:1–2 (*The Story*, p. 215).
9. Hosea 5:4 (*The Story*, p. 216).
10. Hosea 14:1 (*The Story*, p. 217).

CHAPTER 16: THE BEGINNING OF THE END (OF THE KINGDOM OF ISRAEL)

1. 2 Chronicles 7:4 (*The Story*, p. 188).
2. 2 Kings 19:19 (*The Story*, p. 223).
3. 2 Kings 21:1–9 (*The Story*, pp. 231–32).
4. 2 Kings 21:12 (*The Story*, p. 232).
5. 2 Chronicles 33:10 (*The Story*, p. 232).
6. Isaiah 49:23, 26 (*The Story*, p. 228).

CHAPTER 17: THE KINGDOMS' FALL

1. Ezekiel 6:3–5, 7 (*The Story*, p. 236).
2. Jeremiah 4:7; 5:1; 13:17, 19 (*The Story*, p. 240).
3. 2 Chronicles 36:15–16 (*The Story*, p. 241).
4. Jeremiah 21:2 (*The Story*, p. 242).
5. Jeremiah 21:10 (*The Story*, p. 242).
6. Lamentations 1:1–2 (*The Story*, pp. 243–44).
7. Ezekiel 36:25 (*The Story*, p. 246).
8. Ezekiel 36:24–26, 28 (*The Story*, pp. 245–46).

CHAPTER 18: DANIEL IN EXILE

1. *The NIV Study Bible* (Grand Rapids: Zondervan, 2011), 1417.
2. Daniel 3:17–18 (*The Story*, p. 210).
3. Daniel 3:27 (*The Story*, p. 256).
4. Daniel 6:26 (*The Story*, p. 259).

CHAPTER 19: THE RETURN HOME

1. Isaiah 45:1.
2. Matthew 6:33.
3. Ezra 1:1–4 (*The Story*, p. 263).
4. Isaiah 45:1.
5. Isaiah 45:6.

6. Haggai 1:4 (*The Story*, p. 266).
7. Matthew 5:45.
8. Haggai 1:5 (*The Story*, p. 266).
9. C. S. Lewis, "Letter to Dom Bede Griffiths," in *The Collected Letters of C. S. Lewis*, vol. 3, ed. Walter Hooper (San Francisco: HarperSanFrancisco, 2007), 211.

CHAPTER 20: THE QUEEN OF BEAUTY AND COURAGE

1. Proverbs 16:33 NLT.
2. Esther 4:16 (*The Story*, p. 282).
3. Esther 7:4 (*The Story*, p. 285).
4. Esther 4:16 (*The Story*, p. 282).
5. Proverbs 16:33 NLT.

CHAPTER 21: REBUILDING THE WALLS

1. Nehemiah 8:1 (*The Story*, p. 300).
2. Joshua 8:34 (*The Story*, p. 95).
3. Nehemiah 8:9–10, paraphrased (*The Story*, pp. 300–301).
4. Nehemiah 8:12 (*The Story*, p. 301).
5. James 1:22.
6. Nehemiah 8:17 (*The Story*, p. 301).
7. Malachi 3:1; 4:5 (*The Story*, p. 304).
8. Matthew 3:1–3 (*The Story*, p. 321).
9. Isaiah 40:3; Malachi 3:1.

CHAPTER 22: THE BIRTH OF THE KING

1. "353 Prophecies Fulfilled in Jesus Christ," According to the Scriptures.org, www.accordingtothescriptures.org/prophecy/353prophecies.html (accessed September 9, 2016).
2. Isaiah 9:7.
3. Matthew 1:20–21 (*The Story*, p. 312).
4. Matthew 1:21 (*The Story*, p. 312).
5. Matthew 1:22–23 (*The Story*, p. 312).
6. Luke 2:1–7 (*The Story*, p. 312).

CHAPTER 23: JESUS' MINISTRY BEGINS

1. John 1:29 (*The Story*, p. 323).
2. John 4:28–29 (*The Story*, p. 329).
3. John 3:16 (*The Story*, p. 327).
4. John 3:3 (*The Story*, p. 326).

5. John 1:23 (*The Story*, p. 323).

6. Matthew 3:14 (*The Story*, p. 322).

7. Matthew 3:17 (*The Story*, p. 322).

8. John 1:29 (*The Story*, p. 323).

9. John 2:1–11 (*The Story*, p. 325).

10. John 3:16 (*The Story*, p. 327).

11. Merrill C. Tenney, general editor, and Moises Silva, revision editor, *The Zonder-van Encyclopedia of the Bible*, vol. 5 (Grand Rapids: Zondervan, 2009), 289.

12. John 4:25 (*The Story*, p. 328).

13. John 4:26 (*The Story*, p. 329).

14. Mark 2:7 (*The Story*, p. 331).

15. Matthew 11:3 (*The Story*, p. 334).

CHAPTER 24: NO ORDINARY MAN

1. Mark 4:3–9 (*The Story*, p. 335).

2. Matthew 5:3–10 (*The Story*, p. 340).

3. Matthew 6:5, 19–20, 24, 27, 34 (*The Story*, pp. 341–43).

4. Matthew 5:16 (*The Story*, p. 341).

5. Mark 5:30, 34 (*The Story*, p. 345).

6. John 6:29 (*The Story*, p. 349).

7. John 6:53–56, 58 (*The Story*, p. 350).

8. Matthew 14:28 (*The Story*, p. 348).

9. Matthew 14:33 (*The Story*, p. 349).

CHAPTER 25: JESUS, THE SON OF GOD

1. John 8:58 (*The Story*, p. 358).

2. Mark 11:10 (*The Story*, p. 363).

3. Mark 8:27, 29 (The Story, p. 353).

4. John 1:29.

5. John 14:6.

6. Mark 8:29 (*The Story*, p. 353).

7. Mark 8:31 (*The Story*, p. 353).

8. Mark 8:34–36 (*The Story*, pp. 353–54).

9. John 7:15 (*The Story*, p. 356).

10. John 7:40–41 (*The Story*, p. 356).

11. John 7:41–42 (*The Story*, p. 356).

12. John 8:12 (*The Story*, p. 357).

13. John 8:23 (*The Story*, p. 357).

14. John 8:53, 58 (*The Story*, p. 358).

15. Exodus 3:14 (*The Story*, p. 46).

16. Zechariah 9:9.
17. Mark 11:9–10 (*The Story*, p. 363).

CHAPTER 26: THE HOUR OF DARKNESS

1. Matthew 27:64 (*The Story*, p. 374).
2. Matthew 26:45 (*The Story*, p. 373).
3. John 13:21 (*The Story*, p. 368).
4. Matthew 26:39 (*The Story*, p. 372).
5. John 18:11 (*The Story*, p. 373).
6. Isaiah 53:7 (*The Story*, p. 229).
7. Isaiah 53:5 (*The Story*, p. 229).
8. John 19:30, emphasis added (*The Story*, p. 380).
9. Matthew 27:51 (*The Story*, p. 380).
10. Hebrews 10:19–22.
11. John 19:38–42 (*The Story*, pp. 381–82).

CHAPTER 27: THE RESURRECTION

1. Romans 6:23 (*The Story*, p. 434).
2. Luke 24:27.
3. Romans 10:9.
4. Romans 6:23.
5. Isaiah 9:6.
6. Matthew 28:6–7 (*The Story*, p. 383).
7. John 20:15 (*The Story*, p. 384).
8. Luke 24:34 (*The Story*, p. 385).
9. John 20:25 (*The Story*, p. 386).
10. John 20:28 (*The Story*, p. 386).
11. Matthew 28:18–20 (*The Story*, p. 388).

CHAPTER 28: NEW BEGINNINGS

1. Acts 1:7 (*The Story*, p. 389).
2. Acts 1:8 (*The Story*, p. 389).
3. Acts 2:42–47 (*The Story*, p. 392).

CHAPTER 29: PAUL'S MISSION

1. Genesis 12:3 (*The Story*, p. 13).
2. Acts 13:47 (*The Story*, p. 409).
3. Acts 1:8.
4. Acts 8:1.
5. Acts 8:3 (*The Story*, p. 399).

6. Acts 9:1 (*The Story*, p. 399).

7. Acts 9:4 (*The Story*, p. 399).

8. Acts 18:3 (*The Story*, p. 415).

9. Genesis 12:2–3 (*The Story*, p. 13).

10. Acts 13:27–33, 38–39 (*The Story*, pp. 408–9).

11. Acts 13:46–47 (*The Story*, p. 409).

12. Isaiah 49:6.

13. Acts 17:23.

14. Acts 19:19 (*The Story*, p. 422).

CHAPTER 30: PAUL'S FINAL DAYS

1. Romans 8:28 (*The Story*, p. 435).

2. Ephesians 5:1–2.

3. Philippians 1:27; 2:3, 5, 14, 15; 4:4, 5.

4. Ephesians 4:25, 31; 5:3, 4, 18.

5. Ephesians 4:22, 24.

6. Ephesians 4:11–16.

7. 1 Timothy 6:12; 2 Timothy 4:7 (*The Story*, p. 458).

8. 2 Timothy 1:7.

9. 2 Timothy 3:10–13 (*The Story*, p. 457).

10. 2 Timothy 4:6–8 (*The Story*, p. 458).

11. Romans 1:16 (*The Story*, p. 432).

CHAPTER 31: THE END OF TIME

1. Genesis 3:8.

2. Revelation 22:20.

3. John 13:23; 20:3–4 (*The Story*, pp. 368–69, 383).

4. Revelation 21:1 (*The Story*, p. 467).

5. Genesis 1:1 (*The Story*, p. 1).

6. Revelation 21:2 (*The Story*, p. 467).

7. John 14:2 (*The Story*, pp. 369–70).

8. Revelation 21:3 (*The Story*, p. 467).

9. Revelation 22:1–5 (*The Story*, pp. 468–69).

10. Revelation 4:8.

11. Revelation 22:20, emphasis added (*The Story*, p. 470).

TURN EVERYDAY PEOPLE INTO DEVOTED BIBLE READERS

Learn More at TheStory.com

The Story Church-Wide Experience:
Bible Engagement for Adults, Students, and Children

The Story is helping people in churches everywhere experience Scripture like never before. Stories from the Bible are organized chronologically, helping your church understand God's story—from Genesis to Revelation—and how their stories fit into God's one story.

Affordable, flexible, and easy to use, churches are using *The Story* not only as a powerful church-wide experience but also in individual ministries, such as small groups, Sunday School, and youth ministry.

THE STORY WHOLE CHURCH EXPERIENCE INCLUDES:

- Adult books and Bible study lessons
- Student books and Bible study lessons
- Scripture books and storybooks for kids
- Bible lessons for kids of all ages
- Spanish books and Bible study lessons
- Preaching and teaching helps
- Sermon outlines
- Devotionals and more!

Turn your church into a Bible-reading church today! Visit **TheStory.com** to learn how.

THE STORY
POWERED BY ZONDERVAN